Evadne's Odyssey Book One

The Naked Doctor

1 December 2015

Dearest Tiggy

Happy Christmas

Do enjoy this splendid volume!

Love

Neil x

GW00645229

Doctor Evadne Hinge

as told to George Logan

The Naked Doctor

by

Doctor Evadne Hinge

as told to George Logan

ISBN: 9780957624290

GJB Publishing

18 Yeend Close
West Molesey
Surrey KT8 2NY

www.GJBpublishing.co.uk

Dedication

To my partner Luigi Perone, who unselfishly put up with my bad moods, constant abstraction and frequent absences for hours, days and weeks as I struggled to get this thing down on paper.

And to his family, who have become my family.

To Paul Dunford, in recognition of his untiring effort to keep Hinge and Bracket before the public despite the BBC's apparent determination to bury them in an unmarked grave.

To Sue Lavender, for her helpful and heroic proof-reading of early drafts of this book.

To all the loyal fans of *Hinge and Bracket*, young and old.

George Logan

Contents

Foreword

by Doctor Evadne Hinge

7th July 2002

The Croft, Auchterarla, Scotland.

Today is my eighty-second birthday. I have had lots of cards, a small party, and even a cake. How kind people are.

Naturally, I attended Hilda's funeral service in May. She was buried in her beloved West Country, where she had lived happily for the last few years in the cosy little annexe that Julian, her nephew, had arranged for her in the grounds of the home he shares with his friend Greville. 'Annexe' was Hilda's word. I called it a granny flat. She didn't like that much.

Even though she was eighty-four, Hilda's passing was unexpected. In the fifty-seven years we shared a life and a career, I don't remember her having had more than the occasional day's illness. Indeed, neither of us had ever suffered from any major health problems. We were in rehearsal for pantomime when she collapsed and was rushed into hospital.

She was buried in a quiet churchyard near Taunton. The service had been a simple one, following the wishes of her family. This simplicity, I can't help feeling, might not have entirely pleased her. Knowing Hilda as well as I did, I am sure that at the very least she would have anticipated a State Funeral and a corner in Westminster Abbey. However, she would have been pleased, I think, that Julian had arranged for her coffin to be carried by members of the local rugby team, six strapping and handsome young gentlemen. Hilda was in her later years a great fan of rugby. And of strapping and handsome young gentlemen.

It has taken some time to come to terms with the huge changes that her passing has made in my own life. Due to our advancing age we had certainly reduced the frequency of our appearances over the last few years. But neither of us had really considered that a day might arrive when *Hinge and Bracket* would become a memory, a footnote in the annals of British theatre.

Nonetheless, it is astonishing to consider the career Hilda and I forged together since we were persuaded in 1974 to perform in what we anticipated would be a single short season at the Edinburgh Festival. That this was to lead to almost thirty years of further appearances was as unexpected as it was gratifying. During this time we seem to have achieved a celebrity and ubiquity that far outstripped our earlier fame as leading soprano and conductor-in-chief with the

Rosa Charles Opera Company, during the forties and fifties. I had personally never imagined that late in life we would appear together on television, radio, and theatres throughout the land; indeed, throughout the world. Though Hilda, of course, saw this belated recognition as no more than our due. Or no more than *her* due, certainly.

To those who have encouraged me to continue the recital evenings for which Hilda and I were best known, with someone else standing in for my old colleague, I can only say... '*What are you thinking of?*' As if anyone could possibly replace Dame Hilda Bracket. So that is something that is not going to happen. My plan is to retire from the theatre and to devote my remaining years to my first love, music.

* * * * *

It was a chance meeting with a young but close friend, a Mr George Logan, that led to the volume of memoirs you are currently holding. He asked me if I had ever considered that the world might have a certain interest in reading the 'real' story of *Hinge and Bracket*, both on and off stage. The idea seemed absurd to me. Bookshops are cluttered with 'showbiz' biographies, each, in my experience, more tedious than the last. The current cult of celebrity has a lot to answer for. I saw no reason to inflict yet another ego-inflating revelation on the book-buying public.

"Very well," he said. "Point taken. Then how about *your* story? After all, Dame Hilda wrote about her own early years in *One Little Maid* – what about yours?"

At first I was inclined to pooh-pooh the idea. But surprisingly, his suggestion took root, and started me thinking. I had read Hilda's little book many years before, and had found it amusing. Particularly as I couldn't help but be aware, knowing her as I did, that much of it was unashamed invention. And that the rest was being viewed through spectacles that were impenetrably rose-tinted.

"If I did," I said, after thinking his proposition over, "it would have to be the *real* story. No glamorising, no whitewashing, no fables of endless triumphs, adoring fans and a painless passage from nonentity to celebrity. My early life wasn't easy, not at all. And it may well be that the reader who knows only the public face of Doctor Hinge might find my experiences hard to credit, or even shocking."

"But more importantly, there are two major difficulties that stand in the way. One – I have neither the time nor the literary ability to write anything of that sort. And two, some of the people I would have to mention less than flatteringly are still alive. I foresee libel actions, unwelcome correspondence, sagging old faces turning up out of the woodwork, intrusive telephone calls, begging letters, all sorts of repercussions. No, I really don't think it would be a wise move."

Mr Logan explained that the first of my objections was easily overcome. He would 'interview' me over a period of a week or two, and record my words on tape. He would then take the tapes away and himself write up my story. What did I think of that idea?

I gave it some further thought. "Yes," I said eventually. "I can see how that might work. As long as I have *carte blanche* to change anything I feel has not been presented accurately."

"Of course, of course," he said hastily. "I would want it to reflect the real you. You will have the final word as to what goes into the book, always."

"Very well." I hesitated – the idea was oddly appealing. "But what about my second point?"

There was no stopping him. "And as regards upsetting people who would figure in the book – er – unflatteringly, as you put it – you can change some names, surely? Wouldn't that work?"

I considered this. "No," I said eventually. "Then it wouldn't be the real story, would it?"

After further reflection, I said, "But – imagine this. What if we do the book as you suggest? And you don't publish it until after I am dead?" I smiled. "After all, it can't be all that long. My death, I mean, not the book."

He frowned. I don't think he was at bottom at all satisfied with my suggestion. But I refused to be swayed, and eventually he caved in. "OK. If it's the only way, let's do that."

And that's what we did.

Doctor Evadne Hinge

* * * * *

7th July 2014.

Bel Ombrage, Le Dorat, France.

Oh dear. I am ninety-four. Ninety-four years old and still here.

The others are all dead, I imagine. And if by any chance one or two of them are still hanging on, I expect they will be by now completely gaga, or at the least on very heavy medication.

So here it is. I do hope you won't be too shocked, gentle reader, though I venture to hope you will be a little surprised. You may discover that the young Evadne Hinge was a rather different person from the one that you perhaps imagined. You may come to realise that the older Evadne, the one you are familiar with, was to some extent the deliberate creation of her younger self.

I have always been a very private person. In my partnership with Hilda, I quickly learned that any intimate revelations I might be inclined to make to her were liable to be paraded before the public at some later date, and held up to ridicule in the interests of a cheap laugh. This encouraged me to keep my own counsel to a large extent.

And it may be that some of you already suspected this.

One *caveat*. It seems I talked so much and at such length that this story is going to arrive in episodes. That's probably because for the first time in years I was not constantly being interrupted by Hilda. So this volume only covers my life up to the age of eighteen, years before she and I made each other's acquaintance. There is a lot more to come.

You have been warned.

Doctor Evadne Hinge

Foreword

by George Logan

27th October 2014.

Bel Ombrage, Le Dorat, France.

Well, I didn't think I'd ever manage to bring her to the point, but it seems I have finally succeeded. Doctor Hinge has explained her own objections to earlier publication above, and naturally I respect her concerns and her caution. Nonetheless, I was in the end able to convince her that, since her narrative starts almost a century ago, there was little likelihood that any of the people figuring in her account were still around to object; and that even if they were, although she characterises some of her descriptions as 'unflattering', in fact they are rarely that. Rather, they are honest, fair-minded and generally justified by subsequent events.

It may prove rather more difficult to persuade the lady to agree to the publication of the second volume of her memoirs, since this covers a later period, and it is increasingly possible that some of the personages featuring therein are indeed still with us. But it would be tragic if the world were forever to remain in ignorance of subsequent events in the Doctor's history. The astonishing details of her undercover work during the Second World War. Her training at Bletchley Park; her adventures in wartime France and later in occupied Greece (where she first made the acquaintance of a young singer called Mary Callas, who would go on to have a career of some note); and her eventual return to Great Britain after the cessation of hostilities. I did make a point of asking her if these matters, some of them touching the security of the realm, could now be freely discussed. Had she been debriefed, I wondered? "Oh yes, dear. And more than once," she replied with that little secret smile I have come to know so well.

And matters of world import aside, surely everyone will want to know what happened later to lovely Julie, Principessa di Santofiore, trapped in a loveless marriage and in Fascist Italy; to gruff but adorable Mona McCafferty, now reluctant *patronne* of *La Chatte Rose,* notorious *boîte de nuit* catering to specialised tastes in Montparnasse; to Dougal McDougal, sometime hero, sometime villain; to flighty younger sister Lavinia enjoying her own wartime adventure; to vanished older brother Leicester, be he dead or alive; and of course to monstrous Maureen, the Mother from Hell.

And most importantly, just how did that memorable first meeting with young Hilda Bracket occur, and what were the subsequent consequences?

It will take all my powers of persuasion, I am sure. But I live in hope. I have just managed to convince the lady herself to permit the dissemination on the Internet of a filmed interview she gave back in 2002 when this current volume was in preparation.

Evadne (as she prefers to be called these days) has not as yet given me a definite answer, but she joins me in hoping you will take as much pleasure in reading this first book as we did in writing it.

Wish me luck.

George Logan

Prelude

August 1937.

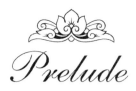

Backstage at The Winter Gardens Theatre, Rothesay, Scotland.

"Fifteen minutes, you lot". The unmistakable adenoidal tones of Shug[1] the call-boy rang out from the corridor. Seated in the shabby dressing room, I gazed into the fly-blown mirror in front of me. '*Who is this stranger*?' I wondered idly, and not for the first time. Short crimped hair of a dazzling if unconvincing gold; eyebrows plucked and pencilled into a fine line; lashes beaded with hot-black; rouged and powdered complexion; lips of a vibrant carmine. I knew who she was, of course. No longer Evadne Hinge, she was Marina Montpellier. 'Rina' to her close friends.

"Pass us the wet-white, angel. I've gone a wee bit patchy." This from my neighbour, Mae Hockshaw, a sturdy lass just as blond as I, and just as painted. The only difference was that Mae favoured a tan, and was compelled to use the disgusting wet-white cosmetic to attain the lily-white skin tone that was *de rigueur* for us ladies of the chorus. No healthy glow for members of the Betty Barnard Beauties. Instead, a corpse-like pallor was the favoured look – unless, of course, we were to be featured in *South of the Border* or the like. On these occasions I was forced to darken any exposed skin artificially, while Mae was happily *au naturel*.

I passed her the bottle of cosmetic and its accompanying sponge, and she began to dab vigorously at the dark patch on her arm. Further down the dressing-room table, Sandra and Phyllis were discussing their adventures of the night before. Apparently the party to which Phyllis had been invited had not turned out to be the up-market society gathering she had anticipated.

"Oh, it wiz a dump, yon, Sandra, Ah'm telling ye. And full of the dregs, a right rough crowd. Two guys gets intae a fight, and the next thing you know, the polis[2] is at the door. Ah says tae Raymond, '*Ah'm out of here right now, Ah've had ma difficulties wi' they lads in the past.*' So we tears intae the kitchen, him an' me, and Ah climbs up ontae the sink and then through the windae, still clutching ma drink. But Ah get stuck halfway oot, so Ray gie's me a shove in the arse, and next thing Ah know, Ah'm oan ma face in the back court. Drink spilt, stockings laddered, heel of ma best shoes broken, dress aw ripped…"

---

1 Shug – the Glasgow pronunciation of the name 'Hugh'. For no discernible reason.

2 Polis - The police

Sandra, pushing a curl or two into place, was suitably sympathetic. "Aw naw, Phyllis – no' yer new dress? The lavender shantung?"

"Aye, the very one – oh, ah wis livid, Sandra. But that's no' the worst – next thing Ah know, Ray lands right oan the top of me, and whit dae ye think he does?"

"Whit?"

"Nae apology, nothing. He says, '*Ah hope that's you, lover*', and kisses me full oan the lips. Oh, Ah wiz *furious*!"

Sandra, peering short-sightedly into the mirror, nodded in agreement. "Ah bet! Ah hope ye gave him hell!"

"Ah did better than that – Ah crossed ma legs and broke his glasses!"

The dressing room erupted in raucous laughter. Even I had to smile.

But Phyllis hadn't finished.

"And *then…*"

I tuned out. I had heard the same or similar conversations many times.

I turned to my neighbour. "Help me into my costume, Mae, will you?"

"Sure angel, nae bother." She stood up and moved to the hanging rail. "Looks like you got the best of the bunch from wardrobe this week. And that green really suits you."

I had to smile. Dear Mae, ever the glass half-full.

With her help I struggled into the unbecoming outfit I would wear for my appearance as Tina Tulip in *The Garden of Beauty*. A full-length skin-tight sheath in a livid green sateen, it had a concealed split at the back to permit some degree of movement, and was topped by a head-dress of brilliant scarlet 'petals' which covered me from the neck to the top of my head. A narrow opening at the front allowed limited vision. Broad, sword like 'leaves' ran from my shoulders to my wrists.

"Wid ye gie's a hand wi mine, angel?" asked Mae, when she had finished forcing the ill-stitched and crooked zip-fastener at the back of my ensemble as far as it would go in the direction of my neck.

"Yes, of course, Mae."

She was equally garishly outfitted to represent Daff O'Dell, with a ruff of yellow petals round her neck. Further down the table Sandra Slack and Phyllis Small were preparing themselves as Lily Valley and Dolly Dahlia, while at the far end Shona McCann and Mary Kelly were clambering into what were allegedly Phoebe Phlox and Chris Anthemum. Frankly, their floral outfits appeared to be modelled on species completely unknown to horticulture. Not that any of our costumes were particularly true-to-life, but as the new girls, they had to make do with what was left over when we 'old troupers' had made our choice.

The Garden of Beauty, indeed! I had forborne from mentioning to our director that a garden, however beautiful, in which tulips, dahlias, daffodils and chrysanthemums bloomed simultaneously would have taxed the talents of Capability Brown himself. I forbore quite a lot these days. I had quickly learned that logic and realism had no place in the Scottish Variety Theatre, and that smart remarks, criticisms and complaints were likely to lead to the sack.

"Five minutes, hoors[1], thank *yew*!" Shug gave the next call with all his accustomed charm.

"So help me, I'll clatter that wee toerag roon' the heid wan o' thae days," said Mae, as she applied an extra layer of colour to her already well painted lips. "Does he no' understand the meaning of the expression 'Ladies of the Chorus', the glaekit[2] wee bugger?"

This was greeted with appreciative laughter. Mae was an outspoken character, always ready with a witty rejoinder, and respecting no-one. If her language could be hair-raising on occasion, she was good-hearted and kind. She was my best friend in the company, and indeed had been instrumental in introducing me to this, my new life.

"Dae ye fancy coming oot for a fish supper after the show, Rina?" she went on conversationally, as she added yet another coat of mascara to her lashes. "Me and the rest of the lassies is goin'; wi' Agnes and Joe and one or two of the stage crew. Then it's back tae oor wee place for a few drinks. Day off the morra, remember? – lovely Sunday! Fancy it, hen? Go on, say ye'll come. Ye're terrible, you – ye never go anywhere – come on, just this once. Ye'll enjoy it."

It was true that I tended to avoid the after-show junketings as a rule, preferring to go back to the flat Mae and I shared and lose myself in a good book. But I was bored. We had been appearing in *Doon the Watter*[3] at the Winter Gardens, Rothesay, for the last three months, two and sometimes three shows a day, and I thought that perhaps a relaxing evening out with the girls would do me no harm. Besides, I had been very grateful for the little party my friends in the company had thrown to celebrate my seventeenth birthday a few weeks before, and didn't want to appear a spoilsport.

"Yes, alright Mae, I will. Why not?"

Mae patted me on the shoulder. "Good for you angel, we'll have a laugh, jist you wait an' see. They're a nice bunch of lassies this year, and that's no' always the way of it."

1 Hoors - Whores

2 Glaekit - Simple-minded

3 Down the Water – suggesting a trip down the Firth of Clyde to some salubrious holiday resort like Rothesay

She was right. All of us girls got on well together, and the easy camaraderie of the dressing room made the repetitive boredom of the job bearable.

"And who knows?" went on Mae with a sly smile, "We might even find ye a fella!"

I grimaced as I re-powdered, and shook my head decisively. "Mae, that's the last thing I'm looking for – I've told you that often enough."

"Aye, ye huv. But Ah'm jist no quite sure Ah believe ye, Rina," responded Mae with a conspiratorial grin.

"Beginners, leg-openers and tarts, please," bawled Shug from the corridor.

"Shut it, ya skelly[1] wee runt," roared Mae. It was true that the vile Shug did have a terrifying squint.

We ladies arose and began the long descent towards the stage.

"Hi Rina – see you later, I hope?" Young Joe Cameron, our second comic, smiled and squeezed against the wall to let us pass on the narrow stairs.

"Yes, Joe, I'll be there," I called over my shoulder. I still occasionally failed to respond to 'Marina' or 'Rina'. My name, indeed my identity, had undergone more than one change in the last twelve months. As I had deliberately arranged.

What did it matter? After all, as they say, *'What's in a name*?'

1 Cross-eyed

Chapter One
Daddy's Girl

1920.

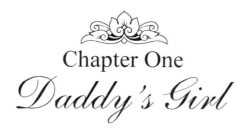

Dean Castle, Ayrshire, Scotland.

Evadne Mona Montpellier Hinge. What's in a name? Well in this case, quite a lot.

My parents married in 1917, near the end of the Great War. Naturally, an embattled Europe discouraged an exotic honeymoon, and a brief perambulation round some of the less scenic spots of the British Isles had to suffice. The result was my older brother Leicester, born in 1918. The international situation being what it was, I imagine my peripatetic parents were pretty much thrown back on their own resources and inventiveness to pass the time.

After the end of hostilities, Father, it seems, decided that he owed Mother a proper honeymoon; so a European trip was arranged in 1919. They must have found the joys of travel particularly stimulating, as I was conceived on this trip, probably somewhere in the Aegean. Father imaginatively decided to name me in connection with some of their more memorable ports of call.

Evadne for the wife of Capaneus, a muscle-bound Greek thug struck dead by Zeus at the siege of Thebes for his arrogance. Father was rampantly philhellenic. His beloved mother had been Greek, and the site of ancient Thebes was the ultimate destination of my parents' journey. The Greek Thebes, that is, home city of Oedipus. Father brought back an Oedipus amphora – he already had the complex.

On the outward leg of their journey was the island of Anglesey, the supposed resting place of King Arthur. *Mona*, to give it its Latin name. And the name by which my mother insisted on addressing me, due to its homophonic relationship to *moaner*. She knew I hated it, and only did it in an attempt to annoy me.

The charming southern French city of *Montpellier* was also on their route. Mother once suggested that this particular part of my name memorialised a moment of togetherness she and Father had shared in the Montpellier rotunda in Cheltenham. Once again, this was simple malice, or 'a bit of fun', as she described it.

I've always been relieved that their itinerary didn't cover Maidenhead or the Virgin Islands.

My older brother had been named less exotically, but after a similar system. Leicester Staines Carlisle. Not *Lester*, but *Leicester*, please note.

Of course, we were stuck with the *Hinge*. Mother could never reconcile herself to it, and continued using her maiden name, McWhirter; unless she was signing an official document – an acknowledgement of a police caution, perhaps, or her discharge papers from one of her clinics. I couldn't really see that McWhirter was any particular improvement on Hinge, but my mother, Maureen, was proud of her family connections; 'McWhirter's Fine Old Scottish Whiskies', a name that can still strike a spark of nostalgic enthusiasm in the breasts of those of an alcoholic persuasion and an undiscriminating palate. I only tasted it once, and that was under unusual circumstances. But Mother loved the stuff, and of course got it free. She and her crony Morag ('*My old school chum*') could put away bottles of it.

Certainly the family was well-to-do. And Mother, as the younger of the two surviving heirs, stood to inherit substantially. Which makes one wonder just what she was doing in a low public house in Glasgow that night when she and my Father met for the first time. She has always been vague on that point.

* * * * *

Father was, of course, Hector Hinge. A highly respected figure in the musical world of his day, he was a composer of vision, a teacher of brilliance, a generous and loyal friend, and a loving father. Born in 1859, he had in his youth studied with the great Franz Liszt, and indeed, had attended Richard Wagner's funeral in the company of his teacher. The style of his music was naturally that of the late Romantic period, and, despite his early successes, by the time we children arrived, his popularity had suffered an eclipse. Like another neglected genius, his friend and fellow composer Joseph Holbrooke,[1] he was compelled in later years to seeing his major works languish unperformed, and was reduced to turning out comparatively trivial pieces for popular consumption. Not that he resented this – his tastes in music were wide-ranging and eclectic. How well I remember him saying to me with a smile, "Well, Evie, it's all one. No masterpiece, maybe, but as long as it has a good wee tune, it's music, isn't it?" He said this often, and it is a maxim I have never forgotten.

Of course he didn't always say it quite like that. A gifted linguist, his languages of choice were French, Classical Greek and 'the Gaelic'. One could never be quite sure which of these he would adopt on any particular occasion.

We children grew up conversant with all the languages Father favoured. Since Mother was also a fluent Gaelic speaker, that or English tended to be the

1 Joseph Holbrooke (1878 – 1958), English composer of 'The Cauldron of Annwn', a Wagnerian-length trilogy of operas based on Welsh mythology.

day to day language of our household. However Mother knew no French or Greek, so Father and I would use one or the other between ourselves if we wanted to speak to each other in confidence, as we often did.

I was always, I think I may fairly say, his favourite child. "You, Evie, are the only person I can talk to in this madhouse. You've a sound head on your wee shoulders, and you say what you think." He was, I think, disheartened that in my early childhood I had shown no particular signs of special musical ability. Indeed, he would wince noticeably as I went carolling round the house. Of course most of us could play the piano after a fashion; but in our household that was considered a fairly minor accomplishment. And Mother, it must be said, always remained something of a philistine where music was concerned.

Initially, it appeared that my brother Leicester would be the one to inherit the musical mantle. He had a resonant baritone voice from a young age, and his rendition of the Prologue from *I Pagliacci* enlivened many of our musical evenings. Father, I am sure, initially had hopes of him. But things were to turn out rather differently.

Father's own family history was a curious one. On his father's side he was a distant collateral descendant of the Dukes of Buccleuch, a title granted in 1663 to the Duke of Monmouth, eldest illegitimate son of Charles II. While I set no great store by hereditary honours as such, it gives me some pleasure to count among my ancestors the 'merry monarch' himself, albeit by way of the wrong side of the blanket. And no doubt it was this distant connection that indirectly inspired Father's comic opera on the life of Nell Gwynne, playfully described as 'a trollop in three parts'. The title was *Sweet Nell of Old Drury; or, The Love for Two Oranges*. How Uncle Sergei (Prokofiev) laughed when Father explained the little *jeu de mots* in which he had indulged![1] And even more so when I, horribly precocious as I was, suggested that we might *entre nous* consider Mother to be '*Sweet Smell of Old Brewery*'; although I did know the difference, even at that age, between a brewery and a distillery.

Father's parents, Hamish Buccleuch Hinge, of immemorial Scots lineage, and Aliki Constantia Paskalis, one time prima donna of the Athens Opera, were long dead when I arrived on the scene. Indeed, the only living relative that Father ever mentioned was a mysterious cousin called Mary McGuire, who had, it seems, been locked away many years previously for some unspecified misdemeanour. No other details were ever revealed.

However, my maternal grandparents, Maxwell and Alma McWhirter, were very much alive, and were a delightful, if eccentric, couple, who thoroughly spoilt us children on the rare occasions they chose to visit. Their relationship with their daughter, my mother, was a strained and uncomfortable one, it always

1 Sergei Prokofiev had enjoyed a 'succès de scandale' with his comic opera 'The Love for Three Oranges' in Chicago in 1921.

seemed to me. Through snatches of overheard conversations, I gathered that she had been, in some undefined way, something of a 'black sheep', and their gratitude to my father for taking responsibility for her was occasionally mentioned.

I realise that all this may give the impression that I did not respect my mother as much as perhaps a dutiful child should. Nothing could be more misleading. I respected her thoroughly; indeed, in my childhood I was rather frightened of her. But her schedule was always so full, she was so caught up with things outside the home, that in my early years I saw very little of her. She was, I suppose, a good mother in a haphazard kind of way – certainly my younger sister, Lavinia, seemed, at least in her early years, to be Mother's favourite. Lavinia arrived some four years after I was born. Mother and Father had spent a weekend with friends in the Trossachs the previous summer, and once again, it appeared, travel had broadened the mind and stimulated dormant passions.

In childhood my sister was thoroughly spoilt, constantly dressed in 'cute' ribbons and flounces. I can still see her aged five as Mother coaxed her through her party piece – *Ma, He's Making Eyes at Me*. Lavinia, as a child, was pretty, in an anaemic, pallid fashion, with blond curls tortured into fat ringlets by Mother or one of her entourage. Father had not much time for her, as she had little musical talent (indeed he occasionally questioned her paternity when in one of his darker moods), and despite Mother's best endeavours, she never succeeded in convincing him that Lavinia was the next Sophie Tucker. As my sister grew older Mother seemed to lose interest in her, and eventually she was treated much as were Leicester and myself, with what Mother would have called 'a healthy neglect.'

Out home was what was referred to by the locals as 'Castle Hinge'. It was properly called Dean Castle, near Kilmarnock, in Ayrshire, Scotland. Owned originally by the Boyd family, it has strong historical connections with many people and events famous in Scottish history. This semi-derelict eyesore was eventually inherited by the wealthy philanthropist, the 8th Lord Howard de Walden (the poet T E Ellis), who commenced its restoration early in the 20th century. 'Tommy' Ellis was also the generous patron and librettist of Father's chum Joseph Holbrooke, and he kindly allowed my father and his family the tenancy of the building during its renovation.

I would not however want to give the impression that we children grew up in luxurious surroundings. Dean Castle was in parts a ruin, it was draughty and virtually unheated, and the constant work involved in the restoration did not make for a comfortable life. Nevertheless, I look back on these years of childhood with almost unalloyed pleasure. For my brother and me it was a fairy-tale existence. The glorious countryside and the grounds were our special realm, and my Father was the Prospero who ruled this enchanted demesne and cast a magical spell over his fortunate subjects.

* * * * *

We are a tall family. Both my parents were above average height. Father at six feet was an imposing figure, with his long iron-grey hair and distinguished features. In later life running a little to *avoirdupois*, in his youth he had been slim, upright and of a notable handsomeness. Some of his early photographs show him to have borne a remarkable resemblance to his teacher, Franz Liszt, on whom I think he modelled himself to some extent. His most prominent facial feature was the splendid Roman nose which dominated everything. Above this, his twinkling blue eyes seemed like a somewhat incongruous contradiction. I am sorry I did not inherit the eyes – mine are brown, as are Mother's – but I am relieved that I also missed that nose!

Mother was only an inch or two shorter than Father. Despite our many differences, no-one could deny that she was a fine-looking woman. In her youth a stunning beauty, she had a slender but voluptuous figure and a piquant face crowned with a mass of chestnut hair. It's no exaggeration to say that Mother had only to enter a room to draw the attention of everyone in it. Perfectly aware of this, she used her personal magnetism shamelessly for her own ends. And usually managed to get her way – indeed the only person who seemed able to resist her was Father – no doubt he had seen her repertoire of tricks only too often. Although no-one could have been more soft and womanly in appearance, her personality was in complete contrast. It was forceful, indeed, adamantine, and her will was of iron. She always felt she knew best, and would stoop to any level to achieve her ends. As will become all too apparent as this narrative proceeds.

My brother and I inherited from both our parents. Alike in general appearance, we were both tall, dark-haired (although I had a glint of Mother's auburn) and of a slim build. Leicester had Father's nose, which luckily had missed me, and his blue eyes. Indeed he grew to resemble Father generally, and was regarded as a very good-looking boy from his earliest years. Beside him I was, I think, considered something of an ugly duckling. I would secretly have liked to look like my mother, but in my childhood this seemed to be a very remote possibility. However, in later years I certainly inherited her figure, and was indeed considered pretty by some. I have never lacked male attention, if that is any criterion.

I was born in 1920, the prelude to the 'Roaring Twenties', although the roar was but a subdued murmur in rural Ayrshire. I entered the world on July 7th, a hot summer, or so Mother maintained. She never tired of reminding me of the endless labour she endured in the ill-ventilated grand bedchamber of the Castle that day.

At the time of my arrival, Father at sixty was already a mature gentleman. Mother was much, much younger, a precocious twenty, but old beyond her years.

This is probably as good a point as any to recount how this spring and autumn conjunction occurred.

As Father told it to me some years later – Mother claimed to have forgotten the details – '*It's all like some dreadful dream*' – it happened in this wise.

* * * * *

Although the vicissitudes of wartime meant that public concerts were few and far between, Father had been invited to visit Glasgow to conduct the first performance of his little *Concertino for Basset Horn and Strings* at the famous St Andrew's Halls. It was after this successful première, while he was relaxing in the artist's withdrawing room, that he was introduced to a flamboyant figure, the great Igor Stravinsky[1]. They fell into conversation (in French, of course – Father, alas, had no Russian) and immediately discovered many mutual interests. Not least that Hector, in his youth, had known Igor's father[2] very well. The reminiscences rolled forth – of lessons in orchestration *chez* the Rimsky-Korsakovs, suicidal evenings spent drinking in the company of Mussorgsky, writing bits of *Prince Igor* when Borodin was too busy, and gay doings on the Nevsky Prospect with Tchaikovsky. All this over a stimulating samovar.

Stravinsky was accompanied by his lady friend, later his second wife, the lovely Vera de Bosset. The irregularity of their relationship (he was already married) had of course caused some scandal and loose talk, and he had actually been booed in puritanical Edinburgh. Glasgow was a more tolerant city, and Father, himself unmarried, was not judgmental in these matters. It was probably his sympathetic attitude, as much as his renown as a composer, that led to the future close friendship of the two men. Stravinsky was at that time – 1917 – working on his *L'Histoire du Soldat,*[3] and apparently decided that Father was just the experienced older musician who could help him iron out a few tricky problems he was encountering in completing the score. They decided to adjourn to a local hostelry to discuss the matter, and there, after several 'snifters', Igor produced a flask of the finest Polish vodka and suggested they make a night of it. Vera insisted they all throw their empty glasses into the blazing log fire in authentic Russian fashion, and they were asked to leave when the bar ran out of glassware. Undaunted, it did not take them long to find a less critical watering hole. And so the evening continued.

---

1 Igor Stravinsky (1882 – 1971), Russian composer of 'The Firebird', 'Petrushka', 'The Rite of Spring' and other major works.

2 Fyodor Stravinsky, for many years a leading bass at the Maryinsky Theatre, St. Petersburg

3 L'Histoire du Soldat' – 'The Soldier's Tale', a theatrical work premièred in Lausanne in 1918.

My Father never had a good head for strong drink. At some point in the evening, Vera sauntered off with her trusty torch and sketching block, in order, she said, to capture some picturesque sailors in the vicinity of *Betty's Bar.*[1] Father and Igor continued their conversation over yet more drinks, and eventually ended up in a seedy establishment in the Broomielaw called *The Croak and Stagger.* It is here that Father claimed his memory became hazy. He remembered the entertainment, an unusual dance performed by a young lady. Probably a strathspey or reel in the Scottish folk tradition – as Father described it, it apparently involved the hazardous control of an improbably located lighted newspaper[2]. He remembered Igor producing yet another bottle from the depths of his overcoat. He remembered being assisted to the facilities by a well-upholstered and friendly redheaded barmaid. And then – nothing. Until he awoke two days later in the 'bridal suite' of a down-at-heel guest house in the vicinity of Gretna Green and became aware that he was not alone. A tousled head emerged next to him from the none-too-clean blankets, and a well-modulated if rather grating voice enquired, "Did you sleep well, Hector, m'dear?" Stravinsky had vanished. Vera had been arrested. And Father was married to Maureen McWhirter.

* * * * *

While Father was an only child with no close relatives other than the mysterious cousin, Mary McGuire, Maureen's family was extensive. However, her only sibling was our uncle Conan, her older brother. He was a great favourite with Leicester and me, a tall, dark-haired, handsome, laughing young man who visited us frequently. I gathered that Conan had led an adventurous life in his youth and had travelled the world in some capacity or other. His exciting stories fascinated us.

"Where else did you go, Uncle Conan?" we demanded to know, all ears.

He smiled. "Oh, I was all over – you name it, I was there."

"The moon?" I asked – I often thought Uncle Conan's stories were a little on the tall side.

"No, not yet. But I'm off there next week, pet." He never minded my little sarcasms. "But everywhere else. Zanzibar, Timbuktu, Tahiti, the islands…"

"Virgin or Caribbean?" I asked, ever pedantic.

"Well," – he hesitated – "let's just say I came back a Caribbean, shall we?"

1 Famous as a home-from-home for sailors on shore leave, where a warm welcome and an empty wallet were guaranteed

2 No doubt as risky in its very different way as the famous Highland 'Sword-dance'

He certainly spent some years in the Navy, and would proudly show us children his tattoos. The one on his left forearm read 'Johnny and Con forever', under a heart pierced by an arrow – no doubt in memory of some friends. And on his right biceps was a portrait of a sailor, who could be made to perform amusing contortions when he flexed his muscles. Conan would have been around thirty when we were growing up, but he would join in our games of make-believe like any other youngster. He was particularly attached to my brother Leicester, and many a time I would find them whispering and laughing together in a distant corner of the old chapel or the attics. Boys and their secrets! When we played hide-and-seek they would manage to elude me for hours. Such was the rambling nature of the Castle and grounds that there were innumerable hiding spots where one could be undisturbed, safely away from the watchful eyes of the adults.

Uncle Conan's relationship with his sister, my mother, always seemed rather unpredictable. On some occasions they could be found laughing together over some shared joke, rather as Leicester and I might. On others there appeared to be an indefinable, veiled antagonism between them. Conan would sometimes make light-hearted jokes about Mother and her behaviour, a habit that Leicester and I both found particularly amusing (and indeed, emulated). Mother, for her part, was generally dismissive of her brother, although from time to time I would catch her staring at him with a peculiar intensity and an expression that was almost regretful.

She and Father seemed to me to have an ideal marriage, in spite of its somewhat unorthodox beginnings. That is to say that they saw very little of each other. Mother was forever dashing off hither and yon to one engagement or another, elaborately gowned and coiffed, ever the belle of the ball. She unquestionably cut a striking figure, with her beautiful auburn hair and voluptuous curves. She was very popular with the local gentry, particularly the male element, and was never at a loss for an escort. The most regular was a certain Ronnie McKenzie. He and his wife Janet ran our little village shop cum post office, which was, among other things, the centre for local gossip. I didn't care much for Mr McKenzie. He had a reputation as a womaniser, and was rather too fond of the whisky bottle. Of course this shared interest only endeared him to Mother.

"After all," she would say, as she posed in the hall for us children in yet another stunning *ensemble*, "someone from this family has to show their face in public from time to time. Our social standing in the neighbourhood is important. My honour's at stake."

"Why bother fighting for a lost cause, eh?" gleefully whispered Leicester in my ear, as Mother headed off to yield to the night, and possibly to Mr McKenzie.

Father quite happily acquiesced in these arrangements. He had no interest at all in the 'social scene', preferring to spend the long summer evenings at home with us children and the servants.

The servants! – if this gives the impression that we were surrounded by a bevy of eager flunkies waiting on us hand and foot, nothing could be further from the truth. Our staff consisted of but four persons. In charge was Old Angus, who looked after the running of our household and waited on at table. His wife Eileen (always Mrs Angus to us children) was our cook and housekeeper, and young Jeannie Dunt, their niece, was officially our maid of all work. Jeannie was, apparently, supposed to clean, and help Eileen Angus with the heavier housework. But she never seemed to do very much.

The most important member of our staff, however, was our gardener, Alec McDougal. Important to us children, that is. Alec lived in a small, stone-built cottage in the grounds of the Castle, along with his son, the imaginatively named Dougal McDougal. Although Alec was a widower, he was a proud housekeeper, and his cottage was always immaculate, spotless and tidy. Leicester and I spent a lot of time there when we wanted to escape the rather stuffy atmosphere of the 'big hoose', as Alec referred to it. Mother would be off to some glittering social event or other, while Father was often shut up in the library for hours working on his latest composition, along with young Jeannie Dunt, who, it was explained to me, assisted him with his music in some mysterious fashion. We children were very sternly warned against disturbing the master at work, as you may imagine!

And so off we would trot to Alec's cottage, where we were always assured of a warm welcome. Alec adored children, but had only one of his own. Young Dougal was a short, stocky, and rather shy young man, four years my senior. He was generally pleasant and agreeable, but I occasionally wondered if he might have been 'drapped on his heid' in childhood, as his behaviour at the age of fourteen was frequently disconcerting. He appeared to have developed something of an attachment to me, and would follow me around with a dog-like devotion, playing 'tricks' to attract my attention; such as jumping out from behind a tree to startle me, or looming up out of an autumn mist when I least expected it. I couldn't help noticing, too, that he seemed to have constant problems with his clothing. On these occasions key items might well be missing, or at best, improperly adjusted.

"Gie us a hand, Eva, will ye? Ah can never get these buttons done up properly."

How often, among other things, did I have to re-tie his shoes!

Like his son, Alec was short and solidly built, but with a ready smile and a bright and cheerful personality. He was always delighted to see 'the weans', as he called us. He would have been, I suppose, in his forties, but he always had time for us children, no matter how busy his schedule of work. I loved to snuggle up on his comfortable lap in front of the roaring peat fire. And how privileged we felt if we were invited to visit his cellar, where he spent a lot of time attending to what he referred to as his 'laboratory'. Mysterious retorts and flasks bubbled and fumed, strange smells and vapours filled the air, and huge glass jars were filled with a mysterious liquid at the end of the process. When I asked him what the purpose of all this activity was, he told me he was in search of the Philosopher's Stone, that fabled material that would turn base metals into gold. An innocent child, I was naturally fascinated – would there be some gold for me when his researches finally bore fruit?

"Aye, hen – as much gold as ye want," smiled Alec. "In the meantime, if ye can get me some of yon empty McWhirter's whisky bottles fae the big hoose, that wid be a help. As mony as ye can find. And not a word tae yer mither, mind."

I was delighted to oblige him, and as Mother got through an considerable quantity of the family product, there was never a shortage of bottles. And there was always a penny for me to spend in the sweetie shop for every delivery.

Leicester too was roped into the bottle business. But somehow he managed to get tuppence or even threepence from Alec, after he had had a little private word with him – no doubt about some childish toy his heart was set on.

My older brother was in many respects an unusual boy. Though he was my elder by two years, he never resented my company, and as children we were virtually inseparable. Blessed with his good looks and an easy-going charm, he found no difficulty in threading his way unscathed through the manifold little hardships of childhood. It was always I who got the blame if we were caught in some youthful misdemeanour – he generally seemed to come out of these situations intact. It is true that I, even though I was the younger, tended to be the leader in our adventures and the more daring in my plans for our activities, so that was probably no more than just.

I remember him explaining to me what he called his 'philosophy'.

"Eva," he said, "there are just two things you need to remember in life. One, always find out what people want, and give it to them if you can. And two, always speak the truth whenever possible. That way you will get a reputation for honesty, so when you need to tell a lie, people will believe you."

Talk about an old head on young shoulders!

I was desolate when, sadly, our friend Alec was dismissed from our service a year or two later. I never found out the reason. Surprisingly, young Dougal, his son, was allowed to remain, and indeed took over his father's cottage and duties. When he was a little older,, at the age of seventeen, he became officially Mother's chauffeur; most of the time she was lacking either the authority or the ability to drive. Frequently both. She and Dougal certainly became very close after his father's departure.

Old Angus, the head of our staff, was a funny, fussy old character. He was considerably younger than my father, but while the latter was an upright and vigorous man, poor Old Angus always looked as though he was on his last legs and might not make it through the night. Ironically, he was to outlive Father by many years. He was devoted to the family, and both he and his wife, Mrs Angus, kept an eye on us children when our parents were otherwise occupied. Eileen Angus was the epitome of the flustered, ever busy housekeeper. Eternally, it seemed, up to her elbows in flour, plump and motherly, always perspiring slightly, she was a complete contrast to her husband. A sensible, down-to-earth kind of woman, she managed generally to keep her edgy, nervous spouse under control when events at Castle Hinge seemed about to overwhelm him.

Their son, Young Angus, one of my regular playmates, took over from his father when the latter reached retirement age, and he himself is now Old Angus. Sadly, there is not a further Young Angus to continue the tradition, as the current Old Angus was gassed during the second war, and proved unable or unwilling to procreate.

* * * * *

I could never warm to young Jeannie Dunt. She, as I have mentioned, was a niece of Old Angus, and our general maid. Short, plump, fair, and on the surface none too bright, she was careless of even the basics of personal hygiene, and was always dressed in what I considered an inappropriately provocative style. Although her overlarge bosom was virtually a deformity, she took every opportunity to display as much of it as possible. She also had what she referred to as a 'bad leg'. By this she meant that it sometimes pained her, not that it was inclined to occasional bouts of disobedience. She would hirple round the house, constantly complaining. I must confess to my shame that naughty Leicester and I sometimes made fun of her.

I remember, one wet afternoon, as Jeannie raised her voice in yet another litany of woe, Leicester asking her, "Jeannie, how much would you charge to haunt a house?" Jeannie replied, with a slightly hopeful expression on her bovine features, "Well, Ah'm no' sure – how many rooms?" On mature reflection, and knowing what I now know, I realise she was far from being as stupid as we thought she was.

She was always very respectful of Leicester, and referred to him as 'the young master'. Indeed, she flirted with him shamelessly in her habitual blatant fashion, tugging her grubby *fichu* an inch or two lower whenever he was around. Me, on the other hand, she treated with a disdain bordering on contempt. She was no doubt what they call 'a man's woman', considering other females to be of little account. She was to learn that she had made a serious error of judgment in my case.

In my early childhood, I couldn't understand what place Jeannie fulfilled in our domestic arrangements. However Father wouldn't hear a word against her, and explained to me when I was rather older that he had found a use for her as an amanuensis in his musical endeavours. In his later years, Father suffered badly from arthritis in his hands, for which he was prescribed special soothing powders, and he had somehow contrived to coach Jeannie in the basics of manuscript writing. He would dictate the names and value of his notes, and Jeannie, it seemed, had become adept at the arcane art of putting these down on paper. This, Father explained, had become her main function in our household.

Mother, too, seemed tolerant of Jeannie. "Well, it spares me the trouble," she said one day when I asked her, yet again, why Jeannie, who never appeared to do much work, was still with us.

But I gradually conceived a hearty dislike of the girl. Looking back, I can see that a quite unjustified jealousy was at the root of my feelings. As children do, I felt that she took up too much of my father's interest. Interest which I felt should have been centred on me.

I racked my brains. I schemed and planned. How could I arrange for Jeannie's dismissal? After all – she was hardly indispensable. Or was she? One had to remember she assisted Father with his music.

Very well – I would learn to do it and render her redundant.

When I make up my mind to something, I don't give up easily. And my plan for getting rid of Jeannie was put into effect promptly.

Secretly, I borrowed some books on the basics of music notation from Father's collection, and spent many, many hours burning the midnight oil in an attempt to master the rudiments. Surprisingly, I found that I seemed to understand almost instinctively what the authors were trying to clarify, and it wasn't long before the curious black marks, hooks and blobs began to make sense to me.

I waited until a Wednesday evening, Jeannie's night off. Father was in the library, orchestrating, when I crept in to see him. He had mysteriously been unable to find his cache of powders, and as a result, his arthritis was troubling him badly. He particularly hated the wearisome process of orchestration, as his poor hands constantly trembled and refused his wishes.

"Hello, Evie dear, it's kind of you to look in on your old dad," he smiled, as I entered the library.

A page slipped from his reluctant hand, and he said a very rude word.

He bent to retrieve it, but was unable to reach. "I'm sorry pet, sorry. But it looks like I'm going to have to leave this job till tomorrow when Jeannie is back. The old hands just won't cope with it, and it needs to be finished by Friday," he sighed, sitting up.

"Can I be of assistance, Father?" I asked timidly. "I might just be able to help with the easy bits."

Father gave his familiar rumbling laugh. "There are no easy bits in a Hector

Hinge composition, pet. And what do you know of music?"

"Father, I…"

He held up his hand,

"And before you say anything, dear, I know that's not your fault, it's mine." He shook his head in mock despair. "Shame on you, Hector Hinge! A daughter of yours unable to even read music, and at eight years of age!"

He patted my knee and winked at me. "Don't worry, Eva, I promise to take your musical education in hand as soon as I have a spare moment."

"Thank you, Father, oh, if only you would!" I hesitated. "But – might I just have a wee look?"

Father smiled indulgently as I picked up the paper he had dropped. "Of course, dear, of course," he chuckled, "but I doubt it will mean much to you".

"What is it you are working on?" I asked, as I scanned the page covered with his minuscule notation.

"It's a new piece for piano and orchestra, *Symphonic Variations on 'Annie Laurie'*. And variation two is giving me a deal of trouble. It looks right on paper. It just doesn't sound right in my head, if you know what I mean."

I took a deep breath. "Father – shouldn't that be a written E flat in the clarinet in A staff, fourth measure, second quaver? Sounding C natural, of course. The A clarinet sounds a minor third lower than written. You've put a D natural, as if you were writing for a B flat clarinet."

Yes, I had been working *very* hard!

"Eh? Let me see!"

I passed the sheet of manuscript back to him. He perused it for some moments, then removed his spectacles and raised his head.

"Yes, yes, you're right, of course it should. But how on earth…"

* * * * *

Jeannie was given notice ('her cards') a week later, and moved back to her parents' crumbling cottage in the nearby village. Unfortunately, we had not seen the last of each other. But for the moment all was well. Father soon claimed that he just couldn't manage without me, and we spent most evenings together merrily transforming his fleeting inspirations onto paper. True to his promise, he began my musical instruction. And the future course of my life was established.

Chapter Two
A Very Talented Young Lady

1928.

Dean Castle.

I was eight years old when everything changed. Although I adored music, and was naturally surrounded by it in my formative years, I had never considered that it might come to be the centre and focus of my life. As father had promised, I was to be thoroughly educated in all its aspects, and every day brought new and delightful discoveries. I was sent to piano lessons, and although I was already able to pick out the more popular pieces by Chopin and Liszt fairly accurately just using my ear, I had to learn that fingers and eyes were more important than ears when it came to the piano. This meant unlearning and relearning, losing all my old bad habits, and virtually starting again from scratch.

I threw myself into this new and exciting world with all the concentration and application of which I was capable. There appeared to be no question that I had an unusual natural facility, but as Father maintained, these gifts needed to be harnessed and refined before I might consider myself to be even an apprentice musician.

I took my first piano lessons with our local teacher, a delightful lady by the name of Miss Euphemia (Effie) Burns. It must be said that dear old Effie was not what one might call a natural musician. But she was strict and pedantic – indeed, something of a martinet – and Father considered that the kind of straight-jacketing she would provide was just what was required at this stage. Father himself had been something of a virtuoso on the piano in his earlier life, but, alas, his infirmities prevented him from undertaking this part of my training himself. Effie would provide the basic physical mechanics, while he, Father, would undertake the even more vital mental and emotional preparation necessary.

I attended lessons with Effie three times a week. Dear old soul, I can see her now, sitting at my side, as I struggled manfully through Liszt's tricky *La Campanella* for the first time – her eternal cigarette firmly clamped between her large front teeth, the blue smoke curling up to the ceiling – her air of intense concentration – her pompadour of white hair stained a distinctive yellow at the front – her eye patch giving her a slightly piratical look. All this is as clear to my mind's eye as if it had happened yesterday.

Effie favoured an 'artistic' mode of dress. Floating draperies were the order of the day, combined with heavy, clanking, barbaric necklaces, the whole topped off by green leather sandals. When occasionally she added to her ensemble a saucy tricorne hat perched on the crown of her head, she looked like a cross between Isadora Duncan and Captain Hook.

She was a great enthusiast of my Father's music, and would occasionally, as a special treat for me, play through one or two of his simpler piano pieces. She had little or no idea of the correct style, but her enthusiasm and her manifest love of playing shone through the numerous wrong notes and misreadings.

After our lesson, her companion, Miss Hodgetts, 'Topsy' to Miss Burns, but always 'Miss Hodgetts' to me, would bring in the tea trolley and we three ladies would gorge on Effie's delicious scones and home-made rock cakes. Short and stout, Miss Hodgetts featured jodhpurs and riding boots extensively, and often carried a smart little gold-topped crop – she was a much-admired horsewoman in Ayrshire, and Master of our local hunt. A jolly, back-slapping character, bluff and hearty compared to the somewhat neurasthenic and wilting Effie, she would roar with laughter at some of my childish remarks, and tell me it was high time I got rid of my little pony, Nelly, a present from Father, and learned to 'clamp my thighs round a sturdy stallion.'

"Don't worry, Evadne, you're a tall, flexible lassie, you won't damage anything vital. After all" – with a wink in my direction – "I've never yet damaged anything, myself!" And off she would go again into gales of uncontrollable laughter.

Effie and Topsy, slightly eccentric as they appeared, were from time to time the target of unkind, mocking remarks from the local children. But Miss Hodgetts was always ready with a withering reply when it was needed.

I remember an occasion when cheeky Alison McKenzie, the daughter of Janet and Ronnie, who ran the village shop, dared to venture an opinion. As a top-hatted Miss Hodgetts passed her, leading Sabre, her favourite stallion, to the water trough, the little brat called out, "Hey, Missis – are you a man or a woman?"

Topsy, turning and looking her up and down disdainfully, replied after a brief pause, "Well, dear, let me put it this way. I'm more of a woman than you'll ever be – and more of a man than you'll ever get."

* * * * *

Father's part in my 'musicalisation' was more intellectual than physical. Firstly, he ensured I was completely familiarised with all the classics. Gramophone records were bought by the dozen, and the library rang to the strains of Beethoven, Mozart and Schubert. Such works as were not available in recorded form Father would himself play on the piano, forcing his poor fingers into the intricacies of Mahler and Wagner just so that I would continue to learn. I'm afraid that he went through a great many of his powders simply in order to continue my enlightenment.

The exact nature of these was something of a mystery. I know he obtained them from our local chemist, Aloysius Jones and Son, but they arrived in twists of brown paper, with no helpful label such as *Askit* or *Seidlitz* to identify them. In later years, alas, they proved no longer efficacious, and Father was compelled to move onto injections of a more stimulating and bracing sort. I quickly learned how to administer these for him, and it soon became just another part of our daily ritual. By great good fortune, Father, despite the arthritic agonies he endured, never showed any outward sign of his problem. Indeed, his white hands and long fingers remained smooth and unmarked by swellings or knots until the day he died.

We listened and we talked. Or, more correctly, I listened, and he talked. This was as it should be – he was the master and I the pupil. I was happy to interject the occasional comment or question at appropriate moments, but otherwise to remain silent. This ability to 'keep my own counsel' has remained with me, and was to prove useful in later years. And Father always considered that the little I did say was to the point, and showed an intelligent understanding of the matter in hand. This, too, is a characteristic I hope I have retained.

And what was the subject of all this talk? Why, music – orchestral, vocal, choral, chamber, instrumental, balletic, operatic.

I was always particularly drawn to opera as an art form. Opera, that 'irrational and exotic entertainment', fascinated me. Fortunately, Father too had a penchant for the opera, or musical drama as he preferred to call it. Many of his greatest works were destined for the stage. The ability of the human voice to express emotion and mood seems to me to be second to none, and the trained operatic voice, be it soprano or basso, to be the ideal vehicle for the transmission of those intangibles. This, at any rate, is my view, and one that my Father shared.

Of course, all work and no play... Please don't imagine that this intensive training prevented me from enjoying the usual childish pursuits. If the sun were shining (as it usually was, or seemed to be, at that happy time) it was not unusual for Father to say, "Come along, Evie, enough for one day, go and see what your brother's up to – some mischief, I've no doubt. Run along and make sure he doesn't get himself into any bother."

And off I would caper, glad to be released for the balance of the day, but with my head still full of the matter of our latest lessons. Perhaps I would wave to Young Angus in the kitchen on my way out, and steal a piece of his mother's delicious shortbread in passing.

The castle grounds were wilderness in some areas and manicured beauty in others. The building itself was a hodgepodge of architectural styles, relics of the mediaeval period cheek by jowl with square Georgian and ponderous Victorian. Outbuildings of all sorts included stables, greenhouses, barns, and even a small and lovely chapel. If I wanted to find my brother I had to search through the grounds and check one after the other his favourite spots.

On one particular rare leisure afternoon, I recall, I found Leicester in the company of Dougal McDougal, for want of any alternative. I suppose I was about ten years old, and Leicester twelve. I'm afraid that Leicester and I had generally very little time for Dougal, and as soon as I arrived, my brother and I would be off and away to play together somewhere else. What a thoughtless, selfish pair we sometimes were, as children of that age can be! Poor Dougal would trail along behind, hoping for some attention, particularly from myself. And I am almost embarrassed to admit that, as we did with Jeannie, we sometimes played unkind tricks on him.

On this occasion, an irritated Leicester, bored with Dougal's company, told him that, if he wanted to belong to our 'gang', he would have to submit to a series of initiation tests. "We've both done them", he insisted, "and so has Young Angus." This was quick thinking, as Dougal at fourteen was a timid and wary young man. My brother obviously had a plan in mind, and so I left it to Leicester's undoubted inventiveness to explain – I was certain that he would come up with some task that Dougal was simply unable or unwilling to fulfil. The boys disappeared off to a distant corner of the grounds and were gone for some considerable time.

When they eventually returned, Dougal was looking rather queasy, and Leicester had a grim, bemused expression on his face. "It's no good, Eva," he muttered. "He managed to do everything I suggested. We'll never get rid of him now!"

"What did you try?" I asked quietly.

"Just the usual things," said Leicester. "With a couple of wee variations because the grass was wet." He heaved a sigh. "Now how do we get out of this?"

"Wait a minute," I whispered, "Let me have a go."

Leicester shrugged and looked off into the distance.

I turned to Dougal, who was by now looking considerably more cheerful.

"Now, there's just one final test, Dougie, and it's an easy one. Here's what you have to do. You have to gather some stinging nettles, quite a handful, and put them down your trousers. Then you have to leave them there for – er – three days."

I was improvising.

"Och no," he said, shaking his head and backing away, "Ah'll get ma hauns aw stung."

"Not at all," said I, drawing my rubber gloves from my skirt pocket. "You can use these."

"That'll never work," sighed Leicester in my ear.

I smiled smugly to myself. He was unaware, or so I believed, that Dougal was generally *sans* underwear.

Dougal donned the gloves, and cautiously proceeded to gather a fair quantity of the nettles that grew abundantly around us. Imagine my astonishment when he then phlegmatically poked them down the front of his trousers with no sign whatever of discomfort.

"Ah'll leave them there for a week, if ye like, they feel quite, er, quite nice," he grinned happily. "So now Ah'm a member of the gang, is that right?"

"Er – yes," I answered weakly, while Leicester frowned in the background.

"I just don't understand it," I said to my brother as we returned home later. "He *never* wears underwear!"

"No, I know," sulked Leicester. "But after I'd initiated him, what with one thing and another, I had to loan him mine."

* * * * *

1930.

Dean Castle.

It was about two years after I started lessons with Miss Burns that she approached my father with some news. She would be unable to continue my piano tuition.

"Really? That's sad news, Effie. So – in your opinion, the lassie has no talent?"

She shook her head vigorously. "No, no, not at all, on the contrary, Hector. She is a *very* talented young lady. If she works at it, she will go far. But there's simply no further I myself can take her. She needs a more advanced teacher, someone who will stretch her. But she's good, very good. I hate the expression, of course, but you might even describe her as something of a child prodigy."

"Really, Effie?" said father, raising his eyebrows. "That good, eh? You *do* surprise me."

"Oh yes, yes. But as you know, Hector, *that* is a dangerous road to go down. Now in my opinion, she should continue her studies a while longer, and then think of a music degree at one of the better Universities."

This seemed a somewhat remote possibility, as I was but ten at the time,

"Lang Hall is the place for her," continued Effie, "my own alma mater. They take them young there. Of course, the final decision is up to you, Hector."

Lang Hall! I had of course heard of the fabled seat of learning in the far north-east, but to think that I, little Evadne Hinge, might be awarded a place there was something I had never dared to imagine.

* * * * *

The matter formed the main topic of conversation at dinner that evening. Lobster bisque was the *entrée*, one of my favourites. Mother, only occasionally *chez nous* for a meal, was rocking Lavinia on her knee, and was entranced by the thought of a child prodigy in the family. She laid aside her own spoon, and took up a fork.

"Think of it, Hector! – What an experience for a young lassie!" she breathed, eyes shining, as she poked a forkful of something disgusting in the general direction of Lavinia's mouth. "Travelling the world with her mother on hand to keep an eye on her… picture it… concerts, parties, social invitations… possibly even a suitable husband eventually. Think of the profits, the glory, the fame. Oh yes, that's just the kind of future I've dreamed of for my wee girl!"

This was worrying. I was not Mother's 'wee girl' on many occasions.

Father smiled indulgently, shaking his head. "Maureen, the child is ten years old. Ten years old! Far too young for that sort of a life."

Mother came back smartly. "And how old was Mozart when he started performing in public? Six!"

She had obviously been doing a bit of homework.

Once again, Father shook his head. "Yes, Maureen, and look how he ended up – dead at thirty five and buried in a pauper's grave. And Evie, talented though she may be, is no Mozart. No, let us hear no more about it. She will continue her studies for another two years as Effie suggests, and then we will apply to the faculty at Lang Hall to see if she has reached the necessary standard."

Leicester too, between slurps, had an opinion.

"Yes, much more sensible, that's what I would suggest myself."

But Mother was unstoppable. "Shut up Leicester, this has nothing to do with you. And stop making that disgusting noise, please. As I was saying, Hector…"

Father raised his hand to silence her.

"That's enough, Maureen." He continued in a more reasonable tone. "It's a possibility, nothing more, that she may give one wee concert just to get her accustomed to public performance. But that's all – no nationwide tours, no international reputation, no nothing. For now."

Mother did not enjoy being balked. She turned up the dial by several notches.

"You mark my words, Hector Hinge; you are making a big mistake.

That child could earn a fortune in a couple of years, and all you want her to do is to study and study, then go off to University, study some more, and end up even more full of her own importance than she already is."

No-one seemed to be interested in my opinion, or even to consider that I might have one.

"God, what an idiot you are, mother," muttered Leicester into his soup.

"I heard that Leicester!" said Father sharply. "If you can't be civil to your mother you can go to your room."

He turned to Mother. "Calm yourself, Maureen, what you said just now is unjust. You couldn't find a more level-headed child than our Evie. And that's the way it's going to stay. I will not have her life ruined by premature exposure. I've made my mind up, so there's no point in you going on and on about it."

Mother was if anything more menacing at lower volume. After rising to her feet for her parting shot, delivered *sotto voce* and in the *basso profondo* register, – "Hector, you have not heard the last of this!" – she swept from the room majestically, and dropped Lavinia on the hard wooden floor in the process.

Father shouted after her amid Lavinia's shrieks, "We will have no infant prodigies in this family, Maureen! And that is my final word!"

He crashed his fist on the table in punctuation. Unfortunately, Old Angus had just laid a platter of *fruits de mer* before him, and a Vesuvian eruption of scallops and mussels ascended into the air. Father was unharmed, but the claw of a rock lobster caught Old Angus under the chin, and he was laid up for a week with blood poisoning.

* * * * *

It was about a week later that Father and I had a very important conversation.

"Now – have I got a surprise for you, Miss Hinge? Guess who your new piano teacher is going to be?"

"Oh, I don't know. Rubinstein? Paderewski?" I was only half joking – Father knew everyone in the musical world of the day.

"No, no dear – you don't want any of these foreigners. No, it's a good, reliable Englishwoman for you. Myra!"

"Myra?"

The only Myra I could think of was Myra 'The Electric Eye' Dennis, as Leicester and I had named her. She was a songstress and comedienne our family had seen at Barfields Pavilion in the seaside resort of Largs during our last summer holiday. Myra might, we had felt, have gone far, were it not for a particularly unfortunate 'lazy eye'. However, as far as I was aware, she didn't teach piano.

"Yes, pet, Myra – Myra Hess!"[1]

"Hess? Isn't that German?"

Father ignored this.

"She's coming up to the Castle for a few days. You will play for her, and if she likes you and thinks you have ability, she may consider taking you as a pupil."

I must confess that at this time the name of Myra Hess was unknown to me – a situation which was about to change.

Father went over to the record cabinet and took out one of the heavy 78 rpm records of which we had an extensive collection.

"Have a listen to this, pet," he said as he crossed to the gramophone, "and see what you think."

All at once the heavenly strains of Myra's famous recording of her own arrangement of Bach's *Jesu, joy of man's desiring* filled the room.

"So what do you think, Evie?" Father asked as the music came to a close.

I was entranced. The deep legato, the even tone and balance of lines, above all, the sheer musicality of the performance, had me captivated.

"Oh yes," I breathed. "*that* is how I want to play."

Father smiled gently. "Aye – as I'm always telling you – Father knows best."

* * * * *

Myra (Miss Hess to me, naturally) arrived at the Castle in September 1930, having taken some time out from her busy schedule to oblige Father. Naturally, I was terrified. I was not confident that I had reached a sufficiently high standard to interest such a renowned figure.

We were introduced just before dinner, and I could hardly manage a morsel, such was the state of my nervous anticipation. Miss Hess turned out to be a lovely brunette, with exquisite manners, and what seemed to me to be a very refined style of speaking. Of course, that was because up to that point I had hardly ever heard an English accent. I resolved that, if by any chance I was favoured, I too would learn to speak like that. I noticed that even Mother's vowels seemed to acquire an unusual clipped sharpness when in conversation with the great lady.

1 Myra Hess was an already established concert pianist by 1930. As popular in the United States as in Britain, she would go on to be awarded the DBE for her sterling work giving lunchtime concerts during the war years, when all concert halls were blacked out in the evening during the blitz.

I remember very little of my audition. Apparently I warmed up with a couple of Chopin *Études* and then started on Liszt's *Mazeppa*. I was only a couple of pages into the latter when Myra interrupted:

"Yes, yes, that's how it should go – very good. Stop, stop dear, I don't need to hear any more."

She turned to Father, eyes shining.

"Hector, you were right. The girl is good. Very good. Still rough round the edges in places, occasionally a little too much enthusiasm at the expense of accuracy, but what musicality! And what big hands! Double octaves, tenths…" She addressed me over her shoulder. "Do you play anything else dear?"

"Well," I answered shyly, turning round on the piano stool, "I have some Beethoven or Prokofiev here." Uncle Sergei had written a tricky little Scherzo just for me.

"No, no, dear. I meant, do you play any other instrument? Or maybe you sing?"

"No Myra, she doesn't sing," Father interjected hastily. "But her brother Leicester…"

Simultaneously, "My little Lavinia has a lovely voice, perhaps I could…" offered Mother.

"Hush Hector, Maureen, please. Let the girlie speak for herself."

Heavens! No-one ever told Father to hush. But amazingly, he did.

"Well, Evadne?" continued Miss Hess.

"I do" – I cleared my throat – "I do play the banjo a bit."

"The banjo?" chorused Father and Miss Hess *ensemble*

"What's a banjo?" Mother wondered.

I hastened to clarify. "Well, yes Father. I've been teaching myself. It's so much easier to carry around than a piano."

"But I *adore* the banjo," enthused Miss Hess. "So ethnic! Come, child, let's have some jolly banjo music."

I retrieved my beloved tenor banjo from the cupboard under the stairs, and the evening ended riotously. Miss Hess accompanied me on the piano, Father joined in with his bagpipes, and Leicester led the singing in endless choruses of *The Camptown Races* and *Polly-Wolly-Doodle*. Even Mother clapped a bit, slightly out of time, and actually managed a smile once or twice.

When bedtime rolled around, I enunciated very carefully in what I considered to be a 'refined' accent, "Good night. And thank you so much for hearing me, Miss Hess."

"Call me Myra, child," said my new teacher. "We're going to have *such* fun!"

* * * * *

1932.

Dean Castle.

My real piano training began then. My two years of lessons with Myra changed me from a talented child into a pianist. It was she, too, who taught me the art of accompaniment.

"You must learn to subdue yourself, if you are accompanying a singer or another musician. That is, you must still maintain your individuality, but it has to blend with that of your colleague."

Myra's busy schedule of concert engagements meant that there were often periods of a week or two when I did not see her. Sometimes I travelled a considerable distance to meet up with her for a lesson. And occasionally she would have a month off from touring and come and stay with our family, during which time it was lessons every day.

The time flew, and it was on my twelfth birthday that Father summoned me to the library.

"Well, Evie, the time has come…"

He appeared to lose his thread for a moment. I wondered if he had had his injection.

"Hm, yes, yes, indeed, the time has come…"

He seemed to be wandering somewhat. I prompted gently, "The time, Father?"

"A quarter past seven, seven-fifteen according to the clock. PM. Happy birthday."

We had already celebrated my birthday at lunchtime. Father seemed to have forgotten.

"Time for your injection, Father, then, I think."

"Yes, no doubt, no doubt it is. What injection's that, pet?"

I was slightly concerned about Father. This was not the first time I had found him to be in a vague and disconnected condition. It crossed my mind (not a long journey, some might say) that perhaps the amount of self-medication he indulged in was having a deleterious effect.

After I assisted him with his treatment, he appeared to regain his composure.

"I have written to Professor Harris, the Dean of Music Studies at Lang Hall, and informed her that we wish to apply for a place there for you. She seems interested – she knows me well by reputation, of course – and suggests that I organise a public concert. I will arrange this. It will probably be in Glasgow. The

SO[1] owes me a favour or two. I shall conduct, naturally, and you must think of your repertoire."

I was horrified at the thought. "But Father – I've never performed with an orchestra before. I won't know what to do – it's too soon!"

Father smiled reassuringly, and shook his head. "Not at all, not at all. There's nothing to it. Just let them know from the start that you are the boss, and it will all go off perfectly. And don't forget, you'll have your old dad next to you on the podium. I will make sure nothing goes wrong."

Somewhat reassured, I said, "But what shall I play?"

He shrugged. "Whatever you like, pet – you're the star of the show. Just let me know what you choose, and I will arrange to get the parts and all the rest."

I considered. "Father," I said hesitantly, "might I be allowed to play your *Annie Laurie Variations*?"

"Really?" Father rumbled. "You want to play that old thing? Of course, it has its moments, but, frankly, it's not one of my best."

I could tell he was moved. The *Variations* had never received a public performance up till then.

"Yes, Father, please say yes. Think of it – a world première."

His eyes lit up. "And why not? – Father and daughter face the world and the critics together. Yes, yes – let's do it! But you will need something else as well – how about the Liszt first concerto? One of my old teacher's best. The plebs will enjoy that one."

That famously difficult *cheval de bataille* held no terrors for me after two years of Myra's iron discipline.

"Good choice, Father," I replied.

It did my heart good to see Father's mounting enthusiasm. He got to his feet.

"Yes, yes. And I will fill out the programme with a couple of lighter orchestral pieces. You should run through my arrangement of *The Flight of the Bumble-Bee*, too, just in case you need an encore."

He stretched out his arms and we hugged each other.

"Now – let's get started, Evie – no time to waste."

It had been some time since I had seen Father so excited. A fugitive unease passed over me when I recalled his earlier confusion. But I swept my momentary doubts to one side. With our heads together, we began to lay the plans for my forthcoming debut.

---

1 The Scottish Orchestra from 1891, later the Scottish National Orchestra, today the Royal Scottish National Orchestra.

* * * * *

If there was ever any chance of me getting a 'swollen head' with all this attention, Leicester, now a young man of fourteen, soon punctured that possibility.

"All this fuss… You're nothing out of the ordinary, Evadne, you know. Fair enough, you play nicely, but I hope you don't think you're anything special," he said, as he examined his nails moodily.

Evadne? "No, of course I don't, Leicester."

What was wrong, I wondered? Leicester was never short or snappy with me as a rule. I wondered if my dear brother was slightly jealous? – he rarely used my full name – and I hastened to reassure him.

"I'm just pleased that Father thinks that there might be something I'm good at. I'm sure he has plans for you too. I've always thought you could be a singer – you have a wonderful voice. And Father would be thrilled to have *two* musicians in the family. Wouldn't you like that? "

He shook his head doubtfully. "I don't think so." He wrinkled his nose. "Never tell him, but I'm not really all that keen on music. Not as a career, anyway. I don't know what I want, really."

He sighed. And after a moment added, "I suppose what I would like to do more than anything is to travel and, you know, see the world."

As I placed an affectionate arm round Leicester's shoulder, I realised I was almost as tall as him.

"Well then that's what you must do, Leicester. I'm sure Father wouldn't object, so long as it's what you really want. When you're older, of course."

"Maybe," Leicester replied uncertainly. "I'm not so sure, myself. The old boy's been a bit off with me recently, don't know why. And travelling is all very well for fun – but what could I *do*?"

I smiled at his obstinacy. "Where's your imagination, Leicester? Study at a University abroad, perhaps? Join an archaeological expedition to the Amazon, if you like. Have an adventure."

Then an idea struck me.

"You should have a chat with Uncle Conan, you know – he's told you what he did when he was eighteen, hasn't he? He entered the Navy."

"Yes, and vice versa," my brother chuckled enigmatically.

Ignoring this, I warmed to my theme. "And of course, if you *did* decide to follow his example, he could give you all sorts of tips. What qualifications you might need, that sort of thing."

His eyes lit up. "Yes, that's an idea. Good thinking, Eva, I'll have a chat to

Conan next time he's here."

My brother was obviously feeling better. I gave his shoulder a quick squeeze.

"And," I added, "I'll have a wee word with Father, and see what he thinks of the idea."

He nodded. "Yes, he will take it better from you. After all, Professor Hinge, you're the golden girl these days."

"Now Leicester, don't start all that again…"

* * * * *

Father's reaction was a little surprising.

"No, I don't think so, dear. Not at the moment. I would hope for something better for Leicester. He's got talent and brains, that boy. But… I just hope I've misread the signs, that he's not… Well, never mind that for now. Let him finish his education first and then we'll see. When that's done, he can travel as much as he wants."

"But father…"

Seeing my look of chagrin, he continued, "Of course, it's that uncle of his who's put all this stuff in his head. They spend far too much time together, in my opinion. And your uncle Conan has always been a bit – well – odd. Strange ideas…"

I acquiesced. "Very well, Father. But I wish you would think of something for Leicester to do. He's not himself these days. And he will need to have a career too."

"Plenty of time for that, pet, plenty of time."

My brother was starting to go through what is generally referred to, I believe, as 'the awkward stage'. Mature for his fourteen years, he had virtually given up our childhood pursuits, and now spent a lot of his time with a group of rowdy older children from the village. I, of course, was taken up day and night with my music, but it saddened me to think that my brother and I seemed to be growing apart. Looking back, and in the light of subsequent events, how I wish I had spent more time with him and tried to find out what was troubling him. And what, if anything, I could do to help.

I remember a visit we made to the home of my maternal grandparents, Maxwell and Alma. They so enjoyed having us children to stay for a few days; and we were thoroughly spoilt by them and indulged in ways we never would have been at home.

Whisky tycoon Grandpa Max McWhirter was, in public, a bluff, hard-headed, no-nonsense sort of man. But he was a different person where his grand-children were concerned. Usually out all day tending to the affairs of the family business, he would arrive home in the evening anxious to see what we had all been up to. Eight-year-old Lavinia, who was present on this visit, adored him, and there is no question that he had a soft spot for her. My younger sister had ceased to be just an irritating little brat, I noticed, and seemed to have developed into a level-headed and sensible child. She idolised our brother Leicester, and had obviously realised that I was no threat to her position in Mother's affections. To me, at least until recently, she had been no more than a rather grating noise in the background. But one particular remark of hers made me think again.

"Lavinia, stop chewing your nails please," I said, during the car journey to my grandparents' house. "You know Mother hates it."

"Oh yes, I know. That's why I do it. I don't really like the taste, but I know it annoys her. Then she forgets about other things, which is useful."

'*Well,*' I thought. '*This is actually a person. How interesting.*'

Grandpa Max had been something of a writer in his younger days, and still maintained a large library of works of esoteric literature. Mother claimed he had once been a member of the 'Golden Dawn'[1], and a friend of Aleister Crowley[2], but I fear she was prone to exaggeration. I do remember that we children were very curious about the contents of a certain locked cabinet in the library, but were never permitted to open it.

His wife, Grandma Alma, was a highly unusual person. I gathered that she had had some sort of religious epiphany in earlier years, and now part of her creed was that she must never leave her bed before five in the afternoon, and that prior to that time she must never be disturbed or exposed to daylight. Leicester, who had recently read Mr Stoker's *Dracula*, would try to scare me by claiming our grandmother was a vampire.

"Oh yes, Eva. Every night she prowls the streets of High Burnside in search of victims; in a low-cut gown, a blazing ruby clenched between her breasts, seductive and smiling."

He looked at me, trying to gauge the effect of his invention.

"But underneath that lovely exterior she is cold and avid, hungering to plunge her fangs into the neck of a hapless innocent."

Her fangs? Grandma Alma wore rather ill-fitting false teeth. She only rarely bothered to fix them in properly, and when she gabbled through grace before

1 The Hermetic Order of the Golden Dawn - A magic order active in Great Britain in the late 19th and early 20th centuries

2 English occultist and mystic, known as The Great Beast 666, and founder of the Abbey of Thelema

dinner it sounded like a castanet recital. As for the seductive low-cut gown and the blazing ruby – he must have read that somewhere. My brother had a very commonplace taste in literature.

I smiled disparagingly. “Really, Leicester?”

He nodded vigorously. “Oh yes, Eva. And every day she is compelled to shun the daylight, and sleep in a coffin on a bed of her native soil, brought at huge expense from distant shores.”

Since I knew perfectly well that Grandma Alma was from East Kilbride, this seemed a rather remote possibility.

Areas of the house were festooned with religious icons and paintings. Some of these were of a rather unpleasant nature, showing unnecessarily detailed illustrations of martyrdoms and the like, and the hall table always bore a sheaf of religious leaflets of one sort or another. Mother had told me that, when she herself was growing up, Alma’s religious mania was at its height. Apparently, that was one of the reasons she, Mother, left home at an early age. I later discovered this was not entirely true. There were other reasons for her departure, unconnected with religion.

My grandmother’s mood seemed to vary unpredictably. One day, she would be given to oracular pronouncements, declaiming passages from the gorier pages of the Old Testament in sepulchral tones. There would be much talk of slaying and smiting, angels with fiery swords and the like. But on other occasions, Alma was just like anyone’s cosy grandma. I remember how she taught Leicester and me to play poker, a game of which Father heartily disapproved. Fortunately, he never found out.

* * * * *

Leicester seemed to be less moody and awkward when removed from the pernicious influence of the crowd he now went around with. Indeed, he was much more like the brother I knew and loved. I decided, therefore, that this might be a good time to have a little heart-to-heart chat with him.

With this in mind, after I had made sure that Lavinia was tucked up comfortably with her favourite teddy, I waited until the house was dark, and crept silently from my bed. I passed along the gloomy corridor and headed towards Leicester’s bedroom. However, on arriving there, I was aware of a murmuring from behind his closed door. At first I thought perhaps he was talking in his sleep, or possibly just saying his prayers, but I gradually recognised the voice of Uncle Conan. I remembered Leicester mentioning that he planned to quiz our uncle on the possibilities of a career in the Navy. I wouldn’t disturb them, I thought, and moved into the shelter of a convenient alcove, out of earshot, to wait.

I had nearly nodded off by the time Uncle Conan emerged and turned off towards his own room. When he was out of sight, I tapped softly on Leicester's door.

"Oh, enough, enough! What now?" my brother sighed. "Go back to bed, I'm busy."

"It's me, Leicester," I whispered, "just wanted to say goodnight."

I opened the door softly, and entered.

The room was in darkness, and at first I couldn't make out where my brother was. Until I realised that the naughty boy was doing something under his bedclothes. I could discern the faint light of a torch.

"Got you," I laughed, as I whipped back the covers. I saw he had been perusing something entitled *Eves Without Leaves*, no doubt one of Grandma Alma's religious tracts. I was relieved to see that he was reading some improving literature instead of his usual comics.

"You shouldn't be doing that under the bedclothes, Leicester," I said wagging my finger roguishly, "you'll go blind."

"Don't worry, Eva," he smiled, "I'll stop when I need glasses. What did you want, anyway?"

I explained that I had felt restless and unable to sleep, and had hoped that he and I might share one of the regular little chats which we used to so enjoy. I was rather disheartened when my brother seemed less than interested.

"What could we have to talk about at this time of night, Eva?" He frowned. "After all – you're just a child."

This was indeed a new and strange Leicester. A little hurt and embarrassed, feeling rejected, I headed towards the door. But realising he had upset me, he called me back to apologise.

"I'm sorry, Eva, really. I didn't mean it. I've got things on my mind. Forgive me?"

"Of course I do, Leicester. I only wanted to help."

"I know you did, Eva. But there are some matters I need to think through myself – you understand?"

Not sure I did, but realising he needed to be alone, "Yes, of course," I said.

"Good." He smiled at me in the old familiar way. "And now, Professor Hinge, be off with you. And if you're having a problem getting to sleep, and want something interesting to read, have a look at this. You might learn a thing or two."

He picked up a weighty tome from beside his bed and turned it towards me. I glanced at the cover – *The Sexual Life of the Savages.*

"No thank you, Leicester." I couldn't conceal a yawn. "You know anthropology has never particularly interested me. See you in the morning then. Good night."

"G'night Eva."

I was disappointed, naturally, that Leicester hadn't wanted to hear what I had to say, but consoled myself with the thought that at least he was studying and not just wasting his time.

"Boys!" I muttered to myself contemptuously.

And I of course had other things to occupy my attention. My concert debut would take place in just one week's time.

Chapter Three

The Best of Times

'Glasgow Herald', Saturday August 27th, 1932

REMARKABLE DEBUT BY YOUNG SCOTS PIANIST

It was your correspondent's pleasure to attend the first public performance, on Friday evening, by young Evadne Hinge, a 12-year-old local girl. Evadne is the daughter of Scotland's premier composer, Hector Hinge, who conducted the Scottish Orchestra on the occasion of his daughter's debut. The concert was sponsored by 'McWhirter's Fine Old Scottish Whiskies', and a surprising amount of this beverage was in evidence not only in the bar, but in the auditorium.

A packed crowd thronged the St Andrew's Halls for the event. A tall, willowy brunette, Miss Hinge appeared somewhat nervous on her arrival on the platform, but seemed to gather confidence when she was accorded a rousing welcome by the audience. Rumours of a paid claque having been employed, are, we are sure, entirely without foundation.

The young pianist launched into her first piece, Liszt's popular Piano Concerto in E flat. It was a surprisingly mature interpretation considering her years, combining delicacy with a remarkable bravura. The orchestra, under her father's guidance, accompanied her to perfection, and a positive storm of applause greeted the cascade of double octaves which concluded the final movement. Miss Hinge was recalled several times. The first half of the concert ended with Sousa's well-known march, 'The Liberty Bell'.

After the intermission, the young star of the evening reappeared, this time to give the world première of a work composed specially for her by her father, the 'Annie Laurie' Variations for Piano and Orchestra. If the general style of the work was somewhat faded and old-fashioned – it could conceivably have been written at the turn of the century – Miss Hinge's sterling advocacy and her utter conviction gave the piece a remarkable appeal. The finale, culminating in a coda of pulverising virtuosity, brought the audience to its feet. We hear that Mr Fats Waller[1]*, who was in the audience, is considering recording the piece.*

1 Fats Waller – noted American jazz pianist and composer, dubbed 'the black Horowitz'. He toured Europe regularly in the 1930s.

The applause for the young virtuoso, who is a pupil of Myra Hess, was happily shared by Miss Hinge with her father, both of them visibly moved by the reception. It is a long time since your critic has enjoyed an evening of music so much. The whisky was good, too.

The 'Daily Record' was more succinct:

'Daily Record', Saturday August 27th, 1932

NICE EVENING

Nice music. The wee lassie played nicely, I thought. An apology for this brevity, but your reviewer is a little under the weather. Something he ate, no doubt. Not nice.

All in all it was a great success. It is true that I was horribly nervous at first, but Father's comforting presence and the manifest good will of the audience soon reassured me. The mention of a rumoured *claque*, that is, a section of the audience paid to applaud, baffles me. Certainly, Grandma McWhirter had ensured that all our friends and family were present under threat of being disinherited, and of course she was anxious to 'oil the wheels' as much as possible, but surely such behaviour is hardly unusual?

I was particularly gratified that Father had shared in this success. Now 73 years of age, his health was beginning to decline, and this was in fact the last occasion on which he would appear on a public platform.

What he had kept from me, however, was the information that the entire faculty of Lang Hall University had been invited to be present at the concert. This was the 'ordeal by fire' which would decide whether or not I was to be considered for admission to its exclusive and limited band of scholars.

Lang Hall! Who remembers it now? Its reputation at that time was second to none, but this seems to have disappeared under engulfing waves of oblivion, just as the waves of the unforgiving North Sea would sweep away the university itself in a few short years. Situated on the north east coast of Scotland between Fraserburgh and Lossiemouth, the original grey granite buildings were on a jutting promontory not far from the little town of Portknockie. A cold and desolate spot in winter, it is often surprisingly lovely in the summer months.

As an educational establishment, Lang Hall barely fitted into any of the accepted categories, even within the idiosyncratic education system of Scotland. Designed from the outset to favour the arts, in the two hundred years since its foundation it had come to restrict its intake to those wishing to graduate in painting, sculpture, dance and all branches of music. Additionally, it allowed pupils to commence their studies from the age of twelve, and tended to attract particularly gifted youngsters. Naturally, as a legal requirement, it also provided courses in the standard subjects that pupils this young were obliged to pursue. However, no degrees were offered in these areas, and indeed they tended to be marginalised in the curriculum.

My general schooling up to that point had been at our local village establishment, but of course, our home life was a haven of literature, poetry and artistic communion. Languages, naturally, presented no problems to me, although mathematics has always been something of a closed book – a fact that was to involve me in some unsavoury rumours, and indeed, legal difficulties, in later years.

It appeared that our visitors from the north east had been suitably impressed with my debut, and Father delightedly informed me that I would be starting my first year of University education within a few short weeks.

It was at that point that, thunderstruck, I realised I would be leaving home! Lang Hall was distant, and the hundred or so pupils came from all corners of the country. The University offered limited accommodation facilities, and the majority of students lived either 'over the shop' or boarded in one or other of the neighbouring towns. I thought on reflection that I might prefer to live at the University itself, but Mother had other ideas.

"No need, no need, Mona. My old school chum Morag lives in Elgin, only a step away. You can stay with her. There's a bus service every day to the University, that'll suit very well. You remember your Aunty Morag, don't you?"

Indeed. How could I forget her? Morag McAllister was a skinny and hatchet-faced 'bottle blonde' of about my mother's age, who had been a regular visitor to our home in earlier years. Mother claimed they had been at school together, although she was surprisingly sparing with the details. Morag had been a less frequent visitor of late. She and Mother had had some kind of a disagreement, concerning what I know not, but apparently that little wound had been healed, or at least bandaged, recently.

I didn't care overmuch for Morag. There was no very good reason for my antipathy, and she had always been very agreeable on the few occasions we had met. But the fact that she aped Mother in always calling me 'Mona' did not endear her to me. Further, when she used to come and stay with us, she and my mother were forever getting into 'wee scrapes', as the latter called them. These usually involved strong drink and dubious gentlemen, and I was of the opinion that Mother and Morag were in general better kept apart. In addition, Morag was incredibly mean. Mother, whatever her faults, was open-handed and generous, whereas her old school friend was the original model for the tight-fisted Scot.

I was uncertain, and decided to talk it over with Father.

Fortunately he was in one of his sunnier moods; there was no sign of the occasional clouding of his intellect which troubled him from time to time.

"I think we should humour your mother in this, Evie. You know she was dead set against this University business, but finally she seems to have come round. Let's not rock that boat, eh?"

I understood that if I objected to Mother's plans, my poor father would probably pay the price for my intransigence.

"I know you're not that keen on Morag, and God knows, she wouldn't be my first choice as a chaperone, but she has a good heart underneath that hard-faced exterior."

How Father had been able to detect this well-concealed soft centre he didn't choose to share with me.

"Give it a term or two, Evie, and see how you get on. Then, if it doesn't suit, we can think again. Agreed?"

"Yes, of course Father, if it's what you want."

"Well, I will rest easier knowing you have a sympathetic adult to keep an eye on you, at least until you settle in."

I forbore to mention that 'sympathetic' was not the first word that sprang to my mind when contemplating 'Auntie' Morag.

And so it was decided.

Uncle Conan was delegated to drive me to Elgin for my enrolment. Father had never driven, and Mother had once again had her license impounded, after a regrettable incident involving a farmer and a bullock.

* * * * *

Leaving was half-exciting, half-frightening. Mother, of course, dismissed my emotion in her usual off-hand manner. However I was gratified to notice that, in spite of her apparent indifference, she had a tear in her eye and a lump in her throat. Or perhaps the former was due to a flare-up of her conjunctivitis, and the latter to a piece of the bannock she was chewing for little Lavinia, all of whose baby teeth had recently fallen out.

Very different was my parting from Father. Seated in the library, he was in a strange mood, almost as if he didn't want me to go at all.

"Of course, fine place as Lang Hall is, there's nothing you will learn there that I couldn't teach you."

This was an unexpected reversal. Up till then, Father had been insistent that my future education should be in the hands of those professionally qualified to oversee it.

"Father," I said, sitting myself down on the arm of his chair, "if you really don't want me to go, there is no more to be said. I will stay here with you."

As quickly as they had appeared, his misgivings seemed to vanish.

"No, no, Evie, I am talking nonsense. Of course you must go."

"Very well. But" – I hesitated – "I'm worried, Father. I can't imagine not having you around when I need you. And what if I'm not good enough?"

"Not good enough?" Father was immediately his usual self. He turned in his seat to look at me. "Evie, you will cut a swathe through Lang Hall the likes of which they have never seen before. Have no doubts on that score. Forget my earlier remark. The truth is, I am going to miss you. This house will be lacking something very important when you have gone."

We both shed a few tears. Finally, he pulled himself together.

"Off you go, pet. It will do you good to get away from this house. There are things happening round here that I don't care for, not at all, and the further away you are, the better I shall like it."

I had no idea what Father was referring to, although later his words would return to haunt me. He explained that young Jeannie would be coming back to help him with his work, since without her assistance he would be unable to transcribe his musical inspirations.

"And she will be able to manage the injections too, so don't you worry. She has a fine hand with a needle, does Jeannie."

I felt some misgivings. Jeannie had acquired something of a reputation in the neighbourhood since leaving our service, and more than once I had seen her and her uncouth cronies in my brother's company.

"But Father, are you sure…"

"No, no, enough for now. You mustn't concern yourself about me. This is your time. This is the start of your great adventure."

He stood up. A vatic mood seemed to come over him. Suddenly his tone changed, he gripped the edge of the piano, his glance turned heavenward.

"You will have a great success, I know it. Indeed, I can see a day when the name of Evadne Hinge will be known throughout the world."

Just as quickly, he resumed his previous matter-of-fact mood. He turned back to me and sat down again. "Well, the civilised part of it, anyway. Off you go, Evie, with all my blessings."

* * * * *

I had to seek out my brother, as he was nowhere to be found in the house. Eventually I discovered him huddled out of the rain inside the little chapel which adjoined the west wing of the Castle.

"So you're off then Eva? Well, good luck, hope it all goes well."

This dismissive attitude was by now familiar to me. Indeed, of late, it had come to characterise Leicester's interaction with me. I suddenly realised that, whatever the cost, I had to try and break through his reserve, to regain even momentarily the closeness we had once shared.

I sat down next to him, and spoke softly.

"Is that all you have to say to me, Leicester?"

He turned to me, a surprised look on his face.

"Well, yes – what do you want me to say?"

He paused. Then, as if it took an enormous effort, he managed, "Of course, it won't be the same around here without you, you know. I will miss you."

"Oh – and how I will miss you too," I cried, and we fell into each other's arms.

After a few moments he withdrew.

"It's good you are going away, Eva. Strange things are going on around here."

Just as Father had implied! What was happening that I didn't know about? But I ignored that for the moment. I had more to say.

"Leicester, do look after yourself. Work hard at school, and" – I hesitated – "maybe you should be a bit more careful about the company you keep. These people are not your sort. They will spoil you."

He smiled dismissively.

"Little sister, where do you get these ideas from? I'm perfectly fine, really I am. Yes, I know the village lot are a bunch of eedjits, but I've got to have some company. I don't like being on my own all the time – who does?"

"I was always here, you know, Leicester. You only had to ask. I've been worried about you. I tried. But you didn't seem interested."

"Yes, I know. I'm sorry, truly. I've had a lot on my mind, one way and another. Really, I'm sorry. You were always the best of the bunch round here. But there are things I can't talk about, even to you. Important things, difficult things."

"Oh Leicester – now I shall worry about you all the more…"

He pooh-poohed my concerns, and gave his old familiar laugh.

"Oh, get off with you, Eva, don't be daft, I'm not serious. Really – have a great time, and do the family proud. Anyway, we'll see each other at Christmas."

And of course, we would.

* * * * *

1932.

Lang Hall, Banffshire, Scotland.

The four years I spent at University were in many ways among the happiest of my life, just as school days are said to be. It was at that time that I perfected and completed the education which would allow me to have a career of some note in the field which I loved. I found new friends, and something more. It was during this period, too, that I lost everything else dear to me.

I arrived in Elgin on a foggy and wet September evening in 1932. Kindly Uncle Conan had kept me entertained throughout the long journey north with his seemingly endless stories, not all of which I understood perfectly. I remember him asking me if Mother, his sister, still attended the AA meetings which had apparently been recommended to her. When I explained that since Mother had lost her driving licence, she had no present use for her membership of the august motoring organisation, Conan burst out laughing.

"No, no, pet, I meant… well, never mind. So – she's given up her Automobile Association membership, then?"

"Well, she's still a member, officially, but obviously, not an active one, at the moment. She's been rusticated." I thought I might essay a small witticism. "She's a Country Member."

"How could I forget?" roared Uncle Conan, seemingly finding my little joke much funnier than I had expected.

"We shouldn't laugh, really," he went on in a more serious tone. "She's all right, Maureen. Oh, I know she drives us all mad sometimes, but really, I often think your mother is a bit of a lost soul. She had a difficult time growing up. Maybe we should all be a bit more considerate of her, you know, make some allowances – what do you think? Shall we make the effort?"

I said I would try. He smiled at me and ruffled my hair. And the lengthy journey seemed to pass in no time at all.

* * * * *

We arrived eventually at *Ballochmyle, A Home Away from Home*, 'Aunty' Morag's gloomy Victorian pile in Elgin. She greeted us effusively and ushered us into the room she referred to as 'the sitting room'. If the welcome was warm, that is more than could be said for the house itself, where the temperature was arctic. Aunty Morag noticed me shivering and asked if I felt cold.

"Just a bit," I admitted.

"Never mind, Mona," said she, sniffing, "you'll soon get used to it. I never have the heating on before December, I don't believe in it. We'll need to toughen you up, m'dear, and get you out of these soft Lowland habits. Just put on another jumper if you're feeling a wee bit chilly – that's what I do. Remember, Mona, I'm a single woman living on my own, and the few shillings I earn with the paying guests don't cover expensive heating bills."

As she spoke I was interested to watch the progress of a drip making its leisurely descent from the tip of her nose in the direction of the thin carpet, and the practised ease with which she swiped her chilblained hands, in fingerless mittens, across her chin to impede its descent.

"I'm sure I will soon adapt, Aunty Morag." This was as good a time as any, I thought, to tackle a major personal issue. "Oh – and would you mind terribly calling me 'Evadne', and not 'Mona'?"

She grimaced. "Very well, if you insist, Mona, if you insist. Evadne – an uncouth name, in my opinion. One of your Father's outlandish notions, I believe? But if 'Evadne' is your preference, then so be it, Mona. And you can call me 'Morag', just plain Morag will do. Or 'Aunty', if you prefer. Although," she sniffed, "I'm rather young to be an aunty, wouldn't you agree, Conan?"

Conan agreed, it appeared. I decided I would call her 'Morag', as she suggested. Plain Morag – she was certainly that.

"And how is your dear mother, Mona?" Sniff. "Not seen her in an age – I hope she's well?"

"She's very well, as far as I know, Morag."

"Glad to hear it, dear, very glad to hear it. Now, I'll just take you upstairs and show you your room, let you get settled in." She turned her attention to my uncle. "Will you stay for a bite of tea, Conan? I've plenty in, with a growing girl to feed and look after." She fluttered her stubby eyelashes winningly in his direction. "It's everybody's favourite tonight, fishcakes and chips…"

Uncle Conan remembered an urgent appointment in Edinburgh and declined the tempting invitation.

"No thank you Morag, I'll be on my way, if it's all the same to you."

He turned to me.

"Look after yourself, young Eva, and study hard. Remember, we are all expecting great things from you."

He kissed me on the cheek and was gone.

"Nice chap," mused Morag, as she led the way upstairs. She shrugged her shoulders and added bafflingly, "Even if he does bat for the other side." Sniff. "Now, Mona, it's just the two of us girls. Your room is on the top floor – follow me. What a time we are going to have!"

* * * * *

And what a time we had. Or rather, what a time *she* had.

Morag took in paying guests. She had four bedrooms on the first floor, which had been converted into bed-sitting rooms. These she let by the night or for longer periods. The bulk of her regular customers were either commercial travellers, who tended to appear for an occasional night and then disappear as quickly, or fishermen who had travelled north for the herring. The latter – the fishermen, not the herring – would be in residence for longer periods, often up to two or even three weeks, depending on the weather. As a non-contributing guest, I found that I had been assigned a large but draughty attic room which appeared, judging from the smell, to have been used for salting cod or some equally odorous purpose. Plain Morag herself was in the bedroom opposite mine, while the guests who actually paid for the privilege of residing in her frigid domains were allocated the rooms on the floor beneath.

On the day of my arrival, I was intrigued to discover that among Morag's current clientele was a young lady who, like me, was a pupil at Lang Hall. She was older than me by a couple of years, apparently, and was about to start her second year of education. I was agog to meet her, and compare notes, but was informed that she was currently out. Morag, of course, had an opinion.

"Odd sort of girl, Julie. Pleasant enough, and very happy to pay three months up front. But there's something not quite right about her, in my opinion. I anticipate wildness, flighty habits and a rebellious attitude. In a word, not really our type, Mona."

We had a 'type'? I decided to reserve judgement.

Morag had resolved that it would be 'fun' for me to help out in the house. It was to be my duty, among others, to serve breakfast to the guests – Aunty Morag would cook while I waited on – and then to help her make up the rooms. How and when I was supposed to find time to study and attend classes was not disclosed to me. I imagine I was expected to fit these lesser matters in around my domestic obligations.

Julie was the last to appear for breakfast the following day. Before then I had served two trawler men, and a gentleman who apparently travelled in ladies' essentials. The former were bluff and hearty, but I have to admit I was somewhat shocked by their uninhibited and salty language. I thought in passing of my dear brother and his sea-faring ambitions. I hoped he would not be subjected to this kind of conversation should he ever achieve his goal, sensitive and delicately reared as he was. The travelling gentleman ('*Call me Eric*') was very affable and well-mannered, although I did not care for the lingering squeeze he gave my hand as I adjusted his cruet.

Eventually, all three left the dining room, and just as I was wondering what could have happened to my fellow student, a resonant voice called from the hallway, "Good morning, Moo-rag…"

And into the dining room strolled Julie. "…you old bag," she muttered over her shoulder.

"Oops," she smiled at me as she sat down, "I didn't see you there, dear. Sorry, but I can't help telling the truth first thing in the morning, it's a shocking habit."

Julie Cotter was a big girl – big in every way. As tall as me (by the age of twelve I topped five feet and seven inches) but whereas I was slim, indeed, skinny, fourteen-year-old Julie was round. She had a very well-developed figure for her age, masses of dark curling hair, and a perfect peaches-and-cream complexion. She was, quite simply, a beauty.

"You must be new, hen, no?" She helped herself to cereal. "It's usually Grace Poole in person who serves breakfast. She doesn't often miss out on a chance to flirt with the male lodgers – don't tell me she has gone to the expense of hiring staff?"

"Well, no, not exactly," I replied, "I'm just helping out. Temporarily."

"Aye, that makes sense. I can't imagine that old skinflint actually *paying* anybody. So you just make sure it *is* temporary. Don't let her wheedle you into working here for nothing – and she will, if she can."

At that moment Morag entered the dining room.

"Ah, there you are Julie – I was just wondering when you would deign to honour us with your presence." She sniffed. I had begun to appreciate that Morag had quite a repertoire of sniffs, one for every mood or occasion. This was definitely an 'it's very inconsiderate of you to keep me slaving in the kitchen till this hour' sniff.

"Anyway, I trust you slept well, dear?" she continued.

"No, not really, Morag," said Julie with a wide yawn. "That Eric chap was banging on my door half the night."

"Surely not!" Morag glanced towards the stairs and drew herself up with a sniff suggesting outraged virtue. "I will be having a very firm word with that young man."

"No need, Morag, no need. I let him out eventually."

For a moment Morag was at a loss. Then her face crinkled into a hesitant smile. "Very amusing, dear, most witty, I'm sure." Sniff. And turning to me, "Look lively Mona – ask Julie what she would like for her breakfast. I can't stand chatting here half the day just because some young ladies choose not to rise until this hour."

"Yes, of course, Aunty Morag, right away."

With a final sniff indicating a general disapproval, Morag turned on her heel and left us alone.

"Oh dear," said Julie. "I'm *so* sorry. I had no idea that the blessed Morag was your aunt."

"Oh no, she isn't," I explained, "not really. She's just a friend of the family who will be looking after me for a while. I'm here to start my first year at Lang Hall, next week."

"No! – So *you're* the new girl, Mona. Sit down, sit down."

I glanced over my shoulder in the direction of the kitchen. Morag seemed to be otherwise occupied, so I joined Julie at the table.

"I had no idea, Mona," said Julie, adding milk to her cereal. "Morag did mention that there was another girl moving in, but she never mentioned how *young* you were. I mean, I'm fourteen, and even then I'm one of the younger students, but you can only be about thirteen or thereabouts."

"I'm twelve." Once again a firm stance seemed advisable. "And – I hope you don't object – would you mind terribly calling me 'Evadne'? After all, that *is* my name." Suddenly I remembered Morag's instructions. "Oh – I'm supposed to ask you what you want for breakfast…"

Julie picked up her spoon.

"Oh, never mind that now, dear, I'm on a diet anyway. Some tea would be nice, and maybe a slice or two of toast. No, wait…" Raising a hand as I made to stand up, she appeared to consider. "Hm – Evadne – yes, I like that." After a moment she added thoughtfully, "So – why does the old battle-axe call you 'Mona' then?" She went back to her cornflakes.

"I don't know, really. It's one of my middle names and I suppose she has just got used to it."

"Mona? Where are you?" came the call from the direction of the kitchen.

Julie shuddered. "Mona! That's *awful*. And 'Evadne' is such a *beautiful* name. From now on we're 'Evadne' and 'Julie'. And we will see if we can't get the old dragon to change her habits, too. You mustn't let people like her get away with things, you know, they'll only take advantage. You have to stand up to them. She's a bully, it's as simple as that. Don't worry, between us we will soon sort 'Aunty Moo-rag' out. It's high time she was educated. No doubt she will let loose with a selection of sniffs before she bows to the inevitable. But trust me, Evadne, bow she will."

As I rose to return to the kitchen for Julie's tea and toast, I thought, *'Goodness! I've already found a friend!'*

* * * * *

Julie was as good as her word. Within a week not only had she cured Morag of the 'Mona' habit ('*It makes you sound ill-bred and stupid, Morag*') and put an end to my household duties ('*The Education Board look very poorly an anything that smacks of child labour or exploitation*'), but she had somehow managed to get me moved from my freezing attic into her own cosy room ('*Well, I have two beds in there and will enjoy the company. And you can now let Evadne's room to some other lonely gentleman who doesn't know any better, can't you, Mo-Mo?*')

The 'Mo-Mo' was a part of Julie's 'educating Morag' project. She thought it would help to make her aware of how irritating her 'Mona' was. Unfortunately, although Morag came to manage 'Evadne' (or occasionally 'Movadne') pretty regularly, she remained 'Mo-Mo' to us in private and occasionally in public if we were feeling audacious.

It was at breakfast a couple of days after we first met that my new friend discovered that I was Evadne *Hinge*, not some other Evadne.

"Evadne Hinge!" she shrieked, nearly causing one of the trawler men to have a heart attack and the other to choke on his toast. "*The* Evadne Hinge? No, it can't be…" She stared at me intently. "But yes, of course, I recognise you now. My dear, I was *there*!"

"Where?"

"At your concert in Glasgow – quite a few of us travelled down for it. You were wonderful, really, amazing. Where on earth did you learn to play like that?"

I explained some of my background to my new friend.

"Ah, I see. Oh, and of course, the old guy is your dad. The conductor, I mean. Seemed a sweet old chap. He wrote that thing you played, isn't that right?"

I admitted that the sweet old chap was indeed my father and the renowned composer of the *Annie Laurie Variations*.

"Terrible old tosh, isn't it?" Julie giggled. "But fun to play, I bet, and it certainly got the audience excited." She assumed a mock-serious style. "Evadne, I had no idea I was breakfasting with a celebrity."

I let the 'old tosh' line pass, and, matching her tone, said modestly that I hoped that this revelation wouldn't stand in the way of our friendship.

"Of course not, Evadne, why should it? And anyway, I'm a celebrity too, you know, in a small way. I gave my first recital when not much older than you – I'm a mezzo-soprano, by the way – and I can modestly claim that it was greeted with considerable success. And when I graduate, I plan to take the opera world by storm, just as I am sure you will the concert platform."

We were enjoying our morning eggs and bacon, served slightly reluctantly by Mo-Mo herself.

"And who," Julie continued, dipping her toast into a greasy and under-cooked egg, "who was that young chap who came on at the end of your evening and sang *On the Road to Mandalay*?"

"Oh, that's my brother, Leicester," I replied. "He's fourteen."

"Well, he's certainly something, isn't he? I'd love to meet him some time. You're obviously a very good-looking family. You'll be telling me next that the busty redhead serving the whisky was your mother."

I admitted that this was in fact the case.

"No! What a family. No wonder you're so pretty."

Me? Granted I was tall and mature-looking for my age, but I had never considered that anyone might find me *pretty*.

"And as for that brother of yours – is he really only fourteen? – I hope he and I will meet up some day."

I said that it was likely that Leicester would visit, and that she would probably see something of him.

"Something?" laughed Julie, "Evadne, my *dear*, I would hope to see *all* of him."

* * * * *

Julie and I grew closer and closer. It wasn't long before I suggested that she might shorten the 'Evadne' to 'Eva', the name that up till than only my close friends and family had used. We could hardly have been more different in temperament. She was certainly the stronger character. Julie appeared to fear nothing and no-one, and was always ready to defend me if she suspected that someone was taking advantage of my youth and naivety. She had a wonderful ability, too, to sniff out anyone's little secrets or weaknesses.

"You know Mo-Mo does extras, Eva, don't you?"

We were in the sitting room, sitting. And studying.

"Well yes, of course." I knew that Morag would occasionally offer a gentleman an extra sausage or a rasher or two at breakfast time if they were on the point of going off.

"Yes – and five bob a time, she charges – can you believe it? Hardly love's young dream, Mo-Mo, is she?"

I had had no idea that Morag was able to get this unimaginable sum for a slice of her black pudding. And what on earth did her looks have to do with it anyway? I looked up from my textbook.

"That seems a lot for a bit of breakfast, Julie. Are you sure? No! Five shillings?"

"A bit of breakfast?" She sighed melodramatically. "Eva, what am I going to do with you? I don't mean extra rations, I mean – well – extras."

None the wiser, I laid my book aside. "What kind of extras?" I asked in puzzlement.

Julie shook her head and cast her eyes heavenward. "Really, Eva, come on – she offers personal evening visits to selected gentlemen. You know – *personal* visits – in their rooms – after lights-out."

I began to have a hazy idea as to what Julie was referring to. I had indeed been aware of certain nocturnal perambulations, creaking stairs and whispered colloquies, but had assumed that Mo-Mo suffered from a delicate bladder. I had wondered idly, too, why the vast majority of her guests were unattached males.

My jaw dropped. "But surely you don't mean…"

Julie was not letting my uncertainty pass unchecked. "It's high time I took your education in hand, hen, you can't go through life without knowing what's what."

It seemed to me that someone was always trying to educate me. But eager to learn as I ever was, I agreed that she might begin lessons as soon as she liked.

* * * * *

Julie did indeed contrive to enlighten me in what she called 'the facts of life', but an even more important lesson was looming – my first day at University.

Both Julie and I were naturally enrolled in the Faculty of Music. Although there were also departments dealing with painting and the other arts in which Lang Hall specialised, each one tended to be something of an independent kingdom, and we only encountered other students in our leisure time or in the holidays.

There were at this time around twenty music students – some singers, others instrumentalists, and finally those who hoped to specialise in teaching, as opposed to performing. I had arranged my course such that I would continue taking lessons in piano, but would also be tutored in the theoretical aspects of my chosen profession. Thus, in my first year I had classes in Harmony and Counterpoint, Musical Form, the Theory of Composition and Basic Orchestration. Additionally, of course, I had to attend courses in English, Languages, Mathematics and Science. A busy curriculum, as you may imagine. As I have implied, these non-artistic subjects were somewhat side-lined at Lang Hall, but even so, one was expected to show one's face from time to time.

The atmosphere was generally easy-going and relaxed. Nonetheless, there was a strong element of competition among the students, and it was unusual for anyone to deliberately miss lectures or tutorials. Julie was a year ahead of me, so we didn't tend to meet up in classes, unless it was an address from a visiting celebrity of the musical world, a not unusual event. However we continued to be inseparable outside working hours, and I generally spent my free time (such as it was) with her and her friends, who were a little older than myself.

There were six other students in my own year, but only one other pianist, a girl named, of all things, Mona McCafferty. Short, tomboyish and dark-haired, at thirteen years of age Mona was, I assumed, headed for the teaching side of the profession. Certainly, what I heard of her pianism left a lot to be desired.

"I only play modern," she maintained, in her gruff baritone, "I've no time at all for all this Beethoven and Brahms."

By this she meant that she specialised in composers of the twentieth century – understandably, given her apparently limited abilities. It's easy enough to smother Debussy under a wash of the sustain pedal, and who can tell how well she played Schönberg[1], when even the right notes sound as wrong as the wrong ones?

Plump fifteen year old Ruby Hall was a formidable violinist. Sweet-natured and motherly, after a brief but highly successful period on the concert platform, she married young, and gave up her career to raise a brood of children. More of Ruby's marriage in its place.

A plain but pleasant girl named Janey Dawson was a fine organist; Janey never went anywhere without her 'special' shoes. These had thick, built-up soles – as she had extremely short legs, it was only when wearing them that she was able to reach the pedal board of the organ.

Then there was little Vicky Dean, a blond and lively Dundee lassie almost as young as me, who was the possessor of a remarkable soprano voice. When she decided to put Mozart's *Queen of the Night* through her paces, Vicky's acuti[2] could be heard as far afield as Cullen or Banff if the wind was in the right direction. Poor Vicky was very sensitive to the cold – how fortunate she was not to be boarding *chez* Mo-Mo! – and her legs were generally encased in thick black woollen tights, her top half in substantial Arran sweaters to keep out the North Sea breezes. Miss Dean was an engaging character, but volatile and unpredictable, and occasionally I feared for her emotional stability, as she was liable to sudden outbursts of unwarranted hilarity or tears at inappropriate moments.

I never cared much for Phil Hanson. A tall and skinny Aberdonian with a drawn and haggard look, he was what Julie referred to as a 'toucher' – one had to be very careful not to be left alone with him. He had apparently been a boy

1 Arnold Schönberg. German composer and founder of the 'Second Viennese School'. His later music followed the 'serial' and 'twelve-tone' (dodecaphonic) systems of composition.

2 Acuti – extreme high notes

soprano of some distinction, but at the age when the voices of most young men start to deepen, his remained in the soprano register, and indeed continued to rise by degrees until his everyday conversation became well-nigh inaudible. I'm told that 'Hanky' later had a successful career as an animal trainer.

He developed an unrequited passion for young Miss Dean, and pursued her relentlessly. Hanky liked to play the junior 'man about town', and was forever inviting Vicky to join him in *The Old Blue Last*, a local bar and restaurant with a low reputation, for what he termed 'an intimate supper'.

He had a taste, too, for practical jokes, and was in the habit of concealing himself in a handy cupboard or closet, from whence his unearthly, disembodied tones would issue in some melody or other just when one thought one was alone. He had a talent for parodying the words of well-known songs, and I remember on one occasion little Vicky tearing out of the library, shrieking in terror, when she was thus serenaded. Apparently what she heard, to the tune of *The Northern Lights of Old Aberdeen*, was:

"The laddered tights of young Vicky Dean are a bonnie sight tae see.

The laddered tights of Vicky Dean hang way down past her knee.

I'd like tae take her out on the town, and show her why I'm so keen.

And hope she'll deign to explain the stain, on the tights of Vicky Dean"

Mr Hanson's practical jokes were eventually to land him in serious trouble and indeed prevent him from finishing his course and gaining his qualifications.

* * * * *

Finally, there was Finlay Clark. Finlay was, in a word, gorgeous – short and compact, blue-eyed, and with an impressive mop of fair hair, worn long, which was his pride and joy. From the moment I saw him I was smitten. I thought he was simply the most handsome man I had ever seen. If he had any physical fault it was a slight tendency to chubbiness. But from our first meeting I idolised him shamelessly, and, inexperienced as I was in such matters, made my feelings all too obvious, I fear. He was kind, and treated me in the indulgent manner one might a younger sister who has overdosed on hero-worship. I vowed to myself that I would one day make him sit up and take notice of me in quite another way. But how to go about it?

Finlay was two years older than me, and played the French horn astonishingly well. My first chance to make a more than sisterly impression on him came when plans were being laid for the concert which traditionally marked the end of the student year. Finlay, it transpired, was trying to find a pianist to join him in a performance of the Beethoven Sonata for Horn and Piano. When he discovered that Mona McCafferty (*'I only play modern'*) was not interested in tackling Beethoven, someone – I suspect it was Julie – suggested he ask me.

"Eva – you'll pardon my frankness, but would you be up to it – musically I mean?" He approached me in the University dining room, his tone ever so slightly patronising. "And if so, would you be interested?"

Would I be interested? I certainly would. And would I be up to it? I, who had romped through a Liszt concerto in the St Andrew's Halls? I could, I felt, encompass a Beethoven sonata without too much difficulty, and told him so in no uncertain terms.

"Pardon my frankness, but 'yes'. And again 'yes'."

In the event, I think I was even more nervous on this occasion than I had been at my début. Terrified of letting the object of my affections down. Hoping that he would somehow see me in a different light after he discovered I could actually play. And all the while not entirely certain of what I wanted from him, if I were to achieve my object of persuading him that I could be more than just another anonymous fellow student.

Our performance at the concert was well-received, and Finlay appeared appropriately impressed. Indeed, backstage, afterwards, he shook my hand in a professional manner.

"Well done, Eva, well done." He tossed back his blond quiff. My knees turned to jelly. "Gosh, I really feel we made something of that, together. I hope we can do it again sometime. What do you think?"

He was still holding my hand!

"I would love to, Finlay, really I would." I hoped I wasn't goggling at him too obviously… I hoped he wouldn't let go…

"Look forward to it, then," he said with a smile. He gave the hand a quick squeeze, and sauntered off, calling back over his shoulder, "Can't believe you're only twelve!"

"Thirteen," I croaked, looking down at the favoured hand unbelievingly. "Nearly."

* * * * *

1933.

Dean Castle.

My studies progressed well for the most part, and I passed the examinations at the end of my first year with notable success. I was able to return home to the family during the inter-term holidays, and was relieved to find that things seemed to have settled down there to some extent. Leicester was much more his old self, and although Father continued to appear occasionally vague from time to time, he was always anxious to hear how I was progressing, and to listen with amusement to my little stories concerning my fellow students. It was a matter of some concern to me, however, to discover that from time to time he would require a double dose of his regular medication to overcome the discomfort occasioned by his condition.

I tried to follow Uncle Conan's suggestion that I should show Mother more consideration. I'm not sure if I was entirely successful. She was, for most of that year, spending an extended period in one of the restful sanatoriums which she favoured. These establishments, according to Father, catered to those suffering from the acute *delirium tremens* that can be brought on by the combination of a nervous disposition and a hectic lifestyle. It was Leicester, however, who made me aware that Father's explanation was not entirely accurate.

"Not at all, it's the drink, Eva. She drinks too much, it's as simple as that. So much that, eventually, she makes herself ill. Then, every so often, she decides to give it up and goes into one of those clinics which deal with her kind of problem."

I had been aware, naturally, that Mother was extremely fond of a glass or two of whisky. But I had no idea that the situation had grown to be such a serious one.

"But why does she drink so much, if it makes her ill?" I wondered.

"Who knows?" answered Leicester. "She claims she drinks to forget. That's what she told me, at least."

"To forget? – to forget what?"

"I don't know. I did ask her, but she couldn't remember."

Leicester and I spent a lot of time together during the long summer break. Our old camaraderie was resumed without any obvious difficulty, and he was particularly attentive to me, as if to make up for his recent coldness. Of course, I had a certain amount of study to do during the holiday, and unending piano practice. But when Father proposed a short break in the Highlands, just himself and us children, we accepted his suggestion with alacrity. Little Lavinia, I couldn't help noticing, now nine years old, had turned into a pleasant and agreeable child, and Leicester and I made a particular point of including her in our plans. It was perhaps an unkind thought, but without anything being said specifically, I think we all appreciated that Mother's absence resulted in a much more harmonious household.

My brother was particularly interested to see a photograph of Julie, Finlay and myself, taken during the end-of-term festivities.

"Hm – pretty girl, pretty boy," he mused. "So when do I get a chance to meet up with them?"

"Oh, one of these days you will, Leicester. You'll like Julie, I'm sure. Leave it to me," I replied airily, though delighted by his reaction.

"And the boy is Finlay, I imagine?" he went on, still gazing at the photo. "The one whose name keeps cropping up in your conversation whether it's relevant or not?" He smiled. "Do I detect a certain *tendresse*, Professor Hinge? Is the studious maiden finally realising that there is a world outside the walls of her ivory tower?"

I was flustered. "I don't know what you mean, Leicester..."

"Oh, I think you do, Eva." He handed the photo back to me. "Well – you'd better get him along here too, so I can decide if he deserves the family seal of approval."

I am sure I blushed, half embarrassed and half delighted.

Peace reigned at 'Castle Hinge'.

Chapter Four
Troubled Times

1933.

Lang Hall.

Some time just after starting my second year at Lang Hall, Julie and I were sitting with Morag in her kitchen having a night-cap – cocoa for Julie and me, and the last of several large whiskies for Morag.

Mo-Mo had improved considerably in the last twelve months, due mainly to Julie's influence. Indeed, after a few glasses, she tended to become positively amiable. We had discovered that the best way to keep her mellow was to indulge her whenever possible, and there was no surer way to a contented and malleable Morag than through the whisky bottle. Indeed, she occasionally became loquacious and confiding to the point of embarrassment. I wondered if it might be time to bring up a question that had always puzzled me.

"You know how you and Mother were friends at school, Morag?" I asked, in a studiedly casual tone, looking down at my cocoa.

"Oh aye," nodded Morag into her whisky, "the best of friends, always – bosom buddies, in fact." She put down her glass and slapped her negligible chest.

I sipped my cocoa before continuing.

"Where was it? The school I mean. Mother has never said. Was it a good school?"

"Oh yes," answered Morag proudly, "the very best. It was" – she sniggered, picking up her glass again – "approved, you know."

I was puzzled. "Oh? Approved? By whom?"

"By everyone. The public, the police, the courts." Morag's whisky sloshed alarmingly from side to side as she gestured extravagantly. "It met with what one might call – a general approval."

I had vaguely heard the expression 'approved school', introduced that very year to replace the older term.[1] But surely…

"She means a Borstal, don't you Mo-Mo?" Julie asked, leaning towards her, intrigued.

---

1 The 'Approved School' was introduced in 1933 as a gradual replacement for the old Borstal system.

Sniff. "Call it what you like. I never liked that word 'Borstal', myself, and I don't care for this new 'approved school' thing either," went on Morag sententiously. "I preferred what we used to call it among ourselves. 'A Home for Wayward Girls'. I've never approved of being approved, though I've never minded being wayward. Much nicer, in my opinion. Quite respectable and Victorian."

I couldn't believe what I was hearing. How could I put this? I took a deep breath.

"You mean that you and Mother were in – a sort of prison?"

Morag raised a finger in objection. "No, no, Mo – sorry – Evadne. Not a prison. More sort of – detention. Like after school, if you've been naughty. But for a bit longer."

"A Borstal," Julie repeated wonderingly, shaking her head from side to side.

"How long?" I asked.

"Well," went on Morag with a shrug, after a bracing sip, "not for long in my case – a few months, maybe. But of course, your mother for much longer."

Suddenly, she seemed to realise that she might have said too much.

"Now, never say a word to Maureen, Mona, promise me. She'd have my guts – well, enough said. But promise me you'll never mention it."

I hastened to reassure her. "No, of course I won't, Morag. I'm just curious, that's all." I had no plans to mention the matter to Mother, that much was true. But I needed to know more.

"So what did you do to end up in the clink, Morag?" Julie asked bluntly

"Me? – oh, nothing at all, just a wee misunderstanding. Of course it *was* late, but I only asked the man if he had the time. How was I to know he was a policeman, and didn't have a watch on? It was rank injustice, really. And me only fourteen…"

She subsided into her whisky. I was not at all interested in what Morag's supposed misdemeanour had been. If my mother had been locked up, I wanted to know why, and what for.

"And Mother," I interrupted, "why was she in this place for so much longer than you? Did she not behave herself or something?"

Morag smiled in reminiscence.

"Oh, she behaved perfectly, everyone there liked her. Lovely manners, your mother, always. No, no. It was because she was in there for" – her voice dropped near to inaudibility – "attempted murder."

"Murder?" gasped Julie and I simultaneously.

"Attempted, attempted. Oh aye. She shot a man. Shot a man, she did."

"Where?"

Morag leaned towards us, whispering with ghoulish enthusiasm, "In the groin, I believe she said."

I shook my head impatiently. "No, I meant – where did this happen?"

She sat back in her chair after looking round for the bottle.

"Oh, I see. In Cambuslang, where your grandparents were living at the time. Justifiable homicide, she described it as. Well – justified and attempted, but unsuccessful, something like that."

"Justified?"

"So she always said. No idea what she meant." Morag found the whisky bottle, filled her glass and once again leaned towards us confidingly. "But why did she have a gun with her in the Post Office, eh, tell me that? It's not as if you have to stage a hold-up to get a stamp. No, there was more to it than that, but justified was what she always claimed it was. Two years she was in there."

My mind was reeling. But I had one more question.

"Why have I never heard about this, Morag?"

She nodded sagely.

"No, you wouldn't have. Big secret. I doubt even your dad knows about it. But it was common gossip at the time. In all the papers, it was. Now" – once again she seemed to become panic-stricken – "not a word to Maureen, Evona – promise me. A dangerous woman, your mother, when she's roused. You promise?"

I crossed my fingers and smiled sweetly. "I promise, of course, Morag, don't you worry. Have another wee whisky. Your secret is safe with me."

* * * * *

In my second year at Lang Hall the courses were harder and expectations higher. I don't know how many exercises I turned in, but it seems I spent my entire time writing fugal expositions, arranging Bach chorales for every conceivable ensemble, and studying the operas of Monteverdi. As is usual, instruction started with the 17th and 18th centuries; not at all my favourite period, but it was explained to us that this was the foundation of 'classical' music, and before we might move on to the great romantics – my own preferred composers – we needed to master Bach, Vivaldi, Handel, Palestrina and the like.

I was now thirteen, and no longer the youngest student at Lang Hall. I had filled out considerably. My chief concern was that I was still growing, and now at five foot nine, I began to wonder if I would ever stop. My pin-up boy, Finlay, the horn player, was a 'wee smout' at five seven, and when we all went out together, I towered over him. Luckily Julie was usually along on these occasions, and as she had kept pace with me as far as height was concerned, I didn't feel too conspicuous. Julie had also given me some advice on appearance, and I had arranged my long hair into what she considered a more becoming style. She was at this stage experimenting with makeup, but I resisted her encouragement to participate. Always having had a naturally clear complexion and fine skin, I decided that such adornments were not for me, or at least, not yet. How little I imagined that before many years had passed I would be plastered in the greasy 'five and nine' cosmetics beloved of the theatrical profession[1]. But all that in its place.

It appeared that my new look was having some effect. Once or twice I thought I caught Finlay scrutinising me in what I interpreted as a slightly speculative manner, while I struggled with some exercise or other. I didn't dare to hope that he was finally starting to see me in *that* way. But I treasured up every little look and word, and spent hours alone wondering about his most innocuous remarks – "What did he mean by *this*?– what was he implying by *that*?"

Julie was my confidante, naturally, and encouraged me to hope that my efforts would bear fruit eventually.

"Don't push it, hen, just let nature take its course. Give it time – he's only human. Boys are a bit slow sometimes – and maybe he's as nervous as you are."

"But what if he meets someone else, Julie? Lots of the girls have their eye on him, I know..."

Julie was dismissive. "Look at the competition, hen. Ruby's fat, Janey's plain and Vicky's half mental. No contest."

Julie could be remarkably blunt on occasion.

"What about Mona, Julie, Mona McCafferty? She's quite attractive, don't you think?"

"Well, yes, she is. Could be a pretty girl, if she dressed like one. But she looks more like a boy than Finlay does, for a start, and anyway, I suspect her tastes don't run in that direction. Relax, hen, it'll all work out, trust Julie."

I remember the occasion when a group of us went to the local cinema to see a film called *She Done Him Wrong*, starring Mae West, at that time a new face to me[2]. I had contrived, abetted by Julie, to be seated next to Finlay, and although I spent most of the two hours in the cinema covertly studying his profile, I was also captivated by the outrageous shenanigans of Miss West on the screen. Here was a woman, I realised, who knew how to handle men. Could I take a leaf out of her book, and adopt a more forward approach? Maybe I could become a

1 Leichner stage cosmetics were in stick form and numbered. Five was a beige shade and nine was a red. They were the standard combination for the base skin tone.

2 'She Done Him Wrong' was Mae West's second film, and a huge commercial success.

platinum blonde – would that work? And most importantly, was the gentle pressure of Finlay's knee against mine intentional, or was it my imagination? A very confusing matter altogether.

Both Julie and I continued to be fascinated with Morag's revelations concerning Mother's past. I had to know more, and it was in Julie's company that I visited the offices of various newspapers in an attempt to pin down the details, or scotch the story entirely. Alas, it was all too true. On the 6th of April 1913, fourteen-year-old Maureen McWhirter, daughter of local distillery tycoon Maxwell McWhirter, had been sentenced to two years Borstal training for grievously wounding a certain Robert McLeod through the discharge of a firearm in a public place. The only differences were that it was not a gun but a rifle that Mother had fired, and that the wound sustained by Mr McLeod was in the left shoulder, not in 'the groin' as Morag had luridly embellished.

* * * * *

If it was taking some time to bring my dream man to the point, not everyone was so backward. As I hurried one wet afternoon through the quadrangle on my way to a class in Harmony, my head full of Finlay, Phil Hanson suddenly leapt from behind a pillar, covered from head to foot in a long opera cloak.

Flinging it wide, he cooed beguilingly, "How about it? Super sex?"

"I'll have the soup, thank you," I responded, which seemed to curb his ardour, at least temporarily. Then as if nothing had happened, he offered to carry my book-bag and we made our way to the lecture together.

"What a very strange young man," I thought, not for the first time.

Later, after the class had finished, I was gathering up my notes when Finlay unexpectedly approached me and, sitting himself down, sprawled attractively in the seat next to mine.

"Hello, Eva," he said, making himself comfortable. "How are things with you – not had a chance to chat to you for a wee while."

I was mortified at the crimson blush that rose to my cheeks. I knew he would see it. I worried he might even feel the heat of it.

"Um – yes, fine, thank you, Finlay," I mumbled, and dropped a large volume of Monteverdi madrigals on the floor in my confusion. "And how are you?"

"Oh, you know, just great."

We both knelt down at the same time to rescue Mr Monteverdi from the floor. Our heads bumped unintentionally and we both laughed, he unselfconsciously and I again pink with embarrassment at my *gaucherie*.

"I was wondering," he said as we both looked up and our eyes met. "There's a new Mae West film on at the cinema this week, and – I know how keen you are on her, and…"

I suddenly realised he was every bit as nervous as I was.

"Yes?" I asked.

"Well, I was wondering – would you like to go and see it. With me?"

Was this really happening?

"Oh – maybe…" I hesitated. No – surely he didn't mean *that*? Think, Eva! What would Mae West do? "Well, I'll ask Julie and Alistair, if you like, and see if they fancy coming along. That would be nice." A double date? – Julie was at that time seeing a lot of Alistair Simmons, a third-year student.

"Yes. Er – no. I meant" – he cleared his throat – "I meant you and me. On our own."

Ah. He *did* mean that.

"I would love to," I barely managed.

Finlay and I both laughed our way through *I'm No Angel*, and when our knees inevitably pressed together, I was fairly sure that this time it was no accident.

* * * * *

It seems to be a truism of educational systems that every set of teachers contains a large proportion of mild eccentrics. Such is the impression one gleans, certainly, from those who choose to recount their experiences while pursuing a course of education. This was certainly the case at Lang Hall.

Professor Murphy, a small, dark-haired lady in her forties, was unmarried, and totally dedicated to her chosen profession. It was her unenviable task to coach we music students in the art of song. It was felt that anyone contemplating a musical career, in whatever capacity, should be able to sing, at least acceptably. One was not expected to reach a professional standard in this area, but, nonetheless, a certain ability to at least carry a tune was the goal.

Singing class, held once a week, was one of the very few occasions when students of all levels came together. We would sit at our desks, about twenty of us in total, our songbooks in our hands, while Professor Murphy ('Wee Ma Murphy' to us students, when the lady herself was not present) attacked the piano and dragged us screaming through such perennial favourites as *The Ash Grove*, *Art Thou Troubled*? and *Linden Lea*.

The songbooks we used were of an unidentifiable age, worn, dog-eared, and decorated liberally with the pencilled comments of former students. Thus one might be invited to turn to *There is a Garden in her Face* to find that some wag had added 'full of weeds' to the title. One might discover that the young lady hymned in *Sweet Lass of Richmond Hill* was not in fact a 'lass' but a portion of the nether anatomy. And that *Trade Winds* described 'Wee Ma' giving vent from a similar location. All very juvenile, of course, but we youngsters found these deathless gems side-splittingly funny. I'm afraid that as a result, a singing class tended to be a rather uproarious event, and to give our Professor her due, she was easy-going and as ready to join in the joke as anyone else.

Occasionally, however, Professor Murphy would decide to take her revenge, and one or other of the class would be invited to give a solo performance to the rest of the group. Naturally, the students of voice, such as Julie, Vicky and Hanky, had no difficulties at all with this. However, the sounds that issued from the throats of such as Ruby Hall, Janey Dawson and even, I regret to say, my beloved Finlay, could be truly appalling.

I can only assume that my own abilities in this field were, at the least, acceptable, perhaps more than that, as I was never once invited to display my prowess in a solo capacity. My conjecture was confirmed when I happened to overhear Professor Murphy telling Professor Liddell, who taught Harmony and Counterpoint, '*Whatever Eva's level of success in her other classes, the voice... Well, words fail me!*' I was much warmed by this remark, although, bless her, I fear she may have exaggerated slightly. And to think they say that those who listen never hear any good of themselves!

Ah, Harmony and Counterpoint! The class that everyone dreaded. Professor Liddell, known to us student as 'OPO' was a huge-bellied, white-haired gentleman, who had a trying time forcing the basics of these skills into our thick skulls. I had to have it explained to me by Julie that his nickname, OPO, stood for 'O Pregnant One', in recognition of his extraordinary girth. He was a determined, if uninspiring, teacher, nonetheless, and gradually, the rudiments of the arcane art of harmonising a melody correctly, or devising a fugue exposition from a three-bar phrase, began to penetrate. It is a theoretical business, and we youngsters considered ourselves 'artistic'. But it was made clear to us that without the firm basis these lessons provided, there was no hope for us, unless we planned to stick strictly to performance. Since I, personally, hoped to combine performance with composition, it was particularly important that I master thoroughly these basic skills, and OPO has my undying gratitude that I finally managed to achieve something more than a competency in the subject.

'Bumbly', or correctly, Professor Cooper, was charged with instructing us in the History of Music. It was not difficult to understand why he was 'Bumbly'. He seemed incapable of stringing the shortest sentence together without tying himself in knots, and his dictates on his subject were liberally larded with anachronistic or periphrastic expressions. His 'oftentimes' and his 'mayhaps' and his 'perchances', all delivered in a broad Glasgow accent, left many of us a little confused, if not completely baffled. However he was a dear and kindly man, and we were all delighted when he finally married Miss Sheridan, the Music Secretary. Their romance had fascinated us all, conducted, as it was, in whispered colloquies outside the staff room, or while leaning companionably over the wrought-iron balcony railing. It was a well-meant gesture, although perhaps a little unkind, when we students clubbed together to buy him a second-hand copy of Doctor Johnson's dictionary as a wedding present!

* * * * *

Christmas 1933.

Dean Castle.

I wrote to Father, as Christmas 1933 approached, to ask if I might be allowed to bring a couple of University friends down to Ayrshire for the seasonal celebrations. He replied, saying that the family would be delighted to welcome a couple of my fellow students to the Castle, and you can imagine with what excitement we three – that is, Julie, Finlay and myself – began to plan our little holiday. Julie was particularly looking forward to meeting Leicester, and I was sure that her sophisticated, womanly charms would make a favourable impression on my brother – such a change from the lumpen local girls who were, his mother and sisters aside, his only experience of the feminine gender up to this point.

All was not well at home. Father had become even more vague and disconnected than he had been on my last visit. He occasionally confused Julie with Dame Clara Butt,[1] a much older singer, and made obscure references to Finlay and his horn – remarks which only Father seemed to find devastatingly funny. Even so, from time to time he would have good days, when he would converse lucidly and entertainingly, and on these occasions my two friends would listen to him entranced, as he regaled us with stories of his past.

A positive note was provided by the fact that Leicester, now fifteen, and Julie, who was the same age, got along famously. Leicester appeared to like Finlay too, and the four of us youngsters enjoyed more than one fun outing. We even allowed nine-year-old Lavinia to join us from time to time, and I was amused to notice that she was already beginning to practice her feminine wiles, currently on Finlay, who received her lingering looks and flirtatious glances with an indulgent amusement.

However, Mother was home for the holidays, and this did cast something of a blight on the proceedings. She was 'dry' – that is to say, not drinking – and this certainly did not improve her mood. I tried to follow Uncle Conan's advice – he

1 Dame Clara Butt (1872 – 1936) Famous deep-voiced English contralto. Standing six feet and two inches, she would have been sixty-one years old at this time.

had suggested that a little more tolerance and consideration would improve our relationship – but she didn't make it easy. For some reason she took a dislike to Julie from the moment they met. Julie made no bones of the fact that she came from a very ordinary background, and Mother decided to play the *grande dame*, adopting a superior and patronising attitude at every available opportunity. The fact that she also referred to Finlay as 'Wee Georgie Wood'[1] was annoying enough. But it was her continual picking on Julie that really aggravated me. I tried to remonstrate with her about this, but she dismissed my complaints airily, maintaining that it was all in my imagination. But it wasn't – the fact is that she was accustomed to being the centre of masculine attention and resented someone else taking the limelight. Julie's bright and positive personality, not to mention her stunning looks, probably made Mother feel her age. She was at this time thirty-four, and still an attractive woman, but the ravages of her lifestyle were just beginning to leave their marks on her appearance, and alongside Julie she looked tired and worn. She had, too, begun to affect an inappropriately youthful style of dress, and the amount of slightly crêpey flesh on display was sometimes a little embarrassing.

In general, Julie received Mother's digs with equanimity and a little smile, but I could tell that she found the continual carping irritating. I apologised to her on my mother's behalf, but she seemed unconcerned.

"She can't help herself, Eva; I understand she's going through a tough time at the moment. If she wants to play the lady of the manor, that's fine with me. Of course, she mustn't be allowed to go too far, that wouldn't be good for her. I'll just wait for the appropriate moment to put her in her place."

I knew that Julie had a sharp tongue when she chose, and hoped that matters would settle down without a confrontation.

The entire family was present for the holiday season, including the McWhirters. Grandpa Max and Grandma Alma had driven down with Uncle Conan. To add to my uneasiness, Grandma seemed to be once more in the grip of her religious obsessions. I was, to say the least, disconcerted, when she stopped me in the hallway on Christmas Eve, and whispered, "He's possessed, you know. No-one else has noticed yet, but I can see it."

"Who, Grandma?" I asked.

"Max, of course. Your grandfather. You look – you'll see. You have the sight, Eva, like me, I can tell. I'm afraid he's always been susceptible to evil influence and it's finally caught up with him again." She sighed. "I may have to have him re-exorcised, it's the only thing that seems to work. Otherwise, it's…."

Raising her eyebrows, she gave me a significant look, and made to move on..

I stopped her. "Surely not, Grandma?"

1 Wee Georgie Wood (1894 – 1979) Four foot nine inches midget music-hall star, awarded the OBE in 1946

She turned to face me. "Oh yes, he bears the Devil's mark, Max, he always has. The stories I could tell you – you wouldn't know about these things of course, pet, but I do, I assure you. Your mother too – she has it."

"Has what?"

"The Devil's mark, of course. They're two of a kind…"

And she carried on into the dining room muttering to herself, "No, no, it can't go on, Desperate measures, that's what's required, desperate measures…"

All in all a baffling and uncomfortable conversation.

Matters finally came to a head over Christmas dinner. We had enjoyed a thoroughly traditional meal, roast goose as I recall, with all the usual trimmings. Everyone was in a relaxed and jovial mood. Father was at his most benign and entertaining, and Leicester and Finlay were joking merrily as boys do. Even Mother seemed for once to have left her high horse tethered in the hallway. Old Angus served the pudding, with a little glass of something special to complement it. I had expected that Mother would avoid this, as up till now she had stayed firmly away from alcohol. However, perhaps inadvertently, she picked up her glass and downed its contents in one.

It was just then that Julie remarked pleasantly, "How delicious – what lovely little éclairs."

Mother smiled in her most condescending manner. "Julie, my dear, I realise you haven't had the benefit of the best upbringing, and are probably not familiar with the more exotic foodstuffs, but even you, surely, can tell the difference between an éclair and a profiterole?"

I could have crawled under the table in my embarrassment. But Julie had had enough.

"Mrs Hinge, I may not know the difference between an éclair and a profiterole. But I do know enough to recognise a tart when I see one." And she continued eating her pudding calmly.

There was a moment of stunned silence; then all hell broke loose. My jaw dropped. Leicester and Finlay stuffed their napkins in their mouths to stifle their guffaws. Alma intoned, "Judge not, that ye be not judged." And Father climaxed the whole issue by saying ruminatively, "Aye, Maureen, the lassie's got your number all right. Well said, Clara."

* * * * *

"You friends will be leaving this afternoon, Mona. I see no reason why I should allow myself to be insulted in my own home and in front of my entire family. Dougal will collect them in the car at two thirty."

Mother had summoned me to her room on Boxing Day morning. She was still in bed, her hair in curlers. I noticed the large glass of whisky on her bedside table.

"Very well, Mother. I shall be leaving too."

"As you choose, Mona." She picked up her glass, and I turned to leave. But she hadn't finished. "Even *you* must understand my reasons. That outburst yesterday was a totally unprovoked and slanderous attack, from a girl to whom I have shown nothing but kindness and consideration. Really, Mona, I wonder at you. How could you make a friend of such a creature?"

I turned back, determined to have my say. "Firstly, it was not unprovoked, Mother," I replied. "Since Julie and Finlay arrived here you have done nothing but insult and belittle them. I'm frankly amazed Julie put up with it for as long as she did. And secondly, it was hardly slanderous. The term 'slander' implies untruth."

Mother was briefly speechless, which gave me some satisfaction. Recovering, and setting her glass down, she continued.

"I don't know what has come over you, Mona. You used to be a quiet, well-behaved girl, never arguing, never rude, always mannerly. What has happened to you?"

"It doesn't matter. I must go and pack."

But Mother had not quite finished.

"Well, before you go, here's something to be considering. Your friend Julie will be leaving Morag's place. She will have to find somewhere else to live. I'm not having my daughter sharing accommodation with such a foul-mouthed and uncouth person."

I stared at her, uncertain.

"Why should she leave? Morag likes her. She won't throw Julie out on your say-so, especially as Julie and I are such close friends."

Mother smiled sweetly.

"But that's where you're wrong, Mona. Morag will do exactly as she's told."

I raised my eyebrows. "Really? And why should she?"

Mother settled herself into a more comfortable position. "Because I know a thing or two about your Aunty Morag and her guest house that you don't." She nodded, exuding self-satisfaction. "Oh yes, the threat of a wee note on my headed paper to Elgin Town Council, informing them of the unsavoury goings-on at Morag's, will soon get her attention. I shall be writing to her this morning, and informing her that, unless Julie is removed forthwith, Morag may find herself without a roof over her head." Self-satisfaction mutated seamlessly into self-righteousness. "Really, it's high time – that place is little better than a bordello."

She smiled contentedly.

"I see, Mother," I said slowly. "You're telling me that the place *you* sent me to the place *you* insisted that I live in, is a house of ill repute?"

Of course this was hardly news to me, but it suited my plan to have Mother think it was.

"If you choose to use such a mealy-mouthed expression, Mona, then yes, it is."

She drew herself up in her bed and continued smugly.

"So what do you have to say to that, eh? You think you are very clever, Mona, don't you? Your foolish father has filled your head with nonsense about how clever and intelligent you are, but you have a long way to go before you are a match for me. Now go and pack – you're giving me a headache."

I turned and reached for the door handle.

"I'm going, Mother." I hesitated. Did I dare?

I turned back. "But I have a question."

Mother yawned. "Very well – what is it? Make it quick."

"I was just wondering… What do you suppose would be the result if the Tennis Club, the Young Farmer's Association and the Ayrshire Hunt were to find out that a highly respected member had spent two years in prison for attempted murder?"

Mother's face was a sight I will long remember.

"What?" she whispered, clutching the bedclothes.

For a moment I panicked, remembering the Post Office and the rifle.

Screwing up my courage, "Yes," I continued. "What if it were to get about that the chatelaine of Castle Hinge was a common criminal? Indeed, a convicted felon?"

A silence. Then, "Get out of here!" Mother hissed.

Her face was as white as her sheets. Indeed, for a moment I worried that she might have a seizure.

"I'm going, Mother. But if I were you, I would leave my correspondence with Morag to another day, when you're more yourself. Just ask how she is – leave it at that. Maybe send her some money? That would be a kind thought. Business is not what it was."

I opened the door, and turned briefly towards her.

"And have another drink, Mother. You look as though you need it."

* * * * *

1934.

Lang Hall.

That was the last conversation I had with my mother for some considerable time. I was invited to spend the Easter break of 1934 with Finlay's family. Then it was time to prepare for my second year examinations, and plan something for the end-of-year concert.

My studies had continued to go well. Harmony and Counterpoint no longer held any terrors for me (as, I must admit, they had during my first year). I was progressing particularly well in composition and orchestration. Indeed, I had already composed some small-scale piano pieces, a set of twelve Studies and three little Caprices on Scottish melodies; I decided it was time to attempt something more ambitious.

I passed my second year exams well ahead of the rest of my year, and Finlay and Julie insisted that we celebrate. I was relieved to discover that I had finally stopped growing, and five foot nine would be my final height. Finlay, thank goodness, had suddenly put on a spurt, and caught up with me. He had lost most of his puppy fat, and had turned into a very handsome young man. Many of the girls at Lang Hall cast languishing glances in his direction, but he appeared to have eyes for no-one but me – indeed, he and I were now officially boy-friend and girl-friend, it appeared. Julie had taken up with a certain Ian Briggs. Ian was one of Aunty Morag's travelling gentlemen. Not one, I hasten to add, who had enjoyed Mo-Mo's dubious favours in earlier days – Ian was nineteen, and had only been on his circuit for a couple of months. He and Julie were emphatically 'not serious' – "I'm far too young to settle down", said Julie. I wasn't sure how serious Finlay and I were, but we certainly spend most of our free time together.

Julie had finally managed to interest me in the art of make-up, although I limited myself to a discreet application of 'papier poudré' and a light coating of Tangee Natural lipstick. To this I would add on occasion a tiny amount of Julie's mascara. Not for me the excesses that my dear friend favoured – I had no need for eyebrow pencil, having naturally well-shaped, dark eyebrows, and my country-bred complexion did not require the assistance of rouge.

I decided that for the end-of-term concert I would prepare a setting of Keats' *Ode to a Nightingale* for voice, horn and piano. The poet's immortal lines would be set for Julie's rich mezzo-soprano, the musical motifs echoed where appropriate by Finlay's French horn, the whole against a delicate tissue of piano support. My work on the piece progressed quickly, and something of a buzz began to go round among our fellow-students in anticipation of the first performance.

Our post-exam celebration, we decided, would be held at Morag's. Julie had recently discovered the 'cocktail', and enjoyed nothing more than coming up with some delicious concoction of her own devising for these occasions. Morag always had ends of various bottles lying around, and it was Julie's self-appointed task to combine these in interesting proportions. It might be a glass or two of ruby port, a few measures of 'Parfait Amour', perhaps a bottle of Ian's favoured pale ale, maybe the dregs of something called 'Absinthe'. Whatever it was, it went into the mix.

I remember that on this occasion the cocktail was something Julie had named 'French Knickers' – she had a vivid imagination and a somewhat saucy vocabulary from time to time. I'm not sure what the ingredients were, but it was certainly potent – so much so that I have a very hazy memory of the end of the evening. But I know that I took a very nasty tumble on my way upstairs to bed, and ended up breaking a small bone in my right wrist. This, although painful, was soon treated, but of course I ended up with a 'stookie'[1] on my forearm. And the first performance of my new composition was due to take place in a few days!

I had no choice but to approach Mona McCafferty, my fellow pianist, to help out, although I had no very high opinion of her abilities. If uninspired, at least she was efficient. She was poring over a score of Berg's piano sonata[2] in the students' common room when I located her, clad in her usual masculine attire – black trousers and a smart snuff-coloured smoking jacket. When I made my request she hesitated for a moment, and puffed pensively on her cheroot.

"Is it *modern*, Eva?" she asked, "You know I only play modern."

"Oh, it's very modern indeed," said I. "In fact it was only finished on Friday."

"OK, I'll have a look at it."

In the event, she performed splendidly, as did both Julie and Finlay. My little piece enjoyed a great success. I was a little surprised to discover that Mona was quite capable of turning in a first-rate performance when the material suited her. Indeed, as I continued to get to know her better, I discovered that I had been perhaps a little too hasty in dismissing her. Her keyboard technique, though idiosyncratic, was a solid one. And during the course of our rehearsals, I discovered that, in spite of her somewhat forbidding exterior, she was an amusing and intelligent colleague. Gradually, we became friends. Even so, I did not for a moment anticipate that she and I, in a few short years, would entertain the cream of the Wehrmacht together as 'Die Beiden Monas – Weltberühmtes Klavierduo'[3], under unusual and terrifying circumstances

---

1 A plaster cast.

2 Alban Berg. Follower and pupil of Schönberg, he used his master's 'twelve-tone' system of composition. He was the composer of 'Wozzeck' and 'Lulu', two of the most highly regarded of 20th century operas.

3 The Two Monas – World Renowned Piano Duo

And so my second year at University came to an end, and I headed for home for the summer break – unaware that a catastrophe of cataclysmic proportions was looming.

* * * * *

1934.

Dean Castle.

"He will marry the lassie, and that's an end of it," Father proclaimed.

"Over my dead body, Hector!" This was Mother.

He nodded absent-mindedly. "Aye, if that's what it takes, Maureen."

Mother again. "Anyway, he's far too young to get married – he's sixteen – and she's twenty-three!"

I had left my cases in the hall, and walked straight into a major family row. Present were Mother and Father, Uncle Conan, Leicester, and, surprisingly, Dougal McDougal, now Mother's official chauffeur. He was standing next to her by the fireplace looking smart and relaxed in his uniform. It had been some considerable time since I had seen Dougal, and I was surprised at the change in his appearance and manner. I found it difficult to associate this good-looking, polished and urbane young man with the timid and agonisingly self-conscious boy I had known only a couple of years ago. He would, I supposed, be about eighteen now.

Leicester, pale and obviously unhappy, was seated on the sofa next to Uncle Conan, and Father was on his feet in front of him.

"What's going on?" I asked.

It was finally explained to me that Jeannie Dunt was pregnant – that didn't surprise me, indeed I would have said it was inevitable. But unbelievably, she was blaming my unfortunate brother for her condition.

"It's not true, it had nothing to do with me, I swear it," insisted Leicester, on the verge of tears.

"And I believe him," said Conan. "I know Leicester well, and he's just not capable of such a thing."

"Of course not," I added. "And anyway, surely it's not possible? He's only sixteen."

Mother rounded on me. "For God's sake, Mona, what do *you* know? If you think a boy of sixteen is not capable, then you had better watch out for yourself."

Father turned to her. "Don't start on Evie, Maureen. She's far too sensible." He turned back to Leicester. "But I wish I could say the same for this idiot here."

He went on, "They will be married as soon as decently possible. That's the way this is going to be handled."

Mother did not agree. "But, Hector, think. There are other possibilities. These things can be – well – dealt with, swept under the carpet, so to speak, got rid of. Or" – she paused – "we could marry her off to somebody else."

Once again Father turned a penetrating gaze on her. "Oh, could we, Maureen? Do you think so? Maybe to young McDougal here?"

"No, no, of course not, Hector, not Dougal." Mother laughed dismissively and, it seemed to me, rather nervously. "Why should *he* take responsibility? He has his own future to worry about, as much as Leicester does. Don't you, Dougie?"

And she smiled at dark-haired Dougal, and gave his hand a little squeeze. He returned both, but did not reply. I noticed that his teeth were white and even.

"Someone has got his feet well under the table," I thought.

Father headed towards the door. "No, Maureen, as you say. So there's no other solution. It will be as I have said."

My poor brother dissolved in tears, while Uncle Conan attempted to comfort him. Mother said a bad word, and Dougal smiled, this time in a self-satisfied manner that made me feel slightly uneasy. I fled in dismay.

* * * * *

Some time later, when I had collected myself, I headed towards Leicester's room, and knocked gently on the door.

"Come in, Eva – I thought it was you," he said as I entered. He was sitting at his desk, looking dejected and unhappy. He turned to face me. "You surely don't buy into this rigmarole, do you?"

I shook my head decisively, and closed the door quietly behind me. "No, of course I don't, Leicester. But Father is convinced; Mother doesn't care one way or the other, just as long as you don't have to marry her." I sat down on the edge of the bed. "But Conan believes you. And naturally, so do I."

He shuddered and wrinkled his nose in disgust. "As if I would have anything to do with that slut! It's ridiculous."

I forgave my brother the coarse epithet, aware of the stress he was under.

"Of course it is." I smiled at him reassuringly. After a pause I went on, "But you must admit, you *have* spent quite a bit of time in her company over the years, haven't you?"

"Yes I have, but that was ages ago. I haven't seen her alone in a year or more. And she's three months pregnant."

"I see. So – who do you think might be responsible?"

He wrinkled his brow.

"Could be anyone – Jeannie's not exactly sparing with her favours – that's well known. It could be McDougal, even."

"Mother says not," I continued, "though I'm not sure how she would know."

"Well, she does if anyone does," replied Leicester. "You'll have noticed how close those two are these days?"

"Yes, I have. What's that all about?"

"Best not to ask, Eva," answered my brother with a crooked little smile. "But the point is, what am *I* going to do? Father's mind is made up. And of course, Jeannie is already seeing herself as the next 'Lady Hinge'. I just don't know where to turn."

I stood up. I could think of only one place. "I can't promise anything, Leicester. But let me see what I can do," I said, as I left him.

It was with some trepidation that I made my way to Mother's room. We had hardly exchanged more than the civilities in the last months. I knew that to ask for her help was opening myself up to all sorts of possible problems. Indeed I almost turned back. However, hurrying through the hall, I ran full tilt into the expectant mother herself. I would have passed her without a word, but she reached out her hand and stopped me.

"Ye'll have heard the news, Miss Eva, Ah suppose? Just think – ye're going to be an aunty! Imagine it – you and me will be sisters. Ah'll just call ye 'Eva', shall I?"

I could have struck her.

* * * * *

Mother was unwontedly cordial when I entered her study. She was seated in a comfy armchair, browsing through a magazine, as if she hadn't a care in the world.

"Come in, Mona, I've been expecting you." She looked up and laid the magazine aside. "How are things with you?"

As if she had ever cared much one way or the other about that. But I decided to take advantage of this unexpected *bonhomie*.

"Good, thank you, Mother. My studies are going really well."

"I'm pleased to hear it. Now enough of that…"

This was more like it.

"…what on earth are we going to do about the situation that your idiot brother has landed us in?"

"Mother, I am as sure as I can be that Jeannie's situation has nothing to do with Leicester, nothing whatever."

She nodded. "Probably not, but in the end it's irrelevant. I am determined ..."

I interrupted. "We thought that maybe Dougal..."

She shook her head. "No, no, you're on the wrong track there Mona – Dougal has – well, let's just say that he has other fish to fry. As I was about to say – I am determined that no son of mine will be trapped into a marriage with that sly-faced slattern, guilty or not. But of course your stupid father has determined that the family honour must be upheld, whatever the consequences. Have a seat, do."

I sat down. "Well, Mother, in that case I don't know what to suggest."

"Don't worry Mona. I have already decided how to tackle this. But I need your help."

My help? I think this was probably the first time that Mother and I had found ourselves on the same side in anything.

I leaned towards her. "Well of course, whatever it takes. If it helps Leicester."

"Good. It will, just as you say. Don't worry, I know exactly what needs to be done."

I wondered if Mother was preparing a loaded rifle for Jeannie? I confess it was not entirely an unwelcome prospect. I actually began vaguely to consider how we might dispose of the body.

She continued, "I'll talk to Conan. Tonight, you must keep your father occupied. Take him into the library, have a wee chat to him about music. He'll need one of his injections – give him a double dose. Tell him all about your studies, ask him about his latest composition, anything at all to keep him occupied. It shouldn't be difficult. I've given Jeannie the night off, and the Anguses are in bed by ten. It should all go smoothly if you just make sure your father isn't around. Can you do that?"

"Yes, of course I can, Mother." The thought of deceiving Father made me uneasy. But what was the alternative? "What is your plan?"

She hesitated. "Best you don't know, Mona. Leave it all to me. Just make sure Hector is kept occupied."

"I will, Mother," I said, "Trust me."

"Funnily enough, I do. You're about the only person around here I *can* trust."

This sounded almost like a compliment.

Mother was ready for action. "Now off you go, there's no time to waste."

I stood up and made for the door, but paused, my hand on the handle. There was something I wanted to say. I turned back.

"Mother – I'm sorry about the way things have gone between us in the past, and that we've not always seen eye to eye."

Mother raised her eyebrows quizzically.

"Oh? Well, I daresay there have been faults on both sides, Mona – no doubt more on yours than on mine. The trouble is we're too alike, you and I."

Alike? For some reason I felt oddly flattered.

I had no trouble persuading Father to join me in the library for a chat. He was only too happy, I think, to forget the cares of the day. Without either of us mentioning it, the whole sad saga was ignored. We talked at length about the subject that occupied us most – music – and he was endearingly interested in looking at the score of my recent composition. If I felt slightly guilty at the deception I was practising, I reassured myself that it was for the long-term good of the family, and that on this one occasion, Father had been wrong. As Mother had suggested, I gave Father a generous double dose of his medication, and when we finally said goodnight at around midnight he was ready for bed, and the house was silent.

* * * * *

Breakfast the next day was a sombre affair. Only Father and I were present. He kept nodding off into his cereal, due no doubt to the extra strong injection he had received the previous evening. Between his naps we chatted desultorily about the musical trends of the day. Then, as we rose from the table, an unearthly shriek echoed through the house. Seconds later, Mother swept into the dining room in her peignoir, clutching a piece of paper.

"This is *your* fault, Hector, all your fault!"

"What is my fault, dear?" Father enquired mildly.

"This is, all of this. Gone, both of them. Gone for ever – and where – eh?"

Father seemed understandably confused. "A?" he went on gamely. "Do I have to guess? Ardrossan, Auchenshuggle, Auchtermuchtie, Addis Ababa? And who has gone, eh?"

So that had been Mother's plan. I smiled to myself quietly – I doubted anyone had gone further than nearby Glasgow.

But Mother was in 'high tragedy' mode, with lots of hand-wringing and hair-tearing. She was rather good.

"Both of them," she replied. "Conan and Leicester. Do you see what you have done, you hard-hearted, unfeeling man?"

"Conan? Leicester? What do you mean, Maureen?" She handed Father the piece of paper she was brandishing. He perused it intently.

Mother was in full flood by this time.

"Come to me, Mona, come, my wee girl, my last remaining child!" And she clutched me to her bosom. This remark, however effective, was rather strong, and not even accurate, unless she had dropped Lavinia down a well.

Father was initially speechless. He rose to his feet, clutching the table for support. He eventually managed a "Leicester? No! Surely not?"

Mother was by now overacting horribly. "A mother's curse on you, Hector Hinge!" she wailed, almost suffocating me in folds of *peau de soie* and clouds of Chanel.

"I can't breathe, Mother," I croaked. When she released me I murmured *sotto voce*, "But why did Conan have to go too?"

Father sank back in his chair, his head in his hands, oblivious.

"You surely don't think I would let a sixteen-year-old boy travel on his own, do you?" Mother whispered indignantly. "Not all the way to Australia?"

Chapter Five
The Worst of Times

Australia? What had Mother been thinking of?

'*My dear father*

I assure you one final time that I am in no way responsible for the present situation. But since only Eva and Mother seem to believe me, I have decided to take the only way out that I can see. Uncle Conan has agreed to help. Don't try to find me. I will return when the truth comes out, as it will one day. Until then I am

Your loving son

Leicester'

Mother did not dare tell Father the facts – that it was she who had organised their flight. So naturally, Father assumed that the plan had been dreamed up by Uncle Conan, and blamed him entirely.

"Kidnap, that's what it is," he raged, storming up and down. "I've never trusted that brother of yours, Maureen. He's been filling Leicester's head with his nonsense for years, giving him ideas about the joys of travel, and I'd rather not think what else. And now, see the result – he's abducted our son!"

"*Abducted?*" Mother smiled deprecatingly. "Really, Hector!" Her tone was placatory. "You must realise, surely, that what he has done is to help Leicester out of an impossible situation – a situation that *you* brought about, with your shotgun wedding notions."

Of course, Father had no idea where the culprits were headed. Leicester's note had given no indication, and for all Father knew they could be in Troon or the Belgian Congo. Mother and I had resolved to keep him in the dark, at least for the time being. When I finally got her alone I asked her what on earth had she been thinking of, sending my brother so far away. She seemed unconcerned.

"It was your Uncle Conan's idea, Mona. And I agreed. Conan knows Australia well; he's been there several times then he was in the Navy, and he has friends there who will help. He thought it best to get Leicester completely out of the way until all this blows over. No doubt he will find a means of getting word to us before too long. But keep that to yourself for now or your father will have every police force in the civilised world after them."

Indeed, Father did notify the authorities of Leicester's flight, but they appeared to be unable to find any useful information. As far as they could tell the fugitives had vanished without trace.

It took Father some time to come to terms with my brother's 'abduction', as he continued to term it. Many times I was on the verge of telling him the truth; but refrained, fearful that a knowledge of the details, and of the deception practised on him by my mother and myself, might send him over the edge.

Weeks went by with no news of any kind. It was with a heavy heart that I returned to Lang Hall to begin my third year.

* * * * *

1934.

Lang Hall.

It was a relief to get away from home. The atmosphere there, with all that had happened, had become gloomy – claustrophobic and stifling. Just seeing my old friends brightened my mood; but best of all, my clever brother had managed to get a letter to me care of Julie, and I finally had some concrete information to pass on to Mother the next time I returned to the family. It was a relief to learn that he and Conan had made the crossing to Australia safely and were currently living in Sydney, where they were posing as father and son. I wrote back immediately and gave him all the news from home. He insisted that Father be kept unaware of his whereabouts until things had settled down, and I agreed to abide by his wishes in the matter, at least for the time being.

My third year at Lang Hall was in truth something of a 'lang haul'. Lessons continued in the usual way; but I found myself less able to concentrate, and was in danger of falling behind, with the constant worries of my home situation and the continuing uncertainty of my brother's position. Indeed I might have come to grief when exam time came round were it not for the support and encouragement of my friend Julie. With her help I managed to pull myself together, and finally made a reasonable showing.

With a single exception, my fellow students were equally successful. That exception was Mr Phil Hanson, who only scraped through by the skin of his teeth. Unsurprisingly, as his entire attention continued to be taken up with his relentless pursuit of Vicky Dean. He never, as far as I was aware, did any studying, but spent all of his time composing elegies, sonnets and the like to his fair lady. For some reason he would occasionally choose me to confide in. I think he sensed that, happy in my own love-life as I was, I felt some sympathy for him. I recall him asking me for my opinion.

"I'm at my wit's end, Eva. Don't know what to do. Nothing seems to work on the girl. How should I approach her?"

I gave the matter some thought. "Light-heartedly would be my suggestion, Phil. You're always too intense. Make her laugh, if you can."

“Make her laugh, eh?” he mused. “Maybe you’re right, Eva. Is she ticklish, I wonder?”

“I’m not sure,” I replied. “You could try. Maybe give her a couple of test tickles?”

“Yes, yes, that’s just my plan,” he groaned as he sank to the ground paralysed with mirth – who knows why?

* * * * *

Speaking of my love-life, that too was causing me some anxiety during this period. Finlay and I continued to be as close as ever, but, as might be expected from any red-blooded male of sixteen, he was beginning to be more pressing in his requests for what I might describe as ‘further intimacies’. Up to this point we had naturally kissed and shared a certain amount of physical closeness, but all too aware, due to recent events, of the pitfalls in the way, I was reluctant to allow matters to proceed any further in this direction. On the surface, he always appeared understanding of my feelings, but it was becoming increasingly difficult to put him off. Particularly as my own inclination was to accede.

How to resist? I summoned up the unyielding discipline instilled in me by Effie and Myra, and applied it here. I discovered it could be as effective in personal situations as in professional ones.

* * * * *

1935.

Lang Hall.

A major change in my lodging arrangements occurred just after the Christmas break in 1934. Although Morag’s general attitude had improved beyond recognition in the years Julie and I had been guests in her little establishment, one thing we had never been able to alter was her steadfast conviction that freezing temperatures and an almost complete lack of heating were somehow beneficial to two growing girls and a variable number of peripatetic gentlemen visitors. If ever we complained, she would assure us in a self-righteous tone that she herself found only benefits in the current regime, and that we needed to ‘toughen up’. The fact that I had on more than one occasion found her warming her blue-tinged hands over the hot plate in the kitchen, when she was concocting one of the dreary dishes with which she was wont to regale us, should have made me realise that there was something of a double standard c*hez* Mo-Mo. But the full extent of her perfidy was not revealed until after the memorable occasion when I found myself being carried down a ladder by a rather jolly fireman, while

Ballochmyle – A Home Away from Home was reduced to ashes behind me. The authorities could find no apparent cause for the conflagration.

But Julie knew better. She had obviously explored the secret life of *Ballochmyle* much more thoroughly than had I.

"Did you not know that Mo-Mo has a very special line in bed-warmers, Eva?"

I assumed Julie was referring to Morag's *penchant* for company in her private quarters.

"No, no, Eva," Julie corrected me. "The blessed Morag has worked out that if she plugs in an electric iron, and puts it inside a Peek Frean's biscuit tin, she can use this contraption to warm the sheets of her virgin couch to a pleasant temperature."

Morag, according to Julie, had been doing this for years without a problem. But, cheeseparing as she was, the frayed cable of the iron had been patched up with sticking plaster so many times that it eventually yielded to the immutable laws of physics and exploded into flames.

Luckily, Julie and I were able to find alternative accommodation at Lang Hall itself, and we soon settled down in a cheerful (and warm) little apartment overlooking the North quadrangle. Why we hadn't opted for this arrangement long before, I don't know. I took a slightly malicious pleasure, too, in allowing Morag to have the use of our freezing box room as temporary lodgings until her insurance claim was arranged. As soon as this was paid out, she purchased a compact three-bedroom cottage in Cullen, just up the coast, and settled in there happily. And it wasn't long before it was 'business as usual' for Morag. I must confess that I rather missed the old bag from time to time.

* * * * *

One awkward complication of our new domestic arrangements was that Finlay was on hand just a few doors away, and it became ever more difficult to avoid his persistence. Julie's advice, if unhelpful, was at least straightforward.

"Just get on with it, hen. Take precautions, of course, but where's the harm? You're nearly fifteen. You and he are obviously going to be an item for life, so don't keep the poor laddie waiting any longer. You never know – keep saying 'No' and he might end up looking elsewhere."

We had no secrets, and sixteen-year-old Julie had, I knew, already advanced much further down that particular path than had I. But something restrained me. Whether it was the memory of my unfortunate brother's fate, or a simple reluctance to take a step from which there was no going back, I can't say. But for the time being, I managed to keep Finlay at arm's length, or at least an inch or two short of his goal.

In February 1935, I received a letter from Leicester. Among his other news, he was excited to tell me that he and Conan were planning a camping trip into the wilds of Australia. They intended to visit Ayers Rock, and to see the many wonders of the mysterious interior of the southern continent. They expected to be gone for a month or two. I was somewhat concerned when I learned of these plans. But I comforted myself with the thought that Conan was a man of experience in such matters, and that he would be bound to keep a strict eye on my brother and look out for his safety. I decided not to mention this news at home for the time being, but wrote back to Leicester asking him to be sure to keep in touch regularly.

Matters with Finlay finally came to a head just before the Easter break. I had continued to fend him off to the best of my ability, but it was becoming more and more difficult. He seemed to have more hands than any human being had a right to. Then, out of the blue, after one particularly stressful tussle…

"OK Eva," he said. "Marry me. You love me. I love you. So marry me."

What? Where had this come from? How to respond? I said the first thing that came into my head.

"But we can't get married – I'm too young."

"Yes, of course you are," Finlay went on. "Stupid law – a few years ago we could have got married right away[1]. That's the way it always was."

"But it's not the way it is now. We need to be sixteen"

"And I already am. And you will be in just over a year. So marry me then. Say you will."

This was certainly a bolt from the blue. While on some level I had imagined that he and I might marry at some unspecified time in the future, perhaps when we were both established in our musical careers, the thought of taking that step at this stage, or even committing to it, seemed ridiculously premature.

I was not so naïve that I didn't take into account that this sudden determination to bestow benefit of clergy on our relationship might have its basis in a rather more mundane matter than a longing for the sound of wedding bells. I had read enough books and seen enough films to understand that promises of marriage could easily lead to a scenario involving mothers and babies in the snow, moustache-twirling and villainous landlords, and fates worse than death.

I wondered how best to respond to his demand.

"Finlay," I replied at length, "We're both far too young to think about marriage as yet. Of course I love you, you know I do. I *will* marry you – who

1 Before the Scottish Marriage Act of 1929, the age of consent in Scotland was twelve for a girl and fourteen for a boy – with no parental consent necessary. In 1929 the age for both was raised to sixteen, but parental consent was still not obligatory. Whence the popularity of Gretna Green for English eloping couples.

else would I marry? – but not yet. When we're older."

He didn't seem too happy with this.

"Oh, I see. When we're older." He hesitated, as if uncertain how to express himself. "I have – well – *needs*, you know, Eva. Men *do*. What am I supposed to do in the meantime?"

"Well," I smiled, "You could just carry on doing whatever it is you've been doing up till now, couldn't you?"

"Oh, Eva, you're *impossible…*"

He was actually sulking like a child. Not an attractive look, I thought.

"On the contrary, Finlay, I am very *possible*. Just not very *probable* right now."

"Oh, I see. Whatever *that* means…"

And he stalked off in high dudgeon.

* * * * *

1935.

Dean Castle.

Easter break that year brought a few surprises. I was pleased to see that Father seemed somewhat improved, at least physically. He had always been an active man, and one of the most upsetting things about his recent decline had been to see him sitting in a chair for hours, staring into space, his mind apparently elsewhere. Now it was a pleasure to find him taking little walks round the grounds, often in my company, and showing a general interest in life which had been noticeably absent for some time.

Inevitably, a frequent topic of conversation at home was Jeannie, who had given birth to a son only a few weeks earlier. I hadn't given Jeannie much thought for a time, being far to occupied with my own concerns, but this recent event was the talk of the village.

I had cause to visit the local grocery store cum post-office for a few provisions for Mrs Angus, and you can imagine my feelings when I saw, along with several other customers, the new mother herself. But this was a very different Jeannie. Indeed, I barely recognised her. Gone were the cheap and flashy clothes, gone the over-familiar and pert attitude. And the baby was simply beautiful. The animated conversation which had been taking place before I arrived subsided immediately. For an instant I wondered, disloyally, '*Is this child possibly my nephew?*' And that question was soon answered.

"Miss, d'ye have a moment?" Jeannie whispered, approaching me. Miss? This was indeed a new Jeannie.

"What do you want?" I responded curtly and clearly, declining to emulate her hushed tone.

She looked round anxiously, embarrassed. "I need to speak to you, Miss," she continued, still whispering. "I need to tell ye the truth. Ah did a bad thing last year, blaming Mr Leicester for ma – for ma difficulties. But – it had nothing to dae wi' him, nothing at all."

My heart leapt. So, at last, the truth. My brother was vindicated. Father would hear the news as soon as I got home, and in a short while Leicester would return to his traumatised family. And to think that all our problems were due to this pathetic creature and her lies. I was at first too taken aback to say more than, "Jeannie – how could you? What kind of woman *are* you to invent such things?"

I have never been of an aggressive temperament. Indeed I despise those who favour violence and yield to its impulses. But then, suddenly, for perhaps the first time in my life I was seized and filled with an overpowering rage. Jeannie tried to speak, but I did not allow her to utter a word. As I leant over her, she cowered away from my superior height and the no doubt threatening expression on my face.

"Get out of my sight, you loathsome, twisted creature," I hissed. "Or I promise you, you will be sorry."

Breathing hard, I turned away. Jeannie burst into a flood of tears.

"Please, Miss, please, let me explain…" She clutched my arm.

I glanced over my shoulder, shaking off her grip. "Do you even begin to understand the misery you have caused?" A mounting anger I had never known myself capable of continued to swell and flame. I would happily have killed her. And it felt intoxicating, liberating. In that moment I was undoubtedly my mother's daughter.

Turning round to face her again, I pushed my face right into hers. "I warn you, Jeannie, one more word and I won't be responsible for my actions. Get out of here, just the sight of you makes me sick."

The rest of the customers in the shop were agog, especially petty-minded Janet McKenzie, the proprietor, our notorious local gossip. Both she and her husband Ronnie, that nasty piece of work and sometime partner-in-drink to Mother, were on tenterhooks for the next revelation.

"I hope you all heard that," I said, turning to them. "Did you get the details of the story spread around by this shameless liar? How she tried to blackmail her way into my family with her fantasies?"

They nodded, open-mouthed, like so many sheep.

And then at that moment, the baby began to cry. Whoever was at fault, it wasn't him. As suddenly as it had arisen my rage was gone. I looked at the weeping girl beside me and felt ashamed.

"Why, Jeannie, why?" I said, trying for and achieving a reasonable tone.

"You must have realised the problems you were causing for us. Why would you do such a thing? How could you hurt us all like that? – haven't the family always been good to you? Father in particular. Don't you know how all this business has made him ill with worry? Why?"

Jeannie ceased to bawl and wiped her eyes. "It wasn't my idea, Miss. Not at all. Ah wid never have thought of such a thing. It wiz Dougal; he put the idea into my heid."

"Dougal?" Aha! Smirking, smug, self-satisfied Dougal McDougal – Mother's dear confidant, and who knew what else? "You mean – *Dougal* is the baby's father?" As I had half-suspected.

But Jeannie shook her head. "No, no Miss, not that. But it was him who had the idea of putting the blame on your brother. He said that, if Ah went along with the idea, everything would work out for the best, for me, for the baby. He planned it, Miss, not me. Ah was just stupid enough to have ma heid turned by the idea."

Dougal, oh Dougal...

"Oh, Jeannie – if you only knew the damage…"

"Ah do now, Miss, Ah do. Ah've no' been able tae sleep thinking aboot it." Her tone became eager, placatory. "But now ye can tell the family the truth, can't ye, and ask them to forgive me? Ah'll come up to the big hoose if ye like, and tell them aw whit Ah've told you."

I thought this was profoundly inadvisable. "There's no need for that Jeannie. You have your baby to consider. And I wouldn't want you to have to face Mother, who might be inclined to do something rash – you know how unpredictable she can be. Leave it to me. I will make sure everyone knows, and before long Leicester will be back home where he belongs."

"Thank you, Miss, thank you," Jeannie said, adding with a watery smile, "You're right, your mother is certainly a fearsome woman. That was why Ah waited tae see you. I thought you might understand, and – forgive me."

I hesitated. "I'm not sure I can go that far, Jeannie. But thank you for telling the truth, however late." I looked into the perambulator. "And the baby is beautiful. You must be proud. No doubt you will have to put up with unkind comments from some people" – I allowed my glance to fall on our audience – "but I am sure Father will help out a little, financially, if you are in difficulties."

Jeannie shook her head. "Thank you – but there's no need, Miss. Ah'm married now – to Johnny Kerr who runs the garage. He's a good man, and he treats the baby like his own."

"I see." The question continued to nag at me. And after what we had all gone through, I had earned the right to ask it. "So Jeannie? – who *is* the baby's father?"

Jeannie glanced towards the listening group.

"For now Ah wid rather no' say, Miss, if ye don't mind. Best if no-one knows that." She turned to face the gathering at the counter. "He's a married man; Ah'll leave it at that."

I nodded and prepared to depart, impatient to share the astonishing news with Mother. But I turned back for a second to our public, who appeared a little disappointed by the reconciliation.

"I do hope you got *all* the details, Mrs McKenzie? If there's anything you missed, you only have to ask."

Janet, practically salivating, actually had the nerve to say, "No indeed, Miss, got it all. You can rely on me to spread the word."

"Oh, I never doubted that for a second, Mrs McKenzie."

I turned back to Jeannie.

"Jeannie – I hope you'll be happy, and I wish you well."

"The same to you, Miss, Ah'm sure."

She bobbed a rather unnecessary curtsey, and left, pushing her pram down what passed for our High Street. I returned home, desperate to astound the family with my news. And for a day of reckoning with Mr Dougal McDougal.

* * * * *

But Mother simply wouldn't accept that the deception had involved Dougal. Amid the relief and exhilaration we all shared, she was adamant on that point.

"Not Dougal, Mona, no – that I'll never believe. What on earth could be his reason? No, not at all, it's a piece of nonsense. The girl may have decided to tell the truth, but no doubt she thought it would sit better with you if she put the blame on someone else. She knows how soft-hearted you are."

And on this point she remained immovable. And certainly, Dougal himself completely denied that the *affaire Jeannie* had had anything to do with him. And we were all too delighted by the outcome to question the facts any further.

* * * * *

Mother and I had to bite the bullet, and explain our deception to Father. I dreaded his response. He and I had always been honest with each other, and his reaction was as bad as I had feared.

He looked at Mother, and shook his head despairingly. "I'm not as surprised as perhaps I should be, Maureen. Not by your part in this, at least. You've always gone to extremes; you jump in without considering the consequences, and don't concern yourself with the effect your actions have on others. Australia? Woman, I sometimes think you're not quite right in the head! And as for you, Eva..."

He turned to me. I didn't dare to look him in the eye.

"You're quite another matter. Sensible, caring Eva. What were you thinking of, lassie? What have I done that would make you lie to me in this way? I can only imagine that somehow you had your head turned by your mother's wild schemes. But that excuses nothing. I'm disappointed in you. I haven't deserved this of you, Eva."

He turned away. I wanted to die of shame and embarrassment. I was all the more mortified to notice the tears in his eyes.

Mother stretched out a hand to stop him. "Hector, don't blame Mona. As you say, it was my plan, all of it. She was just concerned about her brother, and went along with it. Unwillingly, I might add."

I was somewhat taken aback by Mother's defence of my behaviour. It would have been more in character for her to have laid the entire blame at my door. But she could always surprise me, my mother.

But Father was not persuaded.

"I won't accept that. She took a deliberate decision to deceive me and must bear the consequences. She's not a child. This discussion is at an end. Just get the laddie home, Maureen, and we can draw a line under the whole sorry story."

* * * * *

Father was right, of course. And it was with some apprehension that I entered the library some time later to find him sitting in his favourite armchair, staring into space, one hand on his forehead.

"Father..."

"What is it, Eva?"

I had to force myself to speak. "Forgive me. I'm sorry."

He looked up. "So – you think you deserve my pardon, do you?"

I hesitated. "No. I don't think I deserve it. But I hope you will give it, in spite of that."

His little smile was almost undetectable. But it was there.

"A nice humility, Eva. You want me to play Wotan to your Brünnhilde?"[1]

I risked returning his smile. "No, Father, not quite. However you choose to

1 At the end of Wagner's 'Die Walküre', Wotan finally forgives his daughter Brünnhilde for disobeying his godly commands, but punishes her by casting her into a magical sleep.

punish me, I would prefer not to be cast into a magical sleep on a fire-girt rock, if you don't mind."

He laughed gently. "Really? That might be the best place for you. To keep you safe. You know the story – only a hero can pass through the fire and awaken the sleeping maiden with a kiss. Is there a hero on the way, I wonder?"

I blushed. "No, father. No hero."

Father chuckled softly to himself. "Oh, come along now – I think there's a young Siegfried[1] waiting in the wings. Complete with horn. Am I wrong?"

I was utterly astonished. "But Father – how…"

"How did I know? Evie dear, you couldn't have made it more obvious. You barely took your eyes off the boy when he was last here."

I had no idea I had been so transparent. How mortifying. But the 'Evie, dear' did not escape me. Was I perhaps on the way to absolution?

"Now," he changed the subject. "regarding Leicester. Your mother informs me that you are in contact with him."

I explained that I didn't have a current address for Leicester just at present, but that he would be in touch when he and Conan returned from their holiday.

"Hmm. I see. Well, I'm not sure I like the sound of that. But I suppose we'll have to await Conan's convenience, damn the man. Be sure to let me know as soon as you hear from Leicester – it's high time this silly charade was brought to an end."

I couldn't have agreed more wholeheartedly. I would be fifteen in a few months, and perhaps I could celebrate my birthday, Father's forgiveness and Leicester's return at the same time.

* * * * *

1935.

Lang Hall.

I travelled back to Lang Hall for the final term of the year in better spirits. Matters seemed to be improving for our family at last; I had this year's finals to prepare for; and Julie would be graduating at the end of term.

For this year's concert, I had decided to compose something on a rather grander scale than I had hitherto attempted. Since Julie, who was popular with everyone, would be leaving us to go off in search of a career, I thought it appropriate to involve all of us third year students in something that would be a tribute to her, and a farewell gift. Thus it was that what I consider my first major composition was conceived. 'Harmonic Series' was designed from the outset to

1 In the following opera, 'Siegfried', Brünnhilde is finally awakened by the horn-bearing hero Siegfried

include parts for all us third-year students. I also wrote for a small choir composed of half a dozen students from the first and second years. The piece was written partly in a forward-looking style, following some of the precepts of Mona McCafferty's idol, Schönberg, but also incorporating melodious moments in the style of Puccini, a combination which I was sure had never been attempted up till then, and, as far as I know, has never been attempted since.

That I had, as yet, had no word from my brother was causing me a growing concern. His foray into the Australian wilderness should have come to an end, but it was now more than three months since I had heard from him, and I felt uneasy at his continued silence. I knew that Father had already contacted the antipodean authorities to enlist their help in tracking down the missing pair. But so far without success.

My classmates acquitted themselves admirably at the end-of-term concert, particularly my fellow pianist Mona McCafferty, who was fast becoming a friend. She was great company, and in spite of her loud and hearty manner, I detected that, underneath, she was a shy and rather lonely person, and that her eccentric dress and mannerisms masked a sensitive and reserved nature. She too seemed to have become very attached to me, and I readily agreed when she pointed out that, as I would be in need of a new flatmate after Julie's departure, she could fill the vacancy.

Julie had graduated successfully and had already been offered a position with the Carl Rosa Opera Company, playing small roles at first and hopefully moving on to leading parts later. However, she seemed surprisingly reluctant to accept this offer – a worthwhile one for someone of her age – and it was only after much probing on my part that she confided that she had recently met a new man, with whom, it seemed, she was entirely besotted.

"OK, Julie – who is he? When do I get to meet him? You know you are not allowed to involve yourself with any man before I've given my approval."

Julie, usually so forthcoming – indeed sometimes too much so – was oddly restrained.

"Well – it's tricky, Eva. I can't say too much. Delicate negotiations in progress."

This air of mystery only made me all the more determined to get the rest of the story.

"What's his name – come on, tell me that much, at least. Do I know him?"

Julie smiled. "Oh yes – everyone knows him." Suddenly she became serious. "Eva, if I tell you, you must swear *never* to mention it to anyone. Swear it?"

"Of course, if that's what you want, I swear it. Cross my heart and hope to die."

"No need for that, Eva. But *please*...." Her voice dropped to a whisper.

"It's Alberto di Santofiore."

"What?" The Principe Annibale Antonio Alberto di Santofiore, of the minor Italian nobility, was indeed known to me. By repute. His exploits regularly featured in the gossip columns of the newspapers. The original Playboy of the Western World. I was horrified. "But Julie – he's *married*!"

If I expected shocked surprise, I was disappointed.

"Oh yes, I know. But it doesn't make any difference. Don't ask me any more, please, Eva. Can we just leave it there?"

Somewhat taken aback, I would have pursued the issue. But Julie was adamant in refusing to discuss the matter any further.

Finlay and I accompanied her to the railway station after her graduation. The three of us hugged over and over, and many tears were shed. Even Finlay contributed his share, to Julie's amusement.

"Come on, Fin, big boys are not supposed to cry. You're worse than Eva." Then she herself broke into sobs again. "Oh – how I shall miss you both. The Three Musketeers are separated at last. Take care of each other, won't you?"

After we had all calmed down a bit, I had to say, "Julie – do look after yourself. Don't get too carried away with – well, you know." True to my word, I had not told Finlay of Julie's secret.

"Of course I will, Eva, everything will be fine, trust me. Goodbye Eva. Goodbye Finlay."

She kissed us both on the cheek and was gone. It would be many years before I saw her again.

* * * * *

1935.

Dean Castle.

I returned home to Ayrshire for my birthday celebrations, which were a rather muted affair. There was still no word from Leicester or Conan, and the continued absence of news was telling badly on Father. His mind was often clouded, and he began to be increasingly vague and uncommunicative – even with me. More worryingly still, he began to fail physically too, showing little appetite and losing weight. He had always been a healthy man, fit and hale for his years. He was by this time in his mid-seventies and gradually he came to look every year of it. He had composed little of any account for some considerable time, and it was most distressing to see how rapidly his descent into old age took place.

I began to see something of an unexpected side to Mother, however. As Father declined, she seemed to rise commensurately. She devoted herself to our welfare in a manner quite unlike her usual offhand style. It was as though she had finally found a place she could occupy in our family life. She realised, I think, that for possibly the first time she was needed, and her energy and determination to carry us intact through this difficult period aroused my slightly unwilling admiration.

It was near the end of August 1935 we received the dreadful news. Late one night we had a visit from the local constabulary. They told us that they had been contacted by the Australian coast guard to say that, some days earlier, the corpse of a great white shark had been washed up on a Western Australian beach. On opening the body, a portion of a left human forearm had been discovered. Still visible on the remains was part of a tattoo which read '… Con forever'.

Of Leicester there was no trace, but the worst was to be assumed.

Father collapsed when he heard the news and was immediately rushed into hospital. Mother, white-lipped and grim-faced, dealt with the necessary formalities. I retired to my room and wept for what seemed like days.

Finally all the facts came to light. Conan and Leicester had indeed been in the area. Described as father and son, they had apparently set out for a day's leisurely fishing early on the morning of the 23rd July and had not returned. As they were on a travelling holiday and had taken their belongings with them, no alarm was raised, it being assumed that they had simply moved on.

Mother and I conferred in the drawing room. I was due to return to Lang Hall, but didn't feel that I could leave her to handle everything alone. Besides, I had no appetite for study or my carefree student life. My mind was entirely filled with thoughts of my brother, and the remote hope that somehow, somewhere, I would see him again.

"I'm afraid we have to face up to the facts, Mona," Mother said. "You know one or the other of them would have been in contact by now. Conan will be presumed dead, I don't doubt – officially, that is – and as for your brother – well, it does no harm to hope, I suppose."

Quite unexpectedly, Mother dissolved into floods of tears. Something I had never seen before. Or had ever expected to see.

It dawned on me for the first time that Mother's habitual cavalier attitude might actually mask stronger feelings than I had ever credited her with. But to see her like this – Mother, the ever-strong, ever-resilient, reduced to actually showing her emotions? And to me?

In that moment I didn't know what to do, or what to say.

Then I made up my mind. "I won't go back to Lang Hall, Mother. You need me here."

Immediately Mother's tears abated, and her face resumed its customary determined expression.

"What? No, no Mona; of course you are going back. You must. It's your final year. Think of your father, how disappointed he would be. Think of yourself. Think of the family. You have to represent us now."

There was no denying the truth of this, however unexpected the source.

After a brief pause, I agreed. "Yes, of course, you're right. But is there anything else I can do to help, Mother?"

"There is, Mona. Can you find the time to go and see Lavinia, at school? She needs to be told, and frankly, I don't think I'm up to it. She will be heart-broken – you know how she adored her brother."

Lavinia. Poor child, I thought. Packed off to boarding school at ten years of age. I would arrange to see her, and try to find a way to explain Leicester's disappearance without upsetting her too much.

"Of course I will."

"Good. That's one thing I won't have to worry about. I can't do everything around here."

I was slightly cheered to hear her sounding more like herself.

"No, of course not. And you're right, Mother, I must go back. For Father. I'll start packing now."

* * * * *

As Mother had requested, I arranged to pay a visit to Lavinia's school. We met up in a little private sitting room, and I was pleased to see that she looked fit and healthy. "She's going to be the image of Mother," I thought. It was a difficult conversation, and I tried to phrase the information as gently as I could. But there was no way of avoiding the inevitable conclusion. Naturally, she was horrified. But after she had shed a few tears, and we had shared a sisterly embrace or two, she said something that surprised me.

"You know, Eva, Uncle Conan I barely recall. But Leicester… I remember you telling me how, when you were both little, he always seemed to emerge in one piece from whatever mischief the two of you had been up to. Who knows? – maybe he'll manage it this time, too. And anyway – we still have each other, don't we?"

I returned to Lang Hall feeling oddly comforted. But I still waited every day for some news of Leicester, convinced that somehow he had survived.

* * * * *

1935.

Lang Hall.

Things did get slightly better. Slowly. Just the fact of returning to my old routine helped, and having other things to occupy my attention gradually lessened the depressing gloom which resulted from recent events. And Finlay was my saviour. His mere presence comforted me, and he constantly devised little schemes and ploys to keep me interested in my work whenever it looked as though I was sliding back into introspection and misery.

So I was fifteen at the time Finlay and I became lovers. I don't think there was a specific moment when I went from thinking "No, no, not until…" to thinking "Why not?...". With Leicester gone and Father in hospital, I suppose I began to realise how alone I was. And Finlay was there. We loved each other. What was I waiting for? Marriage? Though that might indeed be the ultimate outcome of our relationship, it wasn't going to happen any time soon, as I had made quite clear.

Perhaps another factor influencing my decision was that, since our last discussion of the matter, and Finlay's unexpected proposal, he appeared to have accepted that our level of intimacy was going to stay exactly as it was, and ceased to be as pressing in his demands. Maybe, I thought, he is losing interest in me. But then… Maybe he is *pretending* to lose interest in me, so that I will start to worry, and do what he wants. It was all very confusing.

I decided that, *coûte que coûte*, this Gordian knot must to be cut.

With that in mind, there came a night when I left my little apartment, crept along the deserted corridor, and tapped lightly on his door.

"Eva – what's the matter?" He was half-asleep, rubbing his eyes. "It's late. You should be sleeping." He yawned. "Early class in the morning."

Tousled and rumpled, he looked wonderful.

"We can sleep later," I said, entering and closing the door behind me.

Like most girls of my age, I had devoured books that dared to comment on the intimate details of relations between the sexes. A regularly recurring motif was that the first occasion, whether pre- or post-nuptial, was liable to be a somewhat disappointing and uncomfortable experience. Perhaps I was lucky. Or perhaps I had simply read the wrong books.[1] No need for elaboration. Suffice to say that, after that night, neither one of us was going to die wondering. Our relationship moved onto a new level and I never regretted my decision. Not even when Finlay discovered how much he could irritate me by referring laughingly to

1 Certainly, the writings on the subject by Mr Lawrence (D.H., not T.E.) were at that time unavailable for consultation

my 'unwomanly and wanton behaviour' on the night when I had disturbed 'his virgin slumbers'...

* * * * *

My new flat-sharing arrangement seemed to be working out remarkably well. Dear Mona McCafferty, with her robust humour and her hearty camaraderie proved to be just the tonic I needed to lift me out of my moods. She had asked if she might call me Mona, as she found it extremely funny that we shared a Christian name. Although normally I would have refused point blank, hating the name as I did, I soon got used to her calling me Mona H, while she was Mona M. Very soon that was reduced to simply 'H' and 'M'. It became a little private joke between us, but I warned her on pain of death to say nothing of this to the other students. To Finlay and my close friends I was 'Eva'. To my tutors, 'Miss Hinge', or occasionally 'Evadne'. No-one must call me 'Evie', of course – that was Father's privilege alone.

Finlay was at first a little wary of Mona M. She was so very brusque and masculine that I think she intimidated him somewhat. She also seemed to have adopted a somewhat proprietorial attitude with me, which he found irritating. Worse, she always joshingly called him 'Finlay-boy', which grated on him. But, although I tried, I simply couldn't break her of the habit. Eventually he came to accept it *faute de mieux*, and got his own back by referring to her regularly as 'Mona-girl', which she found equally annoying. Understandably so, as anyone less girlish than Mona would have been difficult to imagine. A *détente* thus arrived at, the three of us finally settled into a mutually tolerant relationship.

We were delighted to receive the occasional letter from Julie. Astonishingly, she had actually *married* His Serene Highness A.A.A. di Santofiore, and was now living in Rome, where she was giving voice lessons. I just hoped that the Prince had remembered to get divorced first, and that Julie hadn't totally forgotten her operatic ambitions.

We three were now in our final year, and without telling me, Finlay had applied for a position in the horn section of the renowned London Philharmonic Orchestra. He had planned to surprise me with the news if he was successful, but couldn't resist a series of hints on which I soon picked up.

"Imagine it, Eva," he said. "If I get the job, we graduate in June, and I move down to London where I will be at the heart of things. I can establish a base there, and then, when I have spied out the lay of the land, you come down and join me. There's nothing in Scotland for us. With all your recent troubles, it would be the best thing in the world for you to get away from here. What do you say?"

"London? Well, yes – possibly. Yes, I can see the advantages in that, of course…"

Finlay didn't seem to register the slight uncertainty in my tone. Things certainly seemed to be moving quickly.

"And then maybe we could think of making our relationship more of a permanent one, if you follow me. Maybe even live together? Maybe even?..."

I kissed him soundly to avoid answering

"We'll see," I said. "And good luck with your audition, my darling. Of course, they would be *mad* to turn you down."

* * * * *

1936.

Dean Castle.

The Christmas break rolled round, and it was once again time to return home. Though there was still no news of Leicester, Father had returned from hospital, and seemed slightly improved. It was a sad festive season, though.

Mother had other problems to occupy her at this time. Her father, Grandpa Max, was involved in a freak motoring accident caused by apparently faulty brakes. Seriously injured, he lay in a coma for several days. Worse, when he eventually regained consciousness, it was discovered that he had suffered a stroke, and it was considered unlikely that he would ever regain his faculties fully. And shortly thereafter his wife, Grandma Alma, was admitted to an institution for the incurably insane. On the one occasion I visited with Mother, Alma didn't appear to know us, and, though she remained physically healthy, her poor mind seemed to have given way completely. She constantly muttered her religious mantras – "God is not mocked," she would whisper ghoulishly, "but the Lord helps those who help themselves."

These tragedies, coming so soon on the heels of my brother's disappearance, would have been too much for anyone less determined and forceful than Mother. But, rallying her strength, she took on single-handedly the running of McWhirter's, the family whisky business. With Conan's presumed death, she was now the only member of the family left to look after it.

It seemed that we had barely recovered from one blow before another sent us reeling. Surely things could get no worse?

Chapter Six

The End of the Beginning

1936.

Lang Hall.

Our family problems were briefly overshadowed by an outside event, when the King, George V, passed away in January. Despite the genuine sadness of the country on the demise of a much-respected monarch, and the national mourning that followed, there was a subtle suggestion of buoyant optimism in the air. His eldest son, David, now Edward VIII, was a popular figure, and great things were expected of him. How false this dawn would prove is, of course, well-known.

Spring term at Lang Hall was to be my last moment of peace for quite some time. And even that brought its surprises. I was now preparing doggedly for my final examinations. In June, I would graduate, all being well, and then in July I would reach my sixteenth birthday. And it was around this time that an event occurred which might have been highly embarrassing, but in retrospect is more amusing than anything else.

Mona M. and I were sitting one chilly March evening, studying, in our cosy apartment. Finlay was very proud of the little second-hand car his parents had purchased for him as an eighteenth birthday present, and had travelled in it down to London for his second audition with the renowned conductor Sir Thomas Beecham. Mona and I were using the time to catch up on our work. She would graduate along with me, and had concerns that she was falling behind in some areas.

"Would you help me out a bit here, H? If we could spend an hour or two revising together, I would be eternally grateful, more grateful than I can say, indeed, so grateful as to be positively embarrassing."

I was accustomed to Mona M.'s occasionally flowery and over-elaborate manner of expressing herself and smiled indulgently.

"Certainly, M, if you think it would help. As it happens, here is a tricky little four-part counterpoint exercise which I have been avoiding, and which I think would be right up your street."

I passed a sheet of manuscript to her and we settled down to work together companionably. Mona's expression changed.

"Oh dear. Counterpoint. Not my favourite. Oh well, I *did* ask, didn't I?" She put on the horn-rimmed spectacles she occasionally affected. “Now – let’s see. Subject in the tenor, countersubject in the bass… Yes, I think that *might…*”

I was well used to Mona’s habit of talking to herself while she worked.

“Yes, brilliant, McCafferty! That’s the way – well done. Now, if the soprano line – no… that’s much too high, unless it were for Vicky… So, down an octave, maybe?...”

Her muttering receded into the background of my consciousness. I was completely engrossed in Berlioz’s fascinating *Traité d’Instrumentation et d’Orchestration,* a copy of which I had recently unearthed in the University library. In the original French, which naturally gave me no problems at all.

After some time I was vaguely aware that both Mona’s monologue and the scratching of her pen had ceased. Suddenly I felt her hand on my arm.

“H, my very dear one. You do realise, don’t you, that I worship at the Sapphic shrine?”

Only half-listening, and without looking up, I remarked that I had not been aware that she possessed any strong religious beliefs.

She sighed. “H, dear, please put down that book and listen to me...”

“Sorry, M,” I apologised, laying my book aside. “Yes, I heard you. Something about a shrine, you said, and worshiping. If you want company, I don’t mind coming along. You know I’m not personally a believer, but I like to keep an open mind.”

To my astonishment, she burst into gales of hearty laughter.

“Evadne Hinge, there really is no-one like you! Here am I, opening my soul to you, but you are so caught up in what you are doing… I’m not talking about a religious cult.” She took off the glasses. “My dear – I’m a lesbian.”

I wasn’t sure what kind of reaction she was expecting. I smiled. “Yes, of course, M. So I always assumed,” I said equably.

Sounding slightly deflated, she said “No! You knew?”

I sighed and resigned myself to the fact that M. Berlioz would have to wait.

“M – the way you dress, the way you speak... You look like a young man; a very agreeable young man; an attractive young man, even.” I smiled again at her look of surprise. “It wasn’t difficult to work out.”

“Attractive? Oh. Do you really think so?” Mona frowned, and ran her hands through her thick, short black hair. “Honestly?” she asked doubtfully.

In truth, Mona resembled nothing more than a pretty young boy masquerading in an eccentric uncle’s clothes.

“Yes, of course I do,” I reassured her, “And I daresay you don’t lack for admirers of your own – er – persuasion”.

“No, that’s true.” Her expression lightened. “I am indeed much admired.

Positively sought after, in fact." Suddenly pensive, she continued, "But, alas, there is room for only one person in my heart. Now I wonder if you can guess who that might be?"

I thought I could. I hesitated. Tact was required, tempered with kindness, but at the same time, a definite and honest response seemed advisable.

"Yes, Mona, I think I can guess. And before you tell me who it is, can I just suggest something? Flattered as this person no doubt would be, in the interest of maintaining a friendly and close relationship, might it not be wise to keep your feelings – what's the word? – sublimated? Though they might be appreciated, they could never be returned. Love at a distance is what I would recommend."

"Wonderful H!" breathed Mona after a moment. "What a unique and extraordinary person you are! Naturally I shall take your advice. I know your own heart is already given elsewhere…"

Not just my heart, I thought. "Well, let us say no more about it," I went on hastily, removing her hand from my arm. "Now – hadn't you better get on with your work instead of chattering nonsense? Oh – and say a little prayer for me at the Sapphic shrine when you're next there. These days I need all the help I can get."

"Naturally I shall," said Mona. "But first I must just express my joy – a joy tempered with regret, of course, but nonetheless, a joy – in music."

She bounded over to the piano and burst into a heartfelt and throbbing rendition of Beethoven's 'An die Ferne Geliebte'.[1]

"Lovely Mona," I said. "Just the thing. Take me to your *lieder*."

I had handled that rather well, I thought.

* * * * *

Father passed away in April 1936. His poor heart, which had been the cause of his earlier hospitalisation, finally gave out. He was seventy-seven years of age, and I suppose one might say that, by the standards of the time, he had had a long and fulfilling life. However, his final years were blighted by the manifold disasters that overtook our family, and it was a source of continual disappointment to him that his own music, once so admired, had ceased to be of interest to the current generation. I believe it was one thought alone – that the family name would continue to be respected and recognised through me – which sustained him towards the end.

On one level, his death was not totally unexpected. His health had been failing for some time. But I was devastated. One by one a malignant fate seemed

1 'An die Ferne Geliebte' - 'To the Distant Beloved', song cycle by Beethoven.

to be removing everyone that I held dear. Father – dead. Leicester – vanished. Grandma – hopelessly insane. Grandpa Max, although somewhat recovered from his stroke, still largely incapacitated.

There remained Mother. But our relationship had never been an easy one. She had many faults. At one moment considerate and kindly, the next raging uncontrollably about some imaginary thwarting of her will; selfish, manipulative, and of a violent and easily roused temper; given to bouts of depression and to a constant dependence on stimulation; thoughtless and hurtful, even deliberately cruel on occasion. However, she had one lonely virtue. She was very brave.

It was she who sent the telegram informing me of Father's death and summoning me home for the funeral. Finlay, who had been thrilled to be finally offered the position with the London Philharmonic for which he had auditioned, accompanied me. Dear Mona M. was only too full of enthusiasm to join us, and offered to play for the funeral service.

"Naturally, H, you will not wish to play yourself – allow me to offer my poor talent. Here is how I see it. Myself on the organ, suitably costumed – perhaps as the 'Phantom of the Opera'? Some Busoni, maybe? – I love his *Fantasia Contrappuntistica*, just the thing for a solemn occasion. Although maybe twenty-five minutes is a trifle long. Or you could get Vicky to sing the *Nuns' Chorus*? – nice wee tune, of its type, if a bit wishy-washy and sentimental. And then to round things off, Gounod's little *Funeral March for a Marionette*. What do you think?"

I thought not. I decided to discourage her attendance, feeling that her *penchant* for the dramatic, not to say the melodramatic, would add an unsuitably jaunty note to the proceedings. Instead I asked my class-mate Janey Dawson, a steady and reliable girl and a fine musician, if she would play for the service, and she readily agreed. Together we discussed her program, and I was able to provide her with the music for two of Father's organ pieces dating back to the beginning of his career. And I was delighted when she agreed to play Widor's famous *Toccata* as the outgoing voluntary. It was always one of Father's favourites.

I will give the briefest outline of the day of the funeral. Suffice to say that all went off as well as I could have hoped. Mother was in an unusually sombre mood. I hadn't expected that Father's passing would have affected her so deeply. But she seemed *distraite* and barely responded to my questions. Lavinia accompanied her. My little sister and I exchanged hugs, and the two of us, along with Mother and the apparently inevitable Dougal McDougal shared the family pew. A sadly reduced Family Hinge.

It was surprising and gratifying, however, to see the service attended by an astonishingly large number of people. Not only the many locals, but visitors from all over the country, indeed all over the world. Musical luminaries – Stravinsky among them – along with conductors, singers, instrumentalists, and a large number of music critics. I was cheered to be reminded just how well-loved and respected my father had been in his chosen profession.

It was arranged that I would return home again after graduation for the reading of father's will, which was scheduled to take place in a couple of months' time. Naturally, Mother would inherit the bulk of Father's estate, such as it was. He had always been somewhat improvident, so it was not expected to amount to a great deal. However, since Mother now controlled her own family business, it was not likely that this would cause any hardship. I hoped that Father had left me his music library, as he had always promised to do.

* * * * *

After saying goodbye to Mother and Lavinia, I returned with Finlay to Lang Hall for our final few weeks. And during this period, an astonishing thing happened. Suddenly, Father's music was being played everywhere. Phrases like 'a neglected genius', 'possibly the finest British composer of his generation' and 'a national treasure' were bandied about. Concerts, radio broadcasts, articles in the press, suddenly the name of Hector Hinge was everywhere. How delighted Father would have been, and how my sorely-missed brother Leicester would have relished the reflected glory of this sudden celebrity.

* * * * *

I graduated from Lang Hall on a sunny June day, along with my class-mates, all of whom had been successful – except for Phil Hanson, who had left a year earlier under something of a cloud. It was all due to his singing habit. Having had no success in his pursuit of little Miss Dean, he next set his sights on an even more unlikely target.

The Faculty of Art was housed in a separate building from our Faculty of Music, and we mixed with the Art students very little as a rule. They were a rather *louche* bunch, in our view, and one of the most notably *louche* was a bohemian lady lecturer called Fulvia Terry. It was rumoured that part of Miss Terry's job was to pose undraped for the Life classes which were an important part of the Arts curriculum. Whether this was in fact the case, I don't know, but this reputation certainly caused her to be a figure of some interest to male students from every department. And particularly to 'Hanky'. The story I heard was that the latter, smitten with an uncontrollable urge, had concealed himself in a supplies store while a Life class was in progress. Then, just at a critical moment, his eerie high soprano burst forth melodiously from his hiding place with '*Ah! Sweet Miss Terr-ee of Life, at last I've found you!*', parodying the famous song from Victor Herbert's *Naughty Marietta*. Naughty Hanky was immediately dismissed from Lang Hall, and subsequently, I believe, found employment with Sanger's Circus.

* * * * *

I was capped and gowned and declared to be a Doctor of Music. Mother had made the trip for the occasion, which surprised me a little. Her somewhat inappropriate heavy mourning struck an incongruous note, but she was playing 'The Widow Hinge' to the hilt and obviously enjoying the attention she received as the relict of 'the great man'. She behaved well generally, and agreed to join our little group for a celebration supper after the ceremony. She enjoyed a tearful reunion there, too, with her 'old school chum', Aunty Morag. They had not met in some time, and the reminiscences flowed. As did the particularly potent punch prepared for the occasion by Finlay and Mona M. When Mother's stories of past escapades threatened to breach the bounds of good taste, and Morag began 'Mona-ing' rather more than I liked, I hastily interrupted.

"I am so pleased you could make it, Mother. And you too, of course, Morag."

Mother raised a glass in the direction of her old friend. "Well, well, Mona – we could hardly stay away, could we Morag?" She turned to me. "And so – you're now Doctor Mona Hinge? I'll know who to come to the next time my chilblains start playing up!"

"Doctor Evadne Hinge, Mother."

"Maybe to you. But you'll always be my own wee moaner, Mona."

I gritted my teeth, smiled and proffered a glass. "Let me give you a punch, Mother."

* * * * *

The time came to bid a fond farewell to Lang Hall, and all my dear friends. A tearful Mona M. promised to keep in touch: "Oh, you haven't seen the last of me, H. We shall meet again, be sure of it." We would; and how much I would come to owe her in the years ahead.

Finlay was due to spend a few days with his family before he set off on the great adventure – his engagement with the LPO was due to commence at the beginning of July. We spent a last night together in his little room at Lang Hall. A few tears were shed, and many promises exchanged.

"I'll write to you as soon as I get there, Eva. Then you must deal with any loose ends here, and join me as soon as you can. First thing I have to do, of course, is to find somewhere for us to live. Big enough for two. Or even three, eventually…"

What? Three? I realised he was referring to the Bad Thing we had spent some considerable ingenuity endeavouring to avoid. Now, it seemed, it was a Good Thing.

"Après la mariage, naturellement," bubbled Finlay.

"*Le* mariage…" My mind was elsewhere.

"Of course, sorry. And you must write back straight away and let me know when to expect you – then I can meet you from the train and conduct you to our little love nest, wherever it turns out to be."

There was no stopping him, it seemed. But eventually I found a way.

* * * * *

On my journey back home I had much food for thought. I realised I had to decide what I was going to do about Finlay. He seemed to have made up his mind about our future. But without really consulting me about it, he seemed to take my acquiescence for granted. He said he loved me, and had certainly told me so, many times. And I loved him. Of course I did.

Didn't I? I was not yet sixteen, what did I really know of love? As I looked back over my life so far, a pattern began to emerge. It seemed I was always under the control of someone else. Naturally, as a young child, my parents made decisions for me. But Mother, for her own ends, and, yes, Father too, with the best of intentions, had continued to guide the course of my life, even from a distance. Later, there was Julie, who, though a dear and loving friend, had taken on the rôle of guardian, forever telling me what to do, what to wear, what to think. And now Finlay, it appeared, was preparing to take charge of my life, which would in future run to his plan. Was this really what I wanted?

These doubts nagged at me. But they were about to be submerged by a more immediate threat.

Mother at this stage knew nothing of these matters. Should I decide in favour of the London move, she would have to be informed, obviously, but that was another task I was not looking forward to. I anticipated objections. But just how strong these would be, and the lengths to which she was prepared to go to thwart me I was yet to learn.

* * * * *

1936.

Dean Castle.

It was all due to Father's will. Unbeknown to anyone, he had made a new one only a few months before his death. To Mother he had left the tenure and contents of Dean Castle. To me, everything else. And, unbelievably, this was an enormous fortune. Ten thousand pounds.[1] Where this huge legacy had come from, no-one appeared to know. But there it was. I was an heiress.

Or I would be. The terms of the will stipulated that I would come into my inheritance on my eighteenth birthday. Until then, the money would be invested by the executor of the will, Father's solicitors, Bartington and Sons. I was utterly bewildered.

But if I was stunned by the news, Mother was incandescent. "The stupid, stupid man!" she raged. "What was he thinking of? Of course, Mona, you were always his favourite. Spoilt and indulged in everything. But I never imagined he would go so far as to leave me, his wife, a mendicant. A pauper, forced to beg my bread from strangers, compelled to depend on the bounty and charity of others. And what about Lavinia, eh? His other daughter? If he wasn't already dead, I would kill him!"

Mother's talent for self-dramatization was in full flow. I forbore from pointing out that if Father wasn't dead, the present situation would not have arisen, and endeavoured to pour on some oil.

"But Mother – there's no need to worry. When I inherit, I'll make sure you and Lavinia want for nothing. And besides – you can hardly be short of funds. You control the family business now, and that must be worth – oh, I don't know – lots and lots of money. I don't see the problem."

"No Mona, as usual, you don't know and you don't see. A wealthy woman? The whisky business? If only you *did* know..." She had resorted to the *sotto voce* tone she adopted when she wished to appear supremely intimidating. It never failed. "You know nothing of my affairs – and indeed, they don't concern you, so why should you? But your father's money *is* my affair. And I will get my hands on it, be very sure of that."

I felt it was time to bring this conversation to a close. I was used to Mother over-dramatising, and knew from experience that there was little point in prolonging the discussion further until she had calmed down.

"Well, I don't see how, Mother, but you must do as you think fit." I kept my tone moderate, as I knew she found that extremely irritating. "I will see you in the morning and we can discuss the matter sensibly."

When I left, I was particularly careful not to slam the door. One of us had to act like an adult.

1 Equivalent to around four hundred and thirty thousand pounds today (2002)

* * * * *

The full scope of Mother's scheming, and the diabolical detail of her invention, were revealed to me the following morning. Summoned to her bedroom, as usual on these occasions, I found her seated at her dressing table attending to her toilette, and in what I at first took to be a mellower mood.

"Have a seat, Mona, make yourself comfortable," she began in a reasonable tone. "This may take a little while."

I sat down in the armchair she had indicated.

"Well, Mother?"

She took a sip from her teacup and gazed into the mirror.

"Would you care for a cup of tea?"

'*Oh yes,*' I thought. '*I know this stunt. The velvet glove, followed by the iron fist. But you're not getting away with it this time.*' I kept my expression neutral.

"No tea, thank you."

"Very well." A pause.

"Now," she continued, "I have decided what is going to happen."

"Then please be good enough to enlighten me."

Mother began applying her lipstick.

"You will get married…"

Married?

"… to Dougal; as soon as you are old enough; in a few weeks."

What nonsense was this? Me, marry Dougal?

With some difficulty, I forbore from laughing. "For heaven's sake, mother, why would I do that?"

But Mother hadn't finished. She set down the lipstick and turned her head to one side to see if she had achieved the desired effect.

"As your husband, he will have control of your money. And when you inherit, he will make sure it ends up in the right place."

I had heard enough. I rose to my feet, preparing to leave.

"I'm going, mother. And I can assure you, Dougal is about the last person I would wish to marry."

She turned to face me

"Sit down, Mona. Your wishes are of no account. Marry him you will."

I believe this time I actually did laugh. "No, I won't. You can't *force* me to marry anyone."

"No, Mona, I can't do that. But I can assure you that when you hear what I have to say you will find that marriage with Dougal will suit you very well – considering the alternative."

Something in her tone made me realise that this was no joke, no wild and impractical ploy, but a carefully meditated plan.

I sat down again.

"I'm waiting, Mother," I said. "Go on."

She paused and lit a cigarette.

"You loved your father, didn't you, Mona?"

I nodded. "Yes, Mother, I did. Didn't you?"

She laughed. "Oh, at one time, possibly. But things change." She rose and moved towards the window, and stood there gazing out, as if considering her next words. "And of course, you must be highly delighted at the sudden fame and adulation that have come his way since he died?"

'*Strange question*,' I thought. '*Where is this going?*'

"Naturally, yes. It's no more than his due. He has been recognised for the genius he was, that's all. It's often the way, it seems."

Mother turned from the window and smiled in a manner that chilled me.

"A genius? Well – who knows, Mona? Maybe. But the point is that this belated recognition is being granted to a person who never existed. The smiling, benevolent *paterfamilias*, pride of Scotland, great composer, husband and father. All that is nothing but a sham."

"What do you mean?" In spite of my increasing unease, I clung desperately to the belief that this was just another example of Mother's shock tactics, designed to throw the listener off-balance and confuse the issue.

She came towards me.

"Just this." She suddenly leaned over me. Her face was close enough for me to notice the lipstick stain on her front teeth. "Your dear father was a drug addict, an adulterer, a swindler, and maybe worst of all, considering his reputation – a plagiarist."

I recoiled from the ugly expression of triumph on her face.

"What?" I laughed shakily. "Who would ever believe such nonsense?"

She withdrew and, stubbing out her cigarette, resumed her seat at the dressing table. She began filing her nails. Her tone was suddenly philosophical, almost sympathetic.

"Nonsense? Oh, Mona, people are always ready to believe the worst, as you may discover one of these days. What a tragedy if your father's belated recognition should be besmirched with the nasty truth, don't you agree?"

"But..."

She replaced the nail file in its case and once again turned to face me. Her voice hardened.

"Listen to me. One – drug addict. His famous powders, his injections? Opium. He was addicted for years."

I rose from my chair in shock.

"But – his arthritis…"

She turned back to gaze once more at her reflection. "Arthritis? Oh no. He never suffered from arthritis, or anything worse than a craving for just a little more."

I moved behind her and we stared at each other in the mirror.

"Two – adulterer. Just who do you think fathered Jeannie's child? It was him. She was his mistress for years. Oh, I knew, always. But it suited me to ignore it."

My head was reeling. Father and Jeannie? If true, I had a brother, not a nephew. But it wasn't true. It couldn't be true...

"Three – a swindler," Mother went on remorselessly. "A crafty one, too. Don't imagine that the money he left to you was come by honestly. It should have gone to his cousin, Mary. But your dear Father contrived to have the poor woman put away years ago, for a crime she didn't commit. I have all the details – and the proof."

A hazy memory returned to me – of the mysterious cousin who had been locked away for some unknown misdemeanour. Mary McGuire… I stretched out a hand.

"Mother – where has this all come from? Why are you trying…"

She interrupted me. But her tone had changed dramatically to a smooth and conversational one. "Of course, these things are family matters, Mona."

Turning back towards me, she rose to her feet and took my hand in hers. She smiled sympathetically. "There's no need for anyone outside these walls to hear a word of all this. And they won't. Provided my dear daughter is a sensible girl."

* * * * *

I didn't sleep at all that night. Why was Mother doing this? Despite all her faults, she was not at all a mean or money-grabbing person. With her family business interests it hardly seemed possible that she was so direly in need of money that she would resort to this ugly and blatant blackmail. A word went round and round in my head – plagiarist. This was a point she had not elaborated on. Impossible, surely, that Father would have resorted to stealing the musical ideas of others! Indeed, there was only too much original inspiration filling his brain – so much so that he had often had barely the time to get his own thoughts down on paper. This was something I needed to tackle Mother about. At worst, I would know everything. Whatever the answer, one thing was certain. I would never marry Dougal McDougal, come what might.

It must have been three o' clock when I decided that I had to make some kind of positive move. After putting on a suitably modest dressing gown and pausing to arrange my hair, I left the house.

* * * * *

I had not had more than a passing conversation with Dougal in many years. Even so, in the course of these, I had noticed that the time spent as Mother's chauffeur-cum-confidant had rubbed the rough edges off his character and the country brogue from his speech.

"Come in, come in." Dressed only in his pyjama bottoms, he stood in the doorway of his cottage. "This *is* a pleasure, Eva. Indeed, an honour." He gave an ironic little bow. "What can I do for you?"

"Dougal," I said, business-like, "I need to speak to you."

"By all means, Eva. But come in, we can't stand here chatting on the doorstep at this hour. Think of my reputation!"

The lightly mocking manner and the polished repartee were unexpected and a little disconcerting.

He ushered me inside and closed the door.

I was vaguely pleased to note that the cottage remained as clean and tidy as it had been during the tenure of Alec, Dougal's father and our one time gardener. However, Dougal's own state of dress – or rather, undress – was rather unnerving. I had seen a male chest before, of course. But rarely in such close proximity.

"Can I get you anything, Eva? A drink, maybe?" He smiled at me companionably, the perfect host.

I avoided his gaze. "You can put some clothes on."

"Oh dear" – the eyebrows rose and the smile widened – "sorry to offend. I'm not used to receiving ladies at this hour. Just give me a moment."

He left the room. I looked around, recognising that the cottage had changed very little since my last visit, many years ago. A happy time, and a safe one. I went to look more closely at the photograph of a smiling Alec on the mantelshelf.

"You remember Dad, of course?" Dougal reappeared, rather more covered than previously, and carrying a tray with a bottle and glasses.

"Yes, of course I do. How is he these days?"

"Well. Very well. Working up north for some grand family or other."

He set the tray and glasses down on the polished oak dining-table that stood in the bay window.

"Sit down, sit down, Eva. Whisky? McWhirter's, naturally."

I shuddered. Anything but that.

"No. I suppose you don't have something like – a cocktail?"

He laughed. "A cocktail, indeed? Very grand. You suppose correctly, Eva. 'Fraid it's whisky or nothing, sorry."

"Oh. All right. Just a small one."

I certainly needed a drink.

"And, sit down, Eva, will you? You're making me nervous."

He poured our drinks, brought them over and we sat either side of the fitfully glowing peat fire. It was warm July, but the nights could be chilly.

"Sláinte, Eva," he raised his glass.

"Er – cheers, Dougal." I sipped the whisky. It tasted delicious, amazingly.

"So," Dougal went on, looking over at me. "What did you want to see me about?"

I drank some more of the whisky. How warming and comforting it was.

No point in prevaricating. "I think you know. All this ridiculous nonsense Mother has come up with. You and I to marry. Is she mad?"

"Oh – she's told you then?" Dougal's familiar disarming grin spread over his features. "And since you ask, yes, I do know, and yes, I do think she is a little mad, sometimes." He hesitated, looking at me fixedly. "But – would it really be so awful, Eva?"

I tried to look at him dispassionately. At nineteen he was a handsome man, certainly. Many girls might have been not displeased by the prospect. But I knew too much about him, and suspected more; and my plans for the future certainly did not include Dougal McDougal.

"I'll be honest. I have no feelings of that sort for you, and never have had. I won't marry you, Dougal."

I drained my glass.

"Then I will be equally frank with you, Eva. You must know I've had a fancy for you since we were children. In spite of the way you and your brother treated me – you remember?" He smiled, and leaned back in his chair, the very picture of relaxed affability. "But none of this is my idea. It's all your mother's doing. You know Maureen – she won't be gainsaid. She has made up her mind to this, and I'm afraid we have no choice."

I frowned. "But Dougal, I don't understand – *you* have a choice." I rose, went over to the table and refilled my glass. "Mother is putting pressure on me, and at present I can't see any way out." I turned back and leaned against the edge of the table. "But you? Why? Just say 'no', for Heaven's sake." I paused. "Or for my sake."

"Oh, I would, I would. I'm not sure I want a wife at all, and I certainly don't want one who hates me, who would? But like you, Maureen has got me just where she wants me. Your dear mother knows everything about everyone. Every little misdemeanour, every shameful thing. She even keeps records, believe it or not – I've seen them. Notes on this one or that one, copies of documents, photographs." He rose from his chair and joined me at the table. "She has made it clear that unless I do what she wants, certain facts about my dad and his – well – his tastes, his activities – will come out."

Dougal's father Alec had long since left our service. With what a fierce nostalgia I recalled those distant days when I would snuggle up on his knee, safe and secure. The visits to his 'laboratory', his insatiable need for empty whisky bottles… The Philosopher's Stone…

"I don't understand – what tastes? What activities?"

Dougal helped himself to another whisky.

"No, no, I'll not say, the details are not relevant. But it seems she has information that could land my old dad in prison, and I won't have that, whatever else happens."

"I see." I looked away. So my malignant mother had us both in an impossible position. Perhaps I had, at least to some extent, misjudged Dougal. What could I do? What had he said?

"I don't *hate* you Dougal? Why would I? But I certainly don't want to *marry* you."

Suddenly a long-ago remark of Mother's came into my mind. *'The trouble is, Mona, we're too alike, you and I.'* Maybe it was time to put that to the test. With a bit of Mother's deviousness, I might manage to come out of this unscathed. And unmarried. I needed more information. I sipped my whisky, and looked back at my host.

"Something else, Dougal. Jeannie Dunt claimed it was you who gave her the idea of blaming Leicester for her pregnancy. You denied it. I want the truth."

He had the grace to look embarrassed.

Eventually he nodded. "Yes, OK. I suppose I owe you the truth. Yes, it was me. Jeannie was desperate, and I wanted to help her." He paused. "I always hated that smug brother of yours, you know. When we were younger, he treated me like the village idiot." His face took on an unusually sombre expression. "And you did too. You Hinges thought you were God's gift, and that the rest of us were just there to laugh at or ignore as you saw fit. You, I could forgive – you know why, I think, even though you were worse than he was, sometimes. But not Lord Leicester. Not him. I swore I'd get my own back."

The accusation was embarrassing. But considering the matter dispassionately, I had to admit it was justified. In our dealings with Dougal – and with Jeannie too, I suppose – Leicester and I had been at best thoughtless and inconsiderate, at worst cruel and heartless. Well, we were certainly paying the price now.

"So," Dougal went on, pulling out a chair and seating himself at the table, "I saw a way to get my own back. I was tickled by the idea of your beloved brother being saddled for life with Jeannie and her brat." He smiled in reminiscence. "I told her what to do. Even though I was well aware that Leicester had nothing to do with it." He gave a bitter little laugh. "Not that it would have been *totally* impossible. All things to all people, that brother of yours – who would know that better than me?"

"You?" I must have looked utterly bewildered by this remark. To cover my confusion, I raised my glass to my lips once more and emptied it. "You?" I said again, as I put it down.

He nodded slowly. "Oh yes, Eva, me." His tone became bitter. "Me, Dougal McDougal, the family stud." What was he suggesting? "Of course you wouldn't have realised. Head in the clouds as usual, Eva." He sipped his drink and gave a nasty little grin. "I suppose there's a kind of poetic justice in the idea of you and I sharing a marriage bed; a sense of completion, a full house." He laughed harshly. "Maybe that's what gave Maureen the idea."

I didn't want to consider for a second the implications of what he said. I looked down at him. I reached again for the whisky bottle. Dougal stretched out a restraining hand.

"Go easy on that stuff, Eva. You're not used to it."

"Don't touch me!" I pushed his hand away, and filled my tumbler to the brim.

Dougal smiled. "OK, OK. But don't say I didn't warn you. That's Maureen's special blend. For family use only, that."

I knocked back the entire contents and banged the empty glass down on the table. I stared at him.

"Oh, I see. So you're *family* now, are you, Dougal?" I moved round the table. "And what's your position? '*The family stud*,' you said? So where do you fit in in the future? How do you see yourself? Not as my husband, certainly. Maybe as my step-father?"

He looked away.

"We won't go into the details, Eva, if you don't mind."

I took another step or two towards him, delighted that I seemed to have dented his imperturbability.

"Oh, but I do mind, Dougal. Indeed, I insist. Yes, Mr Dougal McDougal, the family man." An old idea entered my head. "The father of Jeannie's child, perhaps?"

He roared with laughter and almost choked on his whisky. "Wouldn't that be neat, Eva? And convenient. Me, the villain of the piece. But no, no. Wrong again. I would have had neither the interest nor the energy, as things were. I've no idea who the child's father was – Jeannie would never say."

Deflation. "No, she wouldn't tell me either," I agreed, turning away and taking a step back..

I couldn't have said why, but I believed him. And I had to ask.

I hesitated and looked round again. "Father, do you think? *My* father, I mean?"

He appeared to consider. "The old boy? What gave you that idea? Frankly, I doubt it. But it's possible, I suppose. Jeannie was a popular girl in her fashion." He smiled reminiscently.

There was a long silence.

Then he went on, his tone suddenly serious. "I need to explain. About Leicester. To say sorry. To you, because I can't to him. Please, Eva, sit down"

I did so, a little reluctantly. From the other side of the table he looked at me intently.

"If it makes any difference, I regret what I did to your brother. I was obsessed with that old phrase, '*Revenge is a dish best eaten cold*'. I'd waited a long time. And at first I relished it. Oh yes, I loved it." He appeared to lose his thread for a moment, lost in reminiscence. When he spoke again, it was more quietly. "But I could never get Leicester's face out of my mind, after. That – that – stricken look. Then, of course, his disappearance…" He sighed, almost regretfully. "Old sins cast long shadows, isn't that what they say?"

Then he appeared to rally. "Anyway, that's all in the past. It's you and I who are up against it now. But I don't see any way out of the present situation. Maureen will get what she wants, as usual. Unless we can come up with something between us."

"Maybe. Let me think about it, Dougal." I wanted to go, but hesitated. "And – I'm sorry for the way we – the way I behaved towards you all those years ago. You didn't deserve it." As I stood up, I laid my hand gently on his shoulder.

"I'm sorry too. For many things. For the way things have worked out between us, you and me. For lying to you about Leicester. And for what happened to him. Whatever you may think of me, I know you loved your brother." He reached up and gave my hand a little squeeze. "Shall we agree to forgive each other?"

"Yes," I said, nodding, "Let's do that."

He stood up to show me out. In spite of all my present worries, I had a vague, comforting feeling that some old scores had been settled and some old sins laid to rest. Whatever had happened in the past, Dougal and I were now allies, maybe even friends. Unexpectedly, just before I turned to go, he put his arms round me, pulled me to him and held me tightly. At first I tensed, then relaxed. His dark hair smelled clean and fresh. I was suddenly alarmingly aware of his proximity and his strength.

"Don't worry, Eva," he murmured. "I am here for you, if you need me, always." I somehow found myself returning his embrace. For a moment I seemed to fall into a kind of waking dream. I felt suddenly safe and secure. Then he released me. I was half-relieved and half-reluctant.

His hands still on my shoulders, he held me at arms' length.

"Good night. Sleep well."

I returned to my room feeling oddly confused.

* * * * *

I awoke late, and with a nasty headache, unsure whether my interview with Dougal had answered any of my questions. Or perhaps raised some others. But I had decided how I would deal with the situation, at least until I knew more.

Mother was alone at the breakfast table. Without preamble, she started.

"Well, Mona? You've had some time to think over what I have said. What's your answer? This can't wait; it has to be sorted out as soon as possible."

"You leave me little choice, Mother. I've spoken to Dougal. I will do as you say. For Father."

Her face broke into the sunny smile that had melted unwary hearts throughout the county. "Ah, sensible girl." She became almost jovial. "Come on, it's not such a bad bargain, is it? Fine-looking lad, Dougie. Not the brightest, I grant you…"

Mother's Achilles heel was her inveterate habit of underestimating others.

"…but he has lots of good points."

I was unable to resist. "With all of which, I believe, Mother, you are intimately familiar?"

"Oh well," laughed Mother, without a trace of embarrassment. "Maybe, in the past. But from now on, Mona, he's all yours."

I sat down at the breakfast table and looked at her.

"One thing. Among your other accusations, you described Father as a plagiarist. But you didn't go into that."

She poured some tea. "No, it slipped my mind. But, alas, it seems there's no question of it. Have a look at these."

She went over to the sideboard drawer, and returned carrying a slim pile of printed sheet music.

She placed it in front of me and leaned over my shoulder. "Piano pieces by some Italian composer, apparently, published donkey's years ago. They were in amongst your father's rubbish. I was going to throw them out. But I thought, waste not, want not, Effie Burns might find a use for them. So I gave them to her."

Dear old Effie. My first piano teacher.

I looked up at her. "And…?"

Mother smiled smugly as she moved off and sat down again.

"Well, imagine my surprise, Mona, when she brought them back, and told me that they contain lots of ideas which somehow or other found their way into your father's work. Bits and pieces of them, she tells me, are in his concertos, his operas and I don't know what else. Have a look – you're the Doctor of Music after all, see for yourself."

I picked up the dozen or so sheets with a heavy heart.

But as I leafed through the pages, I smiled.

"Mother, these are all by someone called 'Ettore di Scozia'."

She took out a cigarette. "Indeed; as I was saying. Italian, by the sound of it."

I nodded. "Yes, so you might think. But it's a shame, you know, that your education was so sadly neglected at that up-market school you attended." I prepared to remedy the defect. "*Ettore di Scozia* – Hector of Scotland. These are little pieces *Father* wrote and published while he was very young, travelling in Italy with Liszt. I've seen them before, many times. In fact, Janey Dawson played one of them, this *Andante con moto*, at the funeral service. Didn't you recognise it, Mother? – oh no, of course, music is a closed book to you, isn't it?"

She was frowning up at me as she tried to light her cigarette, her eyes slightly crossed.

"Yes," I went on, putting them back on the table, "Father re-used ideas from some of them later in his career, that's all – it's a common practice. Of course, you wouldn't know that either, Mother, would you?"

The growing uncertainty on Mother's face gave me a pang of fierce joy.

A small step, I thought. But one in the right direction.

* * * * *

Later that morning I sat in my room and considered Mother's accusations. One had been shown to be unfounded. What about the others?

I set off straight away for the local chemist's. Mr Aloysius Jones (or it may have been 'and Son') greeted me affably.

"Good morning, Miss – nice to see you again – how are the studies going?"

"All finished now, Mr Jones – I graduated last week."

He smiled. "Glad to hear it, that's good to know. And please accept my condolences on the passing of your dear dad. Such a charming man and, of course, a regular and long-standing customer of mine."

I hesitated briefly. But I had to know the truth.

"That's what I wanted to talk to you about, Mr Jones. You remember his powders – the ones you supplied him with – his special powders? His injections?"

"Of course I do," he said easily. "I've never known anyone get through so many of them. But they did seem to help a little, and I know the poor man suffered badly with his hands and that. I was only too glad to be of assistance. That's my job, after all."

"What was in them, Mr Jones?" I asked bluntly.

He smiled again and shook his head. "Oh, I'm afraid that's a trade secret, Miss. I would be drummed out of the brownies if I was to tell you."

I dreaded his response. "Opium?"

His face was a study. "Eh? Good Lord, miss, no. What on earth gave you that idea? No, no, they were just a wee concoction of my own. A sleeping powder, basically, a relaxant, with some pain-relieving properties – willow bark, that sort of thing. Nothing harmful at all in them. I experimented with a combination of common ingredients and finally came up with a formula that seemed to do the trick. Mrs Jones – the wife – takes them too, she has a touch of lumbago now and then, and it gives her trouble sleeping. But – opium? Certainly not. I would never hand that stuff out willy-nilly. Not without a prescription. Where did you get the idea that your dad's powders had opium in them?"

"And the injections?" I persisted.

He shook his head. "No, no, the same thing. A wee bit stronger, dissolved in a solution, but no, nothing dangerous or addictive."

With some difficulty, I concealed my sigh of relief, and tried to sound nonchalant.

"Thank you, Mr Jones; it was just a silly idea of mine. Something someone said – I must have misunderstood. Thank you, anyway, for setting my mind at rest."

"Glad to have done so. Good Lord, imagine if it got about that I was handing out something like that…"

"Yes, of course, I'm sorry, it was my mistake."

I turned to leave. Then a notion came into my head. I turned back to the counter.

"Oh – do you think I might have two or three of the powders for myself? I've not been sleeping too well since Father died."

"Of course, Miss. Just wait there for a couple of minutes and I'll make half a dozen up for you. Or …" he hesitated. "Maybe the solution would be better? I know you used to give your dad the injections, he mentioned it a time or two."

No, no, it was the powders I wanted. But, on the other hand…

I smiled winningly. "Well – I don't suppose – just to see which works best – could you…?"

"Yes, of course, Miss – some of each, that the ticket, yes?"

"If you're sure it's no trouble, Mr Jones."

"None at all, Miss, none at all. Five minutes." And the obliging chemist headed off to his dispensing room.

What to make of this? One thing occupied my mind. It was beginning to look as though Mother's elaborate construction might have some rather shaky foundations.

"Something else, Mr Jones," I asked when he returned with the powders and a small bottle. "Where might I find Jeannie Dunt these days?"

He shook his head. "Not around here, Miss. Jeannie moved away, she and her husband. People round here were not kind. I'm not too sure where they went – Edinburgh, I believe, but I couldn't swear to it, sorry."

"It's no matter Mr Jones. Thank you for your help. How much do I owe you?"

"Nothing, nothing at all. You're very welcome. And will we be seeing you around the village, now you've completed your studies?"

"No, I don't think you will Mr Jones."

He smiled as he wrapped the powders for me. "Off to somewhere more exciting no doubt. That's the way of the young, I suppose. And before I forget – how is your dear mother? Well, I hope?"

I took the little parcel he had prepared. "She was very well when I left her. But I suspect she is going to be rather less well in a day or two."

And with this no doubt baffling statement, I left the shop.

Damn! No Jeannie. I would have to put off my investigation of that particular story for the moment. But I returned home filled with new hope, and with the beginnings of a plan.

* * * * *

Mother was full of *bonhomie* when she and I dined together later that evening. I played the acquiescent daughter assiduously, and even started a surreal discussion with her as to where my intended and I might spend our honeymoon. After all, I would be sixteen in a few days, and I deserved some reward for my sacrifice, surely? Mother initially seemed a trifle suspicious of my sudden enthusiasm, but eventually appeared to accept that I had bowed to the inevitable. She downed several large whiskies, as was her habit. Indeed, the bottle was nearly empty by the time she nodded off into a deep, drug-induced sleep, and began snoring loudly and unattractively. I had drunk nothing but water, of course.

I carefully retrieved the bunch of keys that Mother never let out of her sight, and made my way to her bedroom. There was something I had to find. But by the time I had fruitlessly searched through the various cupboards, cabinets and drawers that she always kept locked, I was at my wits' end. There was *nothing*. Nothing of any interest to me, at least. It was only when I accidentally dropped the bunch of keys on the floor and stooped down to retrieve them that I spied the wooden strong-box under her bed. I feverishly tried the keys, one after another. None of them seemed to fit. Without compunction, I took the poker from the fireplace and smashed the lock.

And there they were – half a dozen folders meticulously labelled, stuffed with papers, receipts, documents. Each bearing the name of a person I knew. Father, myself, Alec McDougal and his son, and even Lavinia. Without opening them, and after carefully re-locking all Mother's secret hiding places, I took the entire disgusting bundle into the kitchen, where Old Angus and his family had been enjoying a late supper. Without saying a word, I opened the door of the blazing range, and consigned the lot to the flames.

I made my way to Dougal's cottage. *En route* I dropped Mother's bunch of keys down a convenient drain.

"It's over, Dougal," I said when he opened the door. "Gone – all of it. Mother can't do anything now. You're free."

Briefly, I explained what I had done. We sat side by side as on my last visit. But I had refused his offer of a drink on this occasion. I needed a clear head tonight.

I was full of energy, full of enthusiasm. And full of advice. "The best thing you can do, Dougal, is to get away from here. Away from all this. Away from her."

"No," said Dougal slowly, "I understand why you say that. But I can't, Eva. She needs me. She hasn't got anyone else, you see. Not now you are leaving."

I couldn't believe what I was hearing. "Is this the same person we are talking about? My mother? She doesn't need you. Or me. She doesn't need anyone at all."

He twisted the glass in his hand from side to side and looked down. "You're wrong, Eva. She does. Oh, I know she doesn't show it. But she does. The trouble is, you don't actually know her very well."

"I know her as well as I want to, thank you, Dougal. And how can *you* make excuses for her? You who have been used by her in every imaginable way? – as her errand boy, her go-between, her chauffeur, her lover while it suited her, her lackey when it no longer did. You've told me how she used the information she had acquired to blackmail you. How on earth can you defend her?"

He looked up, scratching his head.

"Yes, you may well ask that, I suppose. But have you never asked yourself *why* she is the way she is?"

"No, I haven't – why should I?"

Not true. The thought had occasionally crossed my mind, only to be dropped when I was unable to come up with any kind of answer.

"Just out of curiosity, maybe? Did you never think to ask her?"

No, I hadn't. My uneasy relationship with my mother had never encouraged cosy mother-daughter chats.

Dougal sensed my hesitation. "As I said, you don't know her very well. But I do. Better than anyone, probably. She talks to me, confides in me. And that's maybe because she never considers me a person of much account."

I wasn't sure I wanted to hear this. I didn't want any doubts raised. In any case, whatever the reasons for Mother's behaviour, nothing – *nothing* – could excuse her latest manoeuvres. And time was passing. I stood up.

"Dougal, I can't stay. Sorry – I must go."

Dougal smiled gently. "Yes, of course you must. Is that maybe because you don't want to know any more?"

For once I was at a loss. He was right. I didn't.

"Before you go, Eva, sit down a moment and think on this. You know, I believe, that she had problems when she was a young girl?" I nodded, yes, and sat down as he had asked. "You've heard the story. Or a version of it, at least. Imagine then what it may have been like for your mother here in this house. Your father the centre of the world. Their children devoted to him, dismissive of her. She may have been lonely, don't you think? Felt isolated and ignored? Maybe she decided that, if there was only one way she could get attention and be listened to, then that was the way she would go."

"Dougal, I don't care. Whatever reasons she may have had, or imagined she had, they can never excuse her recent behaviour."

He sighed. "Yes, I can understand how you feel. But it's different for me."

I took his hand. "Poor Dougal. You care for her, I can see that. Although I can't see why. But for your own sake, go while you can. Before she involves you in yet another of her insane schemes."

He shook his head and sighed. "No. I have to stay here and look after her."

"It's your choice, Dougal." I stood up again. "But *I* can't stay here, not now. And I need a favour."

He rose from his chair. "Anything, Eva, if it's in my power."

"It is. I want you to drive me into Glasgow, now, right away. Before she wakes up and tries something else."

He nodded. "I'll be glad to. Where are you headed?"

"I don't know as yet. You can just drop me in the town centre, I'll make my own way from there."

He was shocked. "What? I can't do that! Leave you on your own in the middle of the city? Anything might happen to you. It's a mad idea!"

I smiled ruefully. "Well, we're all a bit mad in this family, aren't we, Dougal? Really, that's what I want you to do. If you won't, I'll find someone else who will."

Eyeing me dubiously, "Very well, if you're sure," he said.

"I am. And if you have any sense at all, when you've dropped me off, you will keep driving till you're as far away as possible."

I left the cottage and returned to the house.

All appeared to be as I had left it. I wrote a short note to Mother and placed it on the table in front of her. Then I went through her handbag, and removed the sum of money I found there, along with her car keys, her driving licence, her passport and her hip flask.

Upstairs, I hurriedly packed a few personal belongings, then made my way back to the dining room.

I looked at her. She was pale. Some inexplicable impulse made me decide that I should check her pulse before leaving.

As I bent over her, she suddenly stirred, flailed an arm weakly, and muttered something incomprehensible. My heart leapt to my mouth, and for a moment I panicked. Her head rolled to one side. Her eyes opened.

"Mona, dear? Is that you?..." The eyes rolled closed again.

Quick as a flash I dug in my coat pocket and retrieved the little bottle and the syringe I had taken from Father's cache. It was the work of seconds to fill it, I had done it countless times before. I grabbed her arm and plunged the needle in, through blouse and jumper, not caring.

She twitched and gave a little mew like a kitten. A few seconds later she was snoring as loudly as ever.

Just at that moment I heard the crunch of wheels on the gravel drive outside.

I glanced at Mother one final time. She looked oddly defenceless, vulnerable. I threw a tartan rug over her, hoping I hadn't overdone the dose. Then, without a backward glance, I opened the French windows, threw all Mother's junk into the moat, and left my home for the last time.

Interlude

August 1937.

The Winter Gardens Theatre, Rothesay, Scotland.

"Great – look forward to it – it's a pudding supper for me, the rest of you can please yourselves. As you lot tend to do, of course!"

Young Joe Cameron winked at me and continued on his way up the stairs towards his dressing room.

Mae and I, along with the rest of us dancers, continued our descent to the stage to take our positions for *The Garden of Beauty*. *Doon the Watter* had been running successfully for a couple of months now, and by this time we girls were well used to the routine.

The Garden of Beauty was the opening scene of the second half of our show. It was always referred to as *Le Jardin Animé* by Boris, our choreographer and *premier danseur*, nicknamed by me 'Goodenough', in reference to the Mussorgsky opera[1]. Boris Asafiev claimed to have toured with Diaghilev, and had delusions of adequacy. A brief description will give some idea of the exalted level of entertainment *Doon the Watter* provided.

The curtain rose on a darkened stage while the pit band wreaked havoc on Mendelssohn's *Spring Song*. We secondary blossoms were clustered round the recumbent figure of Ruby Rose, played by our boss and nemesis, the lovely Betty Barnard herself. As the music convulsed to a climax, and the stage lighting attempted half-heartedly to portray the arrival of dawn, Betty, spot lit, stretched, yawned delicately and rose on point. The music changed to Ponchielli's *Dance of the Hours* to which we all cavorted merrily for a minute or two. Suddenly, introduced by a motif from Wagner's *Ride of the Valkyries*, a strange black creature leapt on from stage left. Whether he was supposed to be a raven or an owl or some strange hybrid of the two would have been hard to say. Boris (for it was indeed he) proceeded to menace Ruby Rose. She *bouréed* rapidly backward, hands fluttering, away from his advances, the precise nature of which was unclear. Surely he wasn't contemplating a union as unlikely of intent as impossible of consummation? But no, he was merely trying for some unknown reason to tear off her petals. Meanwhile we in the herbaceous border fluttered in helpless alarm. Just in the very nick of time, the Gardener, our Irish tenor Vincent Murphy, entered stage right, and with a commanding gesture banished the interloper to the shadows. The music changed to a gentle strain, and Vincent

1 Boris Godunov

proceeded to intone:

"Come into the garden, Maud

For the black bat, night, has flown"

Ah yes, of course, Boris was a bat. 'The Black Bat, Night', no less.

As Vincent's paean rose to a crescendo, he was joined at the footlights by Maud herself, our soprano and his partner, Lena Lorraine. They then duetted melodiously through *Glamorous Night*, from Ivor Novello's recent hit musical of the same name; and the scene ended incomprehensibly with the drinking song from *La Traviata*, during which we flowers enthusiastically brandished empty champagne glasses and the now tamed 'Black Bat, Night' joined Ruby Rose in a jolly *pas-de-deux*.

All this was the most arrant nonsense imaginable. However, the audiences loved it, and stamped their feet and clapped to the irresistible swing of Verdi's tune.

* * * * *

When the curtain fell, I rushed for the stairs. This was a heavy show for me. As well as supporting the leads in their big scenes, we girls had to assist in all sorts of ways. In our own dance routines, naturally, but one or other of us would often be co-opted to appear in the comics' sketches, where an extra character or two was required. As I had a clear speaking voice, I was often the one chosen for these duties. I was frequently cast as dowagers (the Countess of Muck – Lady Muck, naturally – in *The Road to the Isles*) or French maids (in *Gay Paree* I had to prostitute my flawless French to shriek '*Ooh-la-la – eet ees so beeg*' six or seven times) or even as a simple-minded Highland country girl in *Doon Frae the Hills*[1]. All this meant a few extra pennies in my pay packet at the end of the week, so I wasn't complaining. If, however, the part in question required a more common or specifically Glaswegian style, it would usually be Mae or Phyllis who took the rôle.

In this particular show, *The Garden of Beauty* was followed by a Speciality Act (*Bertram and his Bouncing Budgies* – a grubby little man who did interesting things with budgerigars), and then I was on again in *The Judgement of Paris*, a coarse spoof on the Greek legend. Our tenor, Vincent, played the shepherd Paris, who is asked to award the golden apple inscribed 'For the fairest' to the most beautiful of the immortals. Three goddesses vie for the title, offering Paris various inducements. I was the goddess of wisdom, Athena, a stuffed owl perched on my shoulder; Mae made a buxom Hera, queen of the Gods, complete with peacock; while the deity of love, Aphrodite, was hilariously travestied by

1 Down From the Hills

our leading comic, Tony McLean, in female attire. In our version, however, the bribe offered by Aphrodite to the shepherd is not 'the love of the beautiful Helen, Queen of Sparta', but 'a date doon ra Barraland wi' Hairy Mary frae Gartferry'[1].

And to think we did all this two or even three times a day!

But we were young and full of energy, and as we trooped out of the stage door we chattered away happily, looking forward to our supper and some fun. A sleek elderly gentleman was waiting just outside, and to my surprise, quiet little Shona, one of the new girls, linked arms with him, and with a cheery '*See you on Monday, ladies*', disappeared into the night.

"How nice of Shona's father to come and collect her like that," I said to Mae as we clattered along the uneven pavement. "It shows a proper care, don't you think?"

"Well, it shows something, certainly, Rina," replied Mae, nodding. "But that's no' her father, angel. It's her daddy. Aye, our pal Shona's found herself a wee sugar, by the looks of it."

"A sugar?"

"Yes, a wee sugar; as in 'daddy'.

"Oh – I see," I said.

Mae's eyes gleamed wickedly. "Maybe we can find one for you, Rina – what do you think?"

My look answered her question. Men, rich or poor, were definitely not on the agenda at present.

"Sorry, angel – I forgot – no men is the rule. Yer mental, of course. Young Joe, for example… crazy for you, he is, Joe…"

Another warning look discouraged further speculation.

"Oh – and speaking of men, Danny's doon frae Glasgow, just for the weekend – he'll be meeting us at the chip shop. That'll be nice, won't it?"

Danny was Mae's 'husband', a kindly man, with whom I got on very well. I looked forward to seeing him again. Mae linked her arm through mine and we continued on our way.

We arrived at the fish and chip shop and took seats in the serving area. There were about ten of us in all, and we chattered away light-heartedly while we scanned the menu. After about five minutes the adenoidal waitress came over to take our order.

"Yes?" she sniffed.

"Black pudding and chips, and a coffee," said Joe.

"A fish supper for me," said Mae, passing her menu to me. "Tea, bread and butter."

---

1 A date down at the Barrowland Ballroom with Hairy Mary from Gartferry

I couldn't decide. "Give me a minute," I said.

The waitress looked at Phyllis enquiringly. "Yes?"

"Pissholes and chips for me."

"Eh?" said the waitress with a frown. Conversation at the table died away.

"Pissholes and chips," repeated Phyllis, straight-faced, pointing at her menu.

The waitress bent over and peered short-sightedly at the typed card. After a second she straightened up.

"That's no' a 'P', dear, it's an 'R'," she said patiently, head on one side.

"Oh – sorry," said Phyllis, looking back down at her menu, "ma mistake." She took a deep breath and nodded. "OK, in that case Ah'll have arseholes and chips."

The table convulsed with merriment. Even I had to smile.

Mae's husband Danny greeted me with pleasure and a wink.

"How's it going, hen? Everything OK wi' you? Mae keeping an eye on you?"

"Yes, fine thanks, Danny. Tired, but – you know".

"Not too tired, I hope. Marina, I want you to meet a friend of mine," he went on. I had barely noticed that he wasn't alone. "Marina, this is Rab. Rab – meet Marina."

"How do you do?" I said automatically, stretching out my hand.

It was grasped firmly, and I looked up into an astonishing pair of brown eyes.

"Robert McCarthy," said the eyes. "Hello – and what's your story, hen?"

Chapter Seven
A Fresh Start

July 1936.

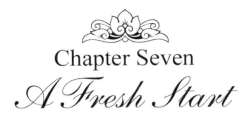

St George's Cross, Glasgow.

What was my story?

It was now just over a year since Dougal had deposited me in the centre of Glasgow, and my plan – to disappear, and to sink below the horizon of everyone and everything that had made up my past life – had succeeded to a degree that not even I had anticipated.

It had been a strange parting. Dougal was understandably reluctant to leave me. Glasgow's reputation at that time was a less than savoury one. I was sixteen and completely alone. When it became obvious that he was determined not to consign me to the streets without at least *some* indication of my plans, I improvised a story of a meeting arranged with a University friend who had invited me to come and stay for a few days.

"But what will you do after that, Eva?"

We sat in his car, parked at St George's Cross, in the city centre, right outside a noisy pub.

"Oh, I'm off down to London in a few days," I said, affecting a breezy manner. "My boyfriend is there already. I will be joining him. He's expecting me."

In truth, I had no intention of travelling to London. But Dougal didn't need to know that.

"Oh, I see. Your boy-friend? So there's a gentleman in the picture?" He glanced at me as he lit a cigarette.

I laughed a little shakily. "A young gentleman, yes."

He wound down the window of the car and looked out. "I hope he's that, Eva." His tone was suddenly serious.

"What – young?" I parried.

"No. A gentleman. A gentleman's what you deserve," he said reflectively. "I wish you luck."

"Thank you." I thought of my dear Finlay, my first love. No doubt busily engaged in setting up a home; booking the church; and furnishing a nursery.

"Anyway, Eva," said Dougal, blowing his smoke out of the window, "Let me know where this friend of yours lives and I'll drive you there."

"There's no need, Dougal, really. I've arranged to meet her here. I'll be fine, Dougal, stop worrying." How to get rid of him? "Hadn't you better be getting back to the Castle? Mother will be wondering where you are. She won't be feeling too great – I *did* give her quite a dose of that stuff. Hadn't you better check on her?"

I could tell he was torn. "Yes, yes, of course. But are you sure you will be all right? How will you live? – what will you do for money?"

"I've got money, Dougal, don't worry. I took some of Mother's, quite a lot. Really, I must go."

I opened the car door.

"Goodbye, Dougal. And thank you."

I leaned over to kiss him. Somehow, what I had intended as a chaste, sisterly kiss turned into something else.

Eventually, I freed myself.

"I have to go," I muttered distractedly. I opened the car door and stepped into the road.

Dougal got out his side of the car, ground his cigarette under his foot, and planted himself on the pavement, immovable.

"I'll wait with you, Eva, just until your friend arrives."

Oh, why wouldn't he *go*?

"No, don't do that, it's really not necessary…"

Suddenly the door of the pub behind him flew open, and a large and patently inebriated gentleman was propelled forcibly from within. He cannoned into Dougal, knocking him to his knees, then fell headlong himself, and vomited copiously over Dougal's shoes.

"Aw, damn it…" said Dougal, looking down.

In spite of this rude introduction, Dougal politely helped the new arrival to his feet, then glanced down again in despair at his ruined footwear. With a resigned sigh, he took a large handkerchief from his pocket.

While his attention was elsewhere, I turned, dashed across the road and rounded a corner. I tore along, desperately looking for somewhere to conceal myself – a doorway, a shop, anything.

"Eva, Eva, come back… Wait…" I heard Dougal's shout, and, seconds later, the sound of the car engine starting up.

There seemed to be nowhere to hide. "Please," I thought, "Please. Let me get away. I have to get away…"

Just at that moment, a crowd of young women, six or seven of them, obviously on a Saturday night junket, laughing and gossiping, came towards me. Thinking quickly, I linked arms with the girl on the end furthest from the road, hoping against hope that they were too engrossed in their private affairs to notice the sudden addition.

What luck! I realised that this was a hen party, and the girl whose arm I had taken merely turned to me and said, "Hey there, hen, welcome. Glad you could make it."

I kept my face down as Dougal's car approached. It seemed to work. He passed us by without a second glance.

At the earliest opportunity, I detached myself from the group.

"Sorry," I said to my new companion, "I have to go."

"Och, Ah know the feeling, hen. Just find a quiet back court – we'll be in the Star, jist roon the corner. Don't be long, it's going to be a great night. How dae ye know Jeanette? From work?"

I muttered something non-committal, and watched the laughing group disappear.

Looking round me, I realised I had no idea where I was. For a moment my nerve failed me.

Then, squaring my shoulders, I plunged into the teeming backstreets of Glasgow.

* * * * *

August 1936.

Maryhill, Glasgow.

Things were difficult at first. Indeed, had it not been for the surprising kindness of strangers, I might not have survived. The small sum – about twelve pounds – that I had removed from Mother's handbag before my departure was soon swallowed up. I managed to find lodgings in a seedy back street in Maryhill for ten shillings a week. A mean little room, with a narrow single bed, an unshaded light bulb hanging from the mildewed ceiling, an ancient gas fire that only worked intermittently, and that only if I had the money to feed the meter – this was my new home. Luckily, I had had the salutary experience of life *chez* Morag to accustom me to surviving in low temperatures. Besides, it was still summer, and Glasgow was enjoying record weather. But the gloom and depressing nature of my new surroundings gradually wore me down. That and the noise.

My landlady, Mrs Scowler (and never was anyone so appropriately named), was a thin, weedy slattern with an unfortunate drooping eyelid. She appeared to have about sixteen children. Since it was impossible to count them (they moved around so much) I can't be sure of that, but they were everywhere, shrieking, laughing, crying, often, it seemed, simultaneously. Add to that the comings and goings at all hours of the various other tenants, the drunken arguments, the constant banging of the front door as one or the other left or arrived. Top it off with the omnipresent warbling of *Me and My Shadow* by my landlady, who appeared to have a pathological obsession with the song, and you will have some idea of the cacophonous torture that I endured. I had been accustomed to the steady pace and muted atmosphere of Lang Hall, or the spacious tranquil surroundings of Dean Castle. This was like living in the anteroom to Hell.

However, I had made my bed, and must lie in it. I had resolved to completely cut myself off from my old life. Well, I had certainly achieved that. How many times was I tempted to contact one or other of my old friends? I even considered Morag at one point, but succeeded in resisting.

I was determined to write to Finlay, explaining my decision not to follow him to the bright lights. Explaining that I had thought long and hard, and though my feelings hadn't changed, marriage at the moment was out of the question as far as I was concerned. Explaining that I needed some time to myself before I came to a definite conclusion.

All this, I fear, no more convincing than I have described it. I shrank from telling him the truth. That I felt our relationship had run its course, that I had to forge my own way on my own terms, and that he should forget me and get on with his own life.

But I didn't have the nerve to be so honest. Shamefully, what I was truly doing was reserving him as an ultimate solution, should all else, including my courage, fail me at the last.

It wasn't until after composing this letter that I realised I had absolutely no idea where to send it. Eventually, I addressed the envelope to Finlay Clark, Horn Section, The Royal Philharmonic Orchestra, London. It was the best I could do. I prayed he would receive it, early or late.

But for now it was imperative that I find work as soon as possible. My little store of money was fast disappearing, and I needed to have an income – one that might allow me above all to find a more congenial place to live.

But I had not realised how completely unsuited I was to the current job market. I was qualified, of course, highly so – but in nothing that would help me to achieve a simple and basic employment. My assumption had been that I would easily find some kind of musical work. And so an interview was arranged with Galt's Theatrical Agency in Sauchiehall Street, at that time the recognised Mecca for those seeking employment in the Scottish entertainment profession. There might be an opening for me in a theatre orchestra or even in a music-hall in the area.

"No dear, sorry, we don't handle musicians. Not as *such*..." The rather superior lady behind the desk stressed the 'such' in an odd manner. If not as *such*, I wondered, did they handle musicians in some other, special way?

"No," she went on, tapping her pencil on her teeth in an irritating fashion, "Not as *such*. We are, you understand, a *theatrical* agency. No, for musicians, you would have to try elsewhere. Maybe down *south*? Yes, that might be best."

"You mean," I asked, "that there is no agency locally that specialises in musicians?"

"No," she drawled, "Not really any *equivalent*. Not really, no. Not for *musicians*. No. They tend to sort it out among themselves, you see. Yes, that's what they do, so they do."

She paused and started to re-arrange some papers on her desk. I rose to leave.

"I understand. Thank you for your time," I said.

"One thing dear, before you go." She looked me over, which was more than she had done up till now. "I don't suppose you *sing*, do you? Or maybe *dance* a wee step or two?"

Father had convinced me that, no, I didn't sing. And I certainly didn't dance. Well, I *had* attended classes in Scottish Country Dancing when much younger, but I doubted if that was the kind of dancing I was being asked about.

"No, I'm sorry, I'm afraid I don't."

"Aw, pity," she went on, winding some paper into her typewriter, "We're short of a girl right now, and Betty likes them *tall*, like you. Anyway, never mind, it was just a thought. Best of luck, dear, I hope you find something."

She began tapping on the keys of her machine in a determined fashion.

"Thank you. So do I." I headed for the door.

Suddenly the clattering stopped.

"Oh – just a wee minute, dear."

I turned back again. "Yes?"

"Now – sorry, it had slipped my mind – and it's nothing to do with the agency, no, not as *such* – but I *did* see a notice in Miss Rombach's window the other day. It seems the restaurant is looking for *somebody*. To play the piano from time to time. Yes, to *play*. Now and then. You might try in there?"

What? I could have kissed her. "Really? Oh, thank you!"

"Nae problem dear, I know how tough the business can be. Good luck." She waved a hand languidly.

I left and hurried towards Waterloo Street. Miss Rombach's Restaurant was a well-known establishment in Glasgow. Catering to a mainly middle-class clientele, it had no pretensions to grandeur, but offered tasty home-cooked lunches and high teas to shoppers and business people. It was always busy, and I had in the past enjoyed an occasional meal there.

* * * * *

I lasted three days at Miss Rombach's. I had assumed that my selection of some of the lighter classics – a delicate Chopin prelude perhaps, or some of Schubert's lyrical pieces – would appeal to the more sophisticated diner. But I soon discovered that such things were not at all to their taste; and that, when they asked for something more in the 'popular' style, they were not expecting *Bonny Mary of Argyll* or *The Road and the Miles to Dundee*, but were anticipating some of the nasty 'jazz' music whose pernicious influence was seemingly everywhere.

"You play beautifully, dear, no question of that," said the elegantly coiffed elderly lady (Miss Rombach herself, perhaps?) who ran the establishment. "I mean, I love a wee bit of Mozart myself. But it's not really the kind of music we need here. Something more lively is what's wanted."

I returned to my dreary bedsit in low spirits. As I entered the hallway, an ancient and withered gentleman, possibly Mr Scowler (or possibly not) spotted me, and called out "Percy – quick – she's here."

Percy?

Mrs Scowler entered the hall from her private domains on the ground floor at a trot, a determined expression on her face.

"So there ye are young lady. It's the rent. You've no paid me yet and it's overdue."

"Sorry, Mrs Scowler, it slipped my mind." I reached into the pocket of my coat and drew out a crumpled ten-shilling note. "Here you are."

"Thank you. I hope you're no' goin' tae make a habit of keeping me waitin' like this?" she grumbled as she pocketed my offering. "Rent is due on Friday and on Friday Ah expect to be paid."

I had forgotten that the one unforgivable sin in this house was not to pay the rent on time.

"No, of course not, Mrs Scowler. I'm trying to find work and it's not been easy. But don't worry; I'll see that you have the rent when it's due, whatever happens."

She appeared to thaw slightly.

"Good." She looked me up and down. "Of course yer very young. Awfy young. Have ye tried the trams? They're always looking for lassies for the trams."

The trams I had *not* considered.

"No, I haven't, Mrs Scowler. Maybe I will. Thank you."

"Anyway," she went on as she prepared to leave, "If ye've nae luck there, there's always other things. There's nae reason why a nice-looking lassie should be wi'oot money. No' while there's a man in the world."

And with a nasty chuckle and a horrid, suggestive wink from her good eye, she retreated to her own quarters.

* * * * *

My stint as a tram conductress, or 'clippie', was even shorter than my engagement as a lounge pianist. I was sacked from the job on my second day. As I have mentioned elsewhere, mathematics is not my *forte.* Although simple addition is not beyond me, the complex calculations necessary to supply a halfpenny one to Auchenshuggle, along with two and two halves to Byres Road, and a pensioner's reduced fare to Partick Cross, left me reeling. Also, the bizarre mechanical device slung round my neck to print the tickets seemed to have a mind of its own. It would insist on either not functioning at all or on spewing out twenty tickets for one fare. Often I would be the target of witty remarks as I struggled doggedly with its handle to make it function. '*Gie it a guid crank, hen*', and '*C'moan ower here, lassie, Ah'll wind yer gadget for ye*', were probably the least offensive of them.

Things were desperate. I had barely two pounds to my name, and the rent was due.

So I gave up eating.

* * * * *

September 1936.

Maryhill.

By the end of August I had virtually abandoned my search for employment. Perhaps I would hear of something tomorrow. I had started sleeping all day, when the house was comparatively quiet, and staying out all night, walking the streets, when the domestic rowdiness was at its height. I would not return to my room until the early hours of the morning. Let me make it clear that, when I say 'walking the streets', I do not mean to imply what my landlady had so evilly suggested; I simply wandered from place to place passing the time, my mind empty.

It was on one of these night time rambles that I discovered the coffee stall. Located at Glasgow's Charing Cross, this all-night mobile café served tea and coffee along with greasy sandwiches filled with eggs, sausages or bacon. It drew the late night crowd like moths to a flame. I could never afford to eat anything there, but did occasionally treat myself to a cup of strong tea. The summer nights were warm still. I would stand on the fringe of the lively throng, but rarely spoke to anyone. Just the human company around me seemed to make me feel a little better and less isolated.

And they were a fascinating collection; generally good-humoured, although occasionally a dispute would break out in the crowd. But it rarely led to anything more than a word from a local constable, and as a rule the atmosphere was lively and friendly. Women who were obviously 'ladies of the night', heavily made-up and provocatively dressed, rubbed shoulders with 'spiv' types and other low-class creatures who might, I imagined, have been petty crooks. A few gentlemen of various ages who appeared to be wearing more than a slight touch of make-up fascinated me most of all. They always seemed to be having a particularly enjoyable time, and their merry laughter rang out constantly.

I was there one Saturday night at the beginning of September, light-headed and faint – I hadn't eaten anything for perhaps three days. Indeed, the pangs of hunger had virtually disappeared. The very last of my money had gone on my rent the previous day, and only a few coppers remained in my pocket. I made my way to the counter and asked for a cup of tea. My mind was composing an orchestral poem to be entitled *Midnight Fantasy*. Yes, that was how it would go… Suddenly I was brought out of my reverie by the voice of a tall, thin middle-aged man standing at my shoulder.

"Are you all right, girlie? You don't look too great."

I turned to my interlocutor.

"Yes, I'm fine, thank you," I said. "Just a bit tired. But thank you for asking."

As a delicious waft of Shem-el-Nessim, 'the scent of Araby', reached my nostrils, I realised that this was one of the discreetly painted gentlemen of whom there were a fair number there that night. I took in a hint of face powder, a delicate blue eye shadow, and more than a touch of mascara. I also saw a kindly, sympathetic expression, and a warm smile.

"Hen, you look as pale as death. Are you sure you're all right? When did you last eat?"

"I don't remember exactly. But I don't eat much. I'm on a diet."

For some reason this struck me as extremely funny, and I laughed weakly.

My neighbour turned to the counter. "Joe, give this lassie a bacon sandwich, on me, to go with that tea."

"Right you are, York, coming up." This was the man behind the counter.

"Oh no, I couldn't possibly…" I protested.

"You'll do as you're told, hen," insisted my new companion with a smile, and a wag of the finger. "Now – what's a wee lassie like you doing out at this time of night? You should be tucked up in bed."

Just at that moment, my sandwich arrived. I devoured it shamelessly. It tasted delicious. As I munched, my saviour went on, "Where do you live? – I'll see you home when you've finished that, and make sure no harm comes to you."

I chewed and swallowed. "That's very kind of you, Mr – er – York. But really there's no need. I've not far to go. I'm in lodgings just off the Maryhill Road, Shakespeare Street."

My new friend looked suddenly shocked. "Not with Percy, surely – Percy Scowler? "

As I finished my sandwich, which I had devoured like a wolf, I realised I was beginning to feel a little peculiar. The food didn't seem to have agreed with me at all. The greasy smell of frying chips, combined with my companion's rather overpowering perfume, was making me feel rather queasy. My vision kept coming and going. What had he just asked me? Oh, yes…

I tried to pull myself together. I nodded. "Yes, that's right, Mrs Scowler. She's my landlady."

He shook his head dubiously. "Oh dear, that's not so good. How do you come to be lodging with that nasty old cow?"

I wiped my greasy lips and grinned weakly. "Just lucky, I suppose." Once again I was convulsed by shaky laughter at my own apparently unending stream of witticisms.

My companion frowned. "It's not funny, hen. Percy Scowler is one to watch out for. She's got the evil eye, that one."

"It's certainly not very attractive," I agreed, giggling. Oh dear. My head was spinning. But something that had been puzzling me suddenly surfaced. "But perhaps you can enlighten me on one point, sir – tell me – why is she called Percy?"

My new friend smiled.

"Yes, it's a bit unlikely, I agree. But you see, her first name is, of all things, Persephone. Did you not know that, hen?" said Mr York.

I almost choked on the last of my tea. Persephone[1] – the queen of the underworld. How Father would have laughed!

Just at that moment a passing black pit yawned wide and I fell gratefully into it.

1 In Greek myth, Persephone, the daughter of Zeus and Demeter, was abducted by Hades, the god of the underworld, and became his queen.

* * * * *

September 1936.

The Palace, Hill Street, Glasgow.

I woke in a haze of delicious warmth, with no idea where I was. Pale sunlight edged the gap at the top of the curtains. I could hear nothing except for the distant ringing of church bells. A beautiful sound. Turning over, I went back to sleep.

The light had faded when I next awoke. A muted murmur of voices came from somewhere close by, and I began to take in my surroundings. I was lying in a large and comfortable double bed in a spacious and beautifully furnished room. Was I somehow mysteriously back at Dean Castle, I wondered? No – the furniture in my own bedroom was old and worm-eaten, and my own bedding could not compare to the soft blankets and embroidered sheets that covered me. Maybe I was in hospital, and a starched and smiling nurse would peep round the door any minute, and ask me if I felt better. I had been ill, I realised. But surely no hospital would provide such comfort for their patients? Weary of trying to solve the mystery, and frankly not really very interested, I thought just a little more sleep was probably what I needed.

Just as I nodded off, there was a gentle tap at the door, and two figures appeared in the gloom.

"Are you awake yet, hen?" a soft voice asked.

"Yes," I said confusedly, sitting up. "Unless I've died and gone to heaven. Which I don't actually happen to believe in; though that's neither here nor there, of course, since I'm obviously not dead."

"I said she was a bit of a character, didn't I?" one figure said to the other. A soft lamp was lit.

The two mysterious figures turned out to be my guardian angel from the Coffee Stall and another gentleman, shorter and plump, who walked with a slight limp.

"Now dear," said the gentleman I remembered as Mr York, "we need to know who you are. Get in touch with your family and so forth. Make sure you get home safely. What's your name?"

I shook my head. "I have no family." This was the simple truth. "But my name is Eva – Eva Lestrange." Where this came from, what novel, what history, I will never know. But I felt that it was important to keep my true identity to myself, however kind and helpful my new friend had been. "And – may I ask – who are you?"

Mr York answered, "I am The Duchess of York, dear, and this is my friend, The Divine Sarah."

The Duchess of York? Was this an avatar of the lovely Elizabeth Bowes-Lyon, wife to the Duke of York, the younger brother of our King, Edward VIII? I knew that *The Divine Sarah* was the sobriquet of the legendary Sarah Bernhardt. But the latter had died when I was a small child. And, at least as far as I was aware, both had been women. Had I somehow moved into one of the parallel dimensions that Mr Einstein assures us exist? I decided to leave that conundrum for the moment.

"Have some soup, dear," said Mr York. "You need feeding up. You've not been well, but in a day or two you will be as right as rain. Sarah, just pop into the kitchen and warm some soup for young Eva."

"Right you are, Elizabeth," and the other gentleman tiptoed out of the room.

Elizabeth?

The thought of delicious soup was irresistible.

"Thank you. You are very kind. But I must get up, really. I need to get back to Maryhill. My landlady will be wondering where I am."

Mr York sat down in a soft armchair next to the bed.

"No need, dear. Sarah's been up to Percy's place and told her you won't be coming back. She collected your stuff. And here's the ten bob you paid for your week's rent."

I took the crumpled note. "Really, I don't know what to say. Except thank you. I should be able to find somewhere else in a day or two, if that's all right."

Mr York smiled, and shook his head. "No thanks necessary, dear. And don't even think of looking for another place. This is your home now. For as long as you decide to stay."

* * * * *

With the resilience of youth, I was up and about again in no time. And I gradually came to know more about my new friends, and to discover a secret side of society of whose existence I had been completely unaware.

But first, I felt, I must make my situation clear. I confided to Mr York some details of my past, suitably edited, and was assured that my revelations would go no further. I explained that, grateful as I was, if I were to stay, I needed to find some kind of work, and contribute somehow to the running of the household.

"Not at all, dear – you can help Sarah and me around the house, if you like – there's always plenty to do. Maybe in a while we can see if we can find you a wee job, if that's what you want. But not until you're stronger. I won't hear of it."

'The Duchess' and 'Sarah', I discovered, ran a bed and breakfast business catering mainly to theatricals. The house was a large one, on three floors, and was in Hill Street, right in the centre of Glasgow, running parallel to fashionable Sauchiehall Street, with its beautiful shops and restaurants. 'The Duchess' always referred to the house as the 'The Palace', no doubt in deference to the other duchess's London home.

It took me some little time to adjust to the mode of address which my new friends considered suitable. At first I was inclined to say 'Mr York' and 'Mr Sarah', which caused some amusement; until one day the Duchess said, "Eva dear, I realise this is all a bit new to you, but really – just call me 'Your Royal Highness' if you're feeling formal, or simply 'Elizabeth'; whichever you prefer. Friends often call me 'York', an intimate abbreviation that I permit; rather as close friends of the Duke of Westminster might call him simply 'Westminster'. Common practice among the nobility, to which of course I belong. Sarah is usually 'Sarah', or occasionally 'the Divine One' if we are talking *about* her and not *to* her. Oh – and stick with 'her' and 'she' in general conversation – you'll find it's easier. Don't worry – you'll soon get the hang of it."

I thought I could manage that. 'Elizabeth', I told myself firmly. 'And Sarah'. Not very complicated. There was one small point however that intrigued me.

"Why is Sarah 'Sarah'? Is he – sorry, she – a great – er – actress?"

Elizabeth laughed. "No, not at all, dear, though no doubt she would dispute the point. She's *The Divine Sarah* because, like the original, she has a wooden leg."

Chapter Eight
The Spice of Life

To the end of my days I shall never forget the kindness I received from my friends in The Palace, as it was always called. I was quickly regarded as a permanent member of the household and was treated with respect and consideration throughout the long period I stayed there. For the first time, it seemed, I was simply accepted for who I was (or rather, for who I claimed to be – I did not reveal the full details of my origins to Elizabeth and Sarah until much later.) No demands were made of me and little advice given. I was simply allowed to be myself.

Incongruous though it first seemed to me, I quickly came to adopt the language and preferred style of my new friends. My hosts were Elizabeth and Sarah, and I soon found that they had a horde of acquaintances of the same persuasion, all of whom were male, but all of whom preferred to be addressed in female terms. Among my many new friends I soon came to number such 'stars', as they liked to refer to themselves, as Myrna Loy and Mary Pickford. Hollywood names seemed to be a popular choice of sobriquet. But there were others of more mysterious origin. I encountered Hieland Kitty, Big Madge, Stella Minge, and most enigmatically, Madam from the Beach.

I was curious, and asked Elizabeth "How are these names allocated? Do they choose them themselves, or what?"

"Well, it depends," Elizabeth answered, after a pause for thought. "Sometimes they do. Other times, someone else thinks of an appropriate name for a newcomer. And often the name has some connection with the 'real' name of the person. For example, I'm really Frederick Lyon. I used to be 'Elizabeth Bowes-Lyon'. Then when the Duke married me, I became 'The Duchess of York' – such an unexpected elevation! Sarah you know about. Mary Pickford was John Fairbanks originally[1]. And so on."

"I see. And what about Big Madge, for example?"

"Oh, simple – have you seen the size of her? Built like an ox. Worked on the bins for a while – that's where the muscles came from, I suppose."

I understood that 'worked on the bins' meant that Big Madge had been employed as what is now termed a refuse disposal officer. "And Madam from the Beach?"

1 Mary Pickford was married to Douglas Fairbanks Snr, and was the mother of Douglas Fairbanks Jnr.

"We just call her that because she's always got a sun tan. Out of a bottle I suspect, though she would deny it."

"I see." It began to make sense. "And Desdemona Drew is – was – oh – Derek Drew – Dennis Drew?

"Close – Desmond Drew, dear."

It wasn't long before I too had a name. I was *Miss Strange* to all and sundry.

Conversations at the many gatherings which took place in The Palace could be somewhat surreal. The guests seemed to move from their real identities to their *noms de guerre* and back again instantly. It could be rather confusing. Occasionally they would appear to assume the style and history of their chosen characters in a realistic way. I remember Sarah holding forth:

"Of course, when Ah played Hamlet it wis a sensation. Jist think – a frail woman like me taking on *the* major Shakespearian hero! It wis a terrible strain, trying tae keep up the masculine manner, as you can imagine. But Ah wis a triumph, of course."

"Of course you were – the part was made for you, hen. Ah've always felt that Hamlet was a bit of a sissy on the quiet." This from ill-natured Mary Pickford.

"Careful, Mary – that's ma fella you're talking aboot." Desdemona Drew was offended. In case I was missing some subtlety, I didn't point out that Desdemona's 'fella' was actually called Othello, not Hamlet.

I soon learned to take my part in these conversations, although in the early days I sometimes made a *faux pas*. As when, on being presented to someone apparently called Ginger Rogers, I said, "How do you do, Ginger. How's Fred?"

"Fred who?" Ginger seemed baffled.

"Fred Astaire, ye daft cow!" said Sarah, indignant. "Ah'm starting tae wonder if you're the *real* Ginger Rogers or not. Keep up wi yer legend, *please*!"

As she was my great favourite, I was curious to know why there was apparently no Mae West in our little entourage. I asked Elizabeth.

She drew in her breath sharply. "Oh, no, hen – that's an unlucky name. I've known two Mae Wests in my time, and they both ended badly. The first one burned to death; set fire to her bed with a cigarette, drunk. The other one had a fight with her man in Union Street and fell under a bus. Tragic." She brightened. "Anyway, one Mae in this house is quite enough."

Sarah added. "She means Mae Hockshaw."

"Yes, that's right. Of course, Mae Hockshaw doesn't really count – she's only a *woman*, not a *real* actress. Oh, sorry, Eva dear, no offence."

"None taken," I smiled.

But the unknown Mae Hockshaw would come to count for a great deal in the future.

* * * * *

After I had spent some time at The Palace, a subtle distinction in our male visitors became evident to me. As well as the 'ladies' who formed by far the larger part of Elizabeth's social circle, there would usually be a couple of 'gentlemen'. Never more than two or three, as a general rule, but these were distinguishable by the fact that their names were simple, ordinary ones, their behaviour and language was masculine, sometimes boyish, and they very obviously eschewed the feminine trappings and mannerisms of the others.

Sarah explained to me that these were the 'husbands' or boy-friends of one or the other of the 'ladies', and made it clear that there was a sharp distinction to be observed between the two.

"As far as the girls are concerned, never the twain shall meet, Eva dear. Not in *that* way, at least. Intimately, that is, if ye follow me. Well, thon's the theory anyway. Ye're either an 'actress' or a 'man', and one of each goes thegither. That's the rule."

I was curious. "And it's never broken? I mean, you wouldn't find Mary Pickford, for example, holding hands with, say, Hieland Kitty?"

Sarah grimaced and shook her head. "No, indeed, Eva. That wid be what's known as 'tootsie trade'. It's heavily frowned upon, that."

"I see..."

She looked at me with a twinkle in her eye. "No' that it disnae happen now and again, in spite of that. There *is* a certain amount of boundary crossing goes on from time tae time. But it's generally disapproved of, and anyone who indulges tends to keep it tae themselves."

"Yes. I suppose it makes sense, in a way." I could see that the 'couples', in spite of their otherwise liberal attitudes, tended to follow the rules of the rest of the world when uniting – one masculine, one feminine.

Sarah appreciated my interest, and had more to impart.

"And of course, between you and me, Eva, it's not unknown for someone tae move from one side tae the other. Some of the younger wans tend to start oot as ladies and wind up as gentlemen, if ye follow me."

I was momentarily confused. "How do you mean, Sarah?" I asked.

"Well," said Sarah, "Have a look over there." She pointed to the sofa where Mary Pickford sat, deep in conversation with an attractive dark-haired young man who was unknown to me.

"That's Mary's husband, Jack Swanson, nice lad. It's a recent union, and not destined tae last long, if Ah'm any judge. Nobody can put up wi' Mary for long, she's a twisted, bad-tempered cow at the best of times."

Certainly the young couple looked happy and contented together, but it was true that Miss Pickford had a somewhat abrasive personality.

"Sorry, Sarah," I said. "I'm afraid I still don't quite understand."

"Well dear, keep it tae yerself, but what Mary disnae know is that her man, Mr Jack Swanson, wis *Gloria* Swanson up tae a year or two ago. Mebbe somebody should tell her, eh?"

Sarah winked wickedly, nudged me, and with a witchlike cackle, hurried back to the kitchen.

* * * * *

There was such a lot to take in.

The company was not always exclusively male. A few guests of my own gender would put in an appearance from time to time. One or two ladies of a decidedly masculine aspect – Mona McCafferty would have fitted in well, I thought – and sometimes a group of what Elizabeth referred to as 'working girls'. I understood what this meant, and indeed recognised one or two faces from my evenings at the Coffee Stall.

The Palace was of course a business establishment, offering bed and breakfast accommodation, mainly to people who were currently appearing at one of Glasgow's many theatres. It soon became my job to act as unofficial housekeeper, for which I was paid a small wage. Since I had no expenses, my board and lodging being free, I even began to be able to save a little money. Sarah was the cook – indeed Sarah the Cook was yet another of her names – and I helped Elizabeth with the endless task of cleaning rooms, stripping beds, washing and ironing. It was easy, mindless work, and never dull when shared with Elizabeth. We laughed, it seemed, from morning to night.

It was a lovely life. My friends, I understood, moved in a world that ran parallel to, but occasionally intersected with, the day-to-day life of 'ordinary' people – indeed, it *was* a kind of parallel universe. They looked on themselves, on one level, as a sort of superior race, far outstripping in intelligence and wit the ordinary mortal. I was aware of the kind of discrimination and abuse they might be liable to receive outside of their private sphere, and could sympathise with their view. Certainly, I have never received more disinterested generosity and support from any other group of people.

I found out that most of Elizabeth's friends had employment in one field or another. Generally, though not always, in their 'real' personae. Prickly, acerbic Mary Pickford worked in the kitchens of Glasgow's Central Hotel, washing dishes, or 'pearl diving', as she referred to it. Big Madge had graduated from 'the bins[1]' to 'the cleansing' – the department of the town council charged with maintaining the pristine appearance of Glasgow's streets.

I hoped that one or another of Elizabeth's friends might be able to help me find a position, as I felt I should contribute to the running of the household at The Palace. But the problem there was that most of them were employed in professions that were essentially masculine. Mary Pickford *did* offer me the opportunity to work under her in her dish-washing empire. It didn't appeal at all, but I was willing to try it. However, Elizabeth advised against it strongly.

"Don't even think about it, Eva. Mary's a crabbit[2] cow, as you must have noticed. She would make your life hell. And it's a horrible job – up to your elbows in dirty greasy water all day long. Besides, I need you here – I'm getting too old to run up and down these stairs every five minutes."

I had to smile to myself – I knew that both Elizabeth and Sarah were no more than forty or thereabouts, and perfectly fit, apart from Sarah's missing leg. But I decided to take Elizabeth's advice, and continued with my duties as unofficial housekeeper.

* * * * *

October 1936.

The Palace.

I tried as far as possible to avoid thinking about my past life. But sometimes at night I would lie sleepless, and inevitably I would start to wonder. Was Mother still scheming endlessly to achieve her imponderable goals? Had Dougal managed to liberate himself from his thraldom to her, now that her leverage over him was destroyed? Had Princess Julie di Santofiore continued with her singing, or was she now simply a pampered member of the minor Italian *nobiltá*? Where was Jeannie Dunt? How was my little half-brother prospering – if such he was? Was Mona McCafferty astonishing and fascinating a roomful of music students with her eccentric mannerisms and unusual attire? And my lost Finlay. What was he doing? Was he enjoying the success he deserved in his new position? Did he ever think of me and wonder where I was? I had received no reply to my letter.

And most importantly – was my brother Leicester still alive somewhere under the sun?

These thoughts tormented me frequently. My consolation was that in a year or two I would be able to claim my inheritance, and then return to the life I had left. I was still convinced that I would one day make a mark on the world of

1 The bins – refuse collection

2 Crabbit – bad-tempered, easily offended.

music. I had studied for four years, I had given up much to achieve my qualifications, I had lost all the people dear to me. I was determined that soon or late the world would hear more of Evadne Hinge.

With this in mind, I had kept in touch by letter with Father's solicitors. I explained that I was currently taking a year or two off to travel, and had no permanent address. They could contact me via a *poste restante* in central Glasgow. When I had reached the age of eighteen I would travel to their offices in Edinburgh to claim what was due to me.

* * * * *

As well as spending time in The Palace, I gradually became accustomed to evenings out with my new friends. We spent many a happy time in one or other of the local hostelries, bars where notices advised sternly that 'Unaccompanied Ladies Will Not Be Served'. As I was always accompanied, and indeed was usually the only lady in the group, this did not present a problem. Although never a heavy drinker, I began to appreciate the occasional glass of something a bit stronger than my customary lemonade. I came to enjoy a sherry, or a sophisticated gin and tonic now and then. I stayed away very strictly, however, from one particular beverage. A cold shudder would rack me if I even glimpsed a bottle of 'McWhirter's Black Label'.

As autumn began to bite, Elizabeth announced that it was now the beginning of the social season. She loved entertaining, and though formal *soirées* would not take place until Christmas time, still two months away, she planned to organise a series of Sunday afternoon teas to get everyone in the mood. These were uproarious events, and unsurprisingly, the rule that the beverages consumed should be restricted to tea and coffee was rarely observed.

As one of these Sundays approached, I found Elizabeth in a rather agitated state.

"Oh no," she exclaimed, brandishing an opened letter, "*she*'s coming on Sunday."

"Who?"

"Her. My mother-in-law."

My mouth must have dropped open. "But – you mean – you're married?"

"No, no, hen. I mean Queen Mary herself. The *old* queen."

I had by this time grown fully accustomed to the mixture of fantasy and reality which could inform our conversations from time to time.

"Oh – the Queen Mother, you mean," I said.

Queen Mary, the widow of King George V, and mother of our present king,

Edward VIII, and yes, mother-in-law to the 'real' Duchess of York.

"Yes, dear, the Queen Mother, as you say. A vile creature."

"But why invite her if you don't like her?" I couldn't understand.

"Royal protocol, Eva; I'm sure you appreciate my dilemma. It would be considered an unpardonable breach of social etiquette if I left her off the guest list. *Noblesse oblige*. But I never for a moment thought she would accept. She hates me as much as I hate her."

It was explained that The Queen Mother was the proprietor of a rival bed and breakfast establishment a few streets away. *She* apparently considered The Palace beneath contempt, with its rather garish theatrical clientele, and maintained that her own superior establishment would never open its doors to such riff-raff. I was intrigued by the prospect of meeting this fabled creature, in spite of Elizabeth's qualms.

* * * * *

The famous Queen Mother proved to be a scruffy, sixtyish, cadaverous scarecrow, pores clotted with powder and rouge. Clad in a worn but still serviceable rabbit fur coat topped with a shabby astrakhan hat that had seen better days, she swept into the cosy salon of the Palace trailing a cloud of Californian Poppy, a scent I have always disliked. After exchanging perfunctory kisses with Elizabeth, Sarah and several others, she ensconced herself in the most comfortable of Elizabeth's armchairs and proceeded to survey the room.

"So nice to see you again, Mother," said Elizabeth affably, "It's been far too long."

"Do you think so, Elizabeth? Really? I was surprised to receive your invitation, to be frank. You were always a disappointment to me as a daughter-in-law. Of course, you were never a true royal. Just a Scottish nobody. Aye, ye can take the girl out of the peasantry, but ye can never take the peasantry out of the girl. I myself, of course, am from ancient German nobility, *der hohe Adelsstand* – quite a different matter. Anyway, let's say no more about it. And yes, I will have a wee whisky, since you're offering."

This was no more than the general badinage which was the common currency in these circles; perhaps a little more acid than most.

Elizabeth continued the slightly uncomfortable fencing match.

"Well of course, Mother, I understand that you live a lot in the past these days, since the old king died, and you were turned off the throne…"

"Indeed. How standards have slipped…"

"… But we will naturally make allowances for your advanced age and decrepit condition."

The Queen Mother did not appear to have a ready answer to this, and raising a lorgnette from the musty depths of her handbag, continued her perusal of the room.

"Is that Stella Minge over there? Good God, I thought she was dead. Oh – I think maybe she is. And dear Mary Pickford. Still washing up after your betters, Mary? How nice. And Madam from the Beach – is that walnut juice you use, dear, or is your dark skin a sign of dubious ancestry?" She folded the lorgnette and returned it to her bag. "Ah must say, yer looking well for yer age, dear, whatever that may be; but of course, who can tell the age of a kipper? Well, what a rare treat to see so many stars out while it's still daylight."

Something about her manner seemed familiar. Suddenly the eyes of the malignant puppet met mine.

"And who, Elizabeth, might this young person be? Another of the waifs and strays you so generously welcome to your lovely home, no doubt."

"This is Eva Lestrange, Mary," said Elizabeth. "Eva, this is The Queen Mother."

"How do you do, Your Majesty?" I hoped I was saying the right thing. One could never be entirely sure.

"Quite well, on the whole, dear. Hm – Eva Lestrange? Strange indeed, if you ask me."

"I don't believe anyone did," I ventured, smiling, teeth gritted.

The eyebrows rose. "Tut! – such rudeness! No doubt the low-class company you keep, dear. Indeed, I have to ask myself what *I'm* doing here. Still, I must try to conceal my true feelings, I suppose. I understand the simple pleasure commoners take in the mere presence of royalty."

And with that the disgusting creature demanded another whisky from our hostess.

I struggled to remember who our guest reminded me of.

The afternoon continued uncomfortably. I wondered that the regulars, not usually backward in stating an opinion and always ready with a withering remark, were prepared to tolerate this poisonous person.

I was in the kitchen with Sarah, preparing more sandwiches, and asked her.

"They're aw frightened of her, hen. She kens all their secrets and disnae care *whit* she says."

Of course – Mother!

"She's got a vicious tongue. But she'll no stay long, don't worry, she never does."

Indeed, when Sarah and I returned to the salon, the royal dowager was just tying the belt of her fur coat.

"So lovely, Elizabeth, if not quite what I'm accustomed to. Second-rate whisky and a shame about the sandwiches. I do hope you didn't splurge *all* your pension on this wee purvey?" She turned in our direction. "Sarah dear, it's been so nice hearing you tapping around on that gammy leg, quite took me back. No sign of death-watch beetle yet? No? So pleased, you had enough trouble with the woodworm."

She perched the worn astrakhan on her head and secured it firmly with a large hatpin.

"Goodbye, ladies, and Miss Strange. It's been a joy."

Just as she prepared to sweep out of the room, the door was thrown open with a crash and a tall, buxom blonde stood framed in the entrance.

This apparition cocked her head back and narrowed her eyes. "Aye, Ah thought it wis your voice, Mary, ya manky old rat bag. Just leaving, ah see? Well, afore ye go ye can get that coat aff yer back – that's mine!"

The Queen Mother paled under the heavy rouge, and raised her lorgnette.

"And just who is this creature, might I ask? Never seen her before in my life."

The newcomer planted her hands on her hips.

"Is that right? Mae Hockshaw's the name, and don't pretend you've forgotten it. Ah left that coat in ma room at your place when Ah wis lodging there. And came hame tae find ye'd changed the locks!"

Maria Regina adopted an unconvincing nonchalance and lowered the lorgnette.

"Oh yes. It comes back to me. You left owing me two weeks rent. This coat went a *little* way to making up for that."

Mae's voice rose.

"Get that coat off right now, ya dirty auld cow. If ye don't, Ah'm coming over there to take it."

Every eye was glued to the unfolding scene, every ear cocked.

"You wouldn't dare, you dirty low gutter," hissed the matriarch. "Remember, I am God's elect. I am royalty."

"Is that right?" Mae nodded her head with determination. "Well, hang onto yer crown, Queenie, 'cos here Ah come."

And incandescent with rage, she tore across the room and grabbed the padded shoulders of the disputed coat. After a brief tug-of war, with the Queen Mother rocketing back and forth like a badly planted maypole, there was a sudden ripping sound, and Mae triumphantly clutched the coat, while Her Majesty stood in the calico lining, still firmly belted round her waist.

But Mae was not satisfied. She glanced down at the coat she held.

"See whit ye've done, ya daft auld hoor? This coat's ruined. Well, for that, Ah'll have the hat and all."

She grabbed the seedy astrakhan from the Queen Mother's head, and threw it straight into the blazing fire. Unfortunately, it had been firmly anchored by the hatpin, and most of the dowager's hair came off with it. Just a few stringy locks on the side remained.

Mae threw the coat on a nearby chair. "Right – now Ah'll just see ye out, shall I, Mary? What'll it be? Window or door? Your choice."

There was the briefest of hesitations. Then, "The door," croaked the ex-queen, devastated.

Mae grabbed The Queen Mother by the scruff of the neck, and without hesitation, propelled her bodily out of the room and down the hallway. Then onwards through the open front door, from where the royal lady tumbled down the unforgiving stone steps of The Palace into a gawping Hill Street.

Mae slammed the street door and returned to the salon, where she was rewarded with a round of applause.

"It was nothing, ladies, really. Now gie's a drink." She collapsed into a chair and kicked off her shoes. "Ma feet are loupin'[1] and Ah'm fair parched."

* * * * *

November 1936.

The Palace.

Mae, I soon learned, was a permanent resident at The Palace. I had not met her before because she had been away working. As a theatrical, she was often absent for long periods, appearing in one of the seasonal presentations which the theatres of the time churned out with clockwork regularity. She had just returned from the autumn show at the Tivoli, Aberdeen, and would be in residence for some time, as she was booked to appear in pantomime at the Metropole Theatre in Glasgow for the Christmas season.

"What does she do in the theatre?" I asked Sarah.

"She's a hoofer, dear."

I was puzzled by the expression. "Hoofer? Something to do with horses, I suppose? Some kind of equestrian act?"

"No, no," Sarah smiled. "She's a hoofer – a dancer, that is. She's a Betty Barnard Beauty."

Though at first I found Mae slightly intimidating, having witnessed her

1 Louping – aching, referring usually to the feet.

summary ejection of the spectre at Elizabeth's feast, I soon came to know her better, and discovered that underneath she was a warm, kindly person. As the only two girls in the house at the time, we became firm friends. Tall and well-built, glamorous in a showy, theatrical way, she was only a couple of years older than me. And though her style of dress tended towards the cheap and flashy, she had a surprising talent for teaming unlikely things together, and the result, though often unusual, she carried off with aplomb. She brimmed with self-confidence and spoke her mind on all occasions.

"Ye need tae smarten yerself up, angel," she said to me. "You're a nice-looking lassie, pretty face, trim wee figure; but oh dear, ye don't make the best of yerself. Here – try this oan."

We were in Mae's room, where she was going through her wardrobe in search of something suitable to wear for an outing she planned with her current boyfriend, Danny, who was, she explained, the front-of-house manager of the Queen's Theatre.

I looked doubtfully at the creation she was proffering – a red two-piece ensemble, dress and jacket, trimmed with sequin appliqué on one shoulder and one hip.

"Fits you a treat," said Mae, as I clambered into it. She stepped back and narrowed her eyes. "Christ, ye've mair bust than me, Eva, under thon sloppy jumpers! Now, with just a tuck here and there" – she pulled the waistline of the jacket in from behind – "it'll be perfect. And with this wee hat…"

I looked in the mirror. Indeed the outfit did fit well, as Mae had said.

"Now" – as she pulled my long hair up – "that's better. You'll have tae get that hair cut, angel. The Virgin Mary look is definitely not in this season." She secured my hair with a couple of pins. "That's it. Look at yerself. Quite the fashion plate, no?"

I was forced to admit that I did indeed look like a young lady of some style, instead of a schoolgirl.

"Have it, angel, the outfit. It's got too tight on me."

"Oh no, Mae, really…"

"It's yours."

She looked me up and down critically. She walked round me, humming to herself. She took a step back, her hand to her mouth, deep in thought. After a moment she said, "Tell me, Eva – have ye ever thought of going into the theatre?"

I looked up as I undid the jacket. "No, I can't honestly say I have, Mae. Why? "

Her look was abstracted. "Just thinking. We're short of a girl right now, for the pantomime – in the dance troupe, I mean. You're tall, and Betty likes tall girls – it makes her look dainty. What d'ye think?"

Unzipping the skirt, I smiled at this outlandish suggestion. "Mae, I can't dance."

Mae laughed heartily. "Any fool can dance a bit. Whit makes ye think the other lassies in the troupe can dae any better? Sure, they can chassis around a bit, and dae a time-step. Dead simple. Nothing Ah couldn't teach ye. Ah'm *good*, Ah am. Ballet, tap, the lot." She took the jacket and skirt from me and hung them on a hanger. "Thanks, angel."

After a moment she returned to her idea. "And with Betty's girls, it's not how ye dance – it's how ye look. In fact, Betty prefers girls who're good enough, but not *too* good. In her eyes, *she* is the dancer – we're just the support."

She hung the ensemble on a rail. "Now, don't forget to take this with you, Eva, will you?" She turned back to me. "Aye – let me think a minute. If ye could manage…"

The idea still seemed ridiculous to me. But two minutes later Mae had me out of my slippers and into a spare pair of her tap shoes, and began humming, of all things, *Me and My Shadow.*

"Right, angel, here's how it goes… Shuffle hop, step, tap, ball-change, shuffle hop, step, tap, ball-change …"

* * * * *

One week later, clad in one of Mae's less extreme outfits, hair cut fashionably short and permanently waved at her insistence, I attended my audition with Betty Barnard, *prima ballerina* of the Betty Barnard Beauties.

I met Miss Barnard for the first time in a seedy rehearsal hall in Renfield Street. Of medium height, probably nearer forty than thirty, with a face that, in Mae's words, 'you couldn't mark with a bottle', and hair drawn back in a severe 'ballerina' bun, she looked me up and down.

"You're awfy young, darling. How old did ye say ye were again?"

"I'm nineteen, Miss Barnard." I was sixteen.

"Okay-dokay, darling. Nice face, nice wee figure. Let's see yer legs."

I raised my skirt to just above my knees.

"Yes, no' bad. Nae obvious deformities. Okay-dokay. Now, let's see ye dance."

Mae had rehearsed with me a simple tap routine to be performed *à deux*. I had not found it difficult to learn, and Mae said I had a natural aptitude and good rhythm. It would have been surprising if I had not had the latter, after all my years of musical study. But of course, Mae was unaware of that part of my life.

In truth, the dance routine I had learned was so simple practically anyone who was able to walk unassisted could have mastered it.

The rehearsal pianist struck up, and Mae and I hit the floor.

When my performance was over Betty called me into her 'office'.

"No' bad darling, no' bad. Okay-dokay, we'll give ye a trial in the panto. Now – what's yer name again?"

"It's – Eva Lestrange, Miss Barnard."

She looked up from her desk and raised her eyebrows. "Eva *Lestrange*? Och, that'll never do. We've got enough strange folk in this business already, some of them stranger than fiction. No, we'll have to come up with something else for you… Any ideas?"

"Well…" I racked my brains. I wanted something that would allow me to be unidentifiable, but I shrank from cutting off all connection with the *real* 'me'. "What about *Marina Montpellier*?" I'd always admired lovely Princess Marina of Kent. "Montpellier was my old granny's maiden name," I lied shamelessly.

"Hm – Marina Montpellier? Yes, ah quite like that. Okay-dokay darling, Marina Montpellier it is."

She became all business.

"Now – rehearsals start in three weeks. Ye supply aw yer own shoes, tap, ballet and Highland. Costumes are provided by the company. The money's two pounds two shillings a week playing, and one pound ten a week rehearsal. If ye have lines in the show it's an extra five bob a week. Three shows a day and ye get Sundays and New Year's Day off. Okay-dokay, darling? Now Ah've got plenty to dae, so off ye go and Ah'll see ye at rehearsals."

* * * * *

After we left the studio, I told Mae about my change of name.

"Marina Montpellier, eh? Like it, hen, it's got a bit of class aboot it. A stage name, a professional name. Wish Ah'd thought of that – *Mae Hockshaw* is terrible, but Ah suppose Ah'm stuck wi' it. OK – from now on, yer *Eva* at home, and *Marina* when we're at the theatre. Or Ah might just call ye *Rina*, if that's OK? Mair friendly, like."

I had no objection. 'Rina' was even further from my real name than was 'Marina'. And further from 'Maureen', too, which resemblance had worried me slightly.

Later, Mae filled me in on some of the background of the Betty Barnard Beauties.

Betty herself had apparently been a ballet dancer of some distinction in her youth. She had appeared as a soloist with the Rambert Dancers, later the Ballet Rambert. Unfortunately a disputative personality and a fondness for the bottle had been her undoing. It seemed that she had made herself thoroughly unpopular with her fellow performers, and had offended many people in the company. One night, someone unknown substituted a real, sharpened sword for the blunt foil usually used for a performance of the famous 'Mad Scene' in *Giselle*. A severed tendon and several months' recuperation had been the result.

Betty was unable to regain full use of her ankle subsequently, and her career languished. Until she had the idea of forming a small dance troupe, made up exclusively of girls, and featuring herself as soloist, which would form the *corps de ballet* in the endless Variety shows of the day. With her partner, Boris Asafiev she set to work, and the troupe became a popular feature in many productions.

All this was long ago, however. By the time I became a Beauty, the glory days had gone. The Betty Barnard Beauties were distinctly number two, and tended to be booked for the lower class theatres and remote outposts.

This suited me very well. I was far less likely to be recognised by any of my former acquaintances if I was playing in music-hall and variety theatres. My circle tended to patronise the more élite theatrical productions, and were unlikely to attend the sort of shows I would be appearing in.

* * * * *

My friends at The Palace were thrilled with my success. Elizabeth was especially pleased for me. Of them all, she was the only one who had any inkling of my past.

"I suppose I'll have to deal with the bed changing and all that on my own from now on," she smiled ruefully. "Sarah can't handle the stairs with her leg."

I felt a twinge of guilt. "I'm sorry, Elizabeth, but – yes, you will. Will you manage all right?"

"Of course I will, dear, I was only kidding. Anyway, Keith will be helping me now."

I was pleased that Elizabeth had recently become romantically involved with a younger gentleman, who was now a permanent fixture in The Palace.

She gazed pensively heavenward, hands clasped together. "Yes, I can see it. Keith and me. We'll be a sort of husband and wife team. Like John and Ethel Barrymore."

I smiled. "Elizabeth, the Barrymores are brother and sister."

She frowned. "Really? Oh yes, of course they are. Well, that's even better – a wee touch of incest, how chic! It'll work out very well. You get off and make a name for yourself. It's time you had a bit of fun with people your own age.

Of course, you'll be keeping on your room here, I hope?"

"Of course I will, Elizabeth. I couldn't imagine living anywhere else."

She reached into the pocket of her kimono. "And take this. Me and the other lassies have clubbed together for a wee present for you."

She handed me three pound notes.

"You'll be needing some money to buy your shoes and such like, no doubt, and we thought this would help."

"Oh Elizabeth..." I burst into tears and threw my arms round her. The kindest person I have ever known.

* * * * *

The thunderbolt of the abdication crisis[1] had very little direct impact on us thespians, although it rocked the nation as a whole. Mae and I took great pleasure in concocting a fake telegram and having it delivered to The Palace, congratulating our dear Elizabeth on the dizzy heights to which she had now risen.

"Thank you, girls," Elizabeth beamed. "How thoughtful of you both. Of course, I've always been a queen, but now We are a Queen! We must have a party. Isn't it wonderful? And the best part is, We hear that the Queen Mother has had to take to her bed in an access of mortification, and has cancelled all her social engagements for the foreseeable future. So she won't be able to come – isn't that splendid?"

"So what do we call you now?" I asked her later. "The Queen? Queen Elizabeth?"

"No, no, nothing of the sort, Eva. I've been the Duchess of York for years, and that is what I will stay. It's a kind of unwritten rule in our society that you stick with your original name, no matter what changes occur outside. And I've already broken it once – I couldn't resist moving up from Elizabeth Bowes-Lyon to The Duchess of York. But I fear if I were to lay claim to further advancement, I might be considered to have overreached myself, and be seen as a snobbish social-climber. No – it's The Duchess of York for good and all. And of course, still 'Elizabeth' to you and all my other dear friends."

---

1 Edward VIII abdicated on December 11th 1936 in favour of his younger brother, the Duke of York.

* * * * *

January 1937.

The Metropole Theatre, Glasgow.

The name of the pantomime in which I made my theatrical debut was *Goody Two-Shoes*. Not a subject that one sees nowadays, but a popular one at that time. It tells the story of a poor girl, an orphan with only one shoe. Eventually, through her apparently inexhaustible goodness, she receives every imaginable benefit and a happy ending. And a second shoe.

Of course, as is usual in pantomime, the bare bones of the plot were just a peg on which to hang what was, essentially, yet another variety show. Jugglers, acrobats, comedians, singers and dancers all featured, and the simple story rather disappeared under the weight of the 'turns'.

We started rehearsals at the beginning of December, and the show would open on Boxing Day, as was traditional at that time, and run for ten weeks. I was nervous, as this was a completely unknown field to me, and I was on tenterhooks in case I would be simply unable to do what was expected of me. Mae however was reassuring.

"Never worry, angel – I've explained tae Betty that this is yer first professional engagement, and she'll gie me the steps of the routines, and Ah'll teach them tae ye oan the quiet."

There were eight of us girls in the dance troupe, and what a mixed bunch we were. Helen Talman and Irene Loudfoot (an unfortunate name for a dancer, I thought) were, like me, new to the Beauties. They were friends from ballet school, and were rather grand. Sandra Slack and Phyllis Small were bosom buddies, regular members of the team, and old acquaintances of Mae. As were the other two girls, Deirdre Campbell and Mairi McGibbon.

How we worked! True to her word, Mae ensured that I didn't get left behind at rehearsals, and indeed, I soon became accustomed to interpreting Betty's shouted instructions, as she improvised yet another terpsichorean gem from her apparently inexhaustible repertoire of steps.

"*Pas de basque, pas de basque, entrechat*, ladies – two, three four – *arabesque penchée*, – five six seven eight – *penchée* please, Deirdre, are you deaf? – now *pas de chat* twice and forward into yer pose, Marina and Phyllis on the ground, Mairi and Helen *en attitude derrière* – no, no, no, Irene, yer too far forward..."

And so on.

The whole production was of a very high standard. A cast of forty-five and an orchestra of eighteen made up the company. Costumes were beautiful, and the scenery and special effects amazing. In all, a high-class presentation.

The Metropole Theatre had been originally the Scotia Variety Theatre, and was a huge house seating over three thousand. Although cinema was generally decimating theatre audience numbers, the majority of our performances were sold out. Pantomime then, as it continues to be, was a big draw, perhaps because it was suitable for children as well as adults. The humour was rowdy but never coarse. I would notice a marked change of style when I went into my first Variety season later in the year.

We dancers were heavily used in the pantomime. If it wasn't a Highland Fling – no problems there for me with my Scottish Country Dancing lessons – it was the ballet sequence *The Mists of the Glen*, with Betty B. as the Spirit of the Glen. I generally tried to stay at the back during anything requiring balletic skill, as Mae had taught me only the rudiments. She herself was something of an expert in this area, and had the knack for turning a set of sixteen *fouettés en tournant.*[1] This feat would often elicit spontaneous applause from the audience, but after the first few performances Betty had Mae's little solo cut. Apparently it held up the flow of the scene. Or so she said, anyway. "Cow," was Mae's reaction.

Then it would be the Can-Can sequence, over which it is perhaps best to draw a veil. I had hoped I might be asked to deliver some lines as a character in the pantomime, but apart from the occasional 'Hooch!' as we struggled through the Highland Fling, I was mute in my first theatrical season.

* * * * *

I soon settled into my new life. Because I was always on time, and never complained, Betty Barnard seemed to take a liking to me. She assured me that she would be happy to use me again if I was interested. I had found the pantomime fun, if very hard work, and happily signed a contract for a spring show in the Queen's Theatre, at Glasgow Cross, which would open only two weeks after the pantomime closed. There was just one stipulation. I would have to become a blonde, as we were to be billed as The Betty Barnard Blondes. Hopefully we would still be Beauties.

I had no rooted objection to this suggestion. Indeed, I felt it could only aid my incognito – I was firmly determined that no-one from my previous life should be able to find or recognise me until I decided the time was right. So with Mae's help I was transformed into a blonde one wet afternoon at The Palace. Everyone seemed to agree that the transformation was a success. I was not so sure. There was no question – I *was* a kind of pale strawberry blonde. But the harsh chemicals had not been kind to my hair, and it felt dry and coarse. Luckily

1 A series of rapid turns on one foot, the extended working leg whipping round between each. From the French 'fouetter' – to whip

Mae was able to recommend appropriate remedies for this – she herself had been bleaching her hair for years – and gradually my hair began to resume something of its accustomed shine.

On a Saturday in March we packed up our suitcases and left the Metropole Theatre. On Monday we would start rehearsals for the spring show at the Queen's. I was excited, and looking forward to my appearance in *The Skirl o' the Pipes*.

Chapter Nine

The Men in My Life

March 1937.

The Queen's Theatre, Glasgow.

As Mae West has it, *'It's not the men in my life that counts – it's the life in my men'*. More of that later.

The Skirl o' the Pipes proved to be a very different matter from the pantomime. These variety shows were the bread-and-butter end of the theatrical market. Here, the overwhelming popularity of the cinema had eroded attendances mightily, and as a result, wages were lower and standards considerably less elevated. The cast consisted of no more than twenty souls, including us six dancers, and the band in the pit was reduced to seven or eight musicians. There would be a lead comedian and his 'feed'[1], and a second comedian who was known as the 'front-cloth comedian', as most of his routines were performed in front of a drop curtain near the front of the stage area, to allow the following scene to be set up behind. There was always a vocal duet, tenor and soprano, and one or two 'specialities', acrobats or animal acts, usually. The show would consist of musical scenes interspersed with comedy sketches and the 'spesh' acts. The first half always started and ended with the entire company onstage for an ensemble number, and the Grand Finale would feature some sort of surprise item or scenic effect, frequently something known as Currie's Dancing Waters. This consisted of a trough at the back of the stage which produced jets and cascades of water cunningly illuminated to represent maybe *The Falls of Ben Lomond*. This very popular attraction could prove something of a hazard, and more than once we girls threw ourselves into our Highland Fling while almost ankle deep in water. How we were never electrocuted, considering the rather primitive lighting systems of the day, is a mystery. If such a scenic spectacular were not featured, then the finale always introduced a novelty of some sort, perhaps the Braemar Lady Pipers, four or six sturdy kilted lasses with out-puffed cheeks leading the company in *Scotland the Brave* or another patriotic number.

As the cast was comparatively small, it was often the case that extra personnel were required from time to time to play scenes with the comics, in small roles with just perhaps a line or two. Betty Barnard, great *artiste* that she was, disdained to be a 'talking woman', so it generally fell to us dancers to

1 Feed – the 'straight man' who leads the comic into his gags

undertake these parts. I was particularly favoured if the part in question was the *grande dame*, a regular feature, and a type that people thought I played well, due to my 'posh' accent, and the fact that I could manage words of more than two syllables without apparent difficulty. For the more common characters, either Mae or Phyllis was co-opted. Sandra had a pronounced lisp, Deirdre couldn't read and Mairi suffered from crippling stage fright if she was asked to do anything other than shake her legs about. These extra duties meant a little bonus in my weekly wage, which was welcome, and also alleviated the boredom of the endless dance routines.

Helen and Irene, the two ballet girls, had left us – they felt that, while pantomime might be just about acceptable to trained but unemployed ballet dancers, common variety shows were simply one rung too far down the theatrical ladder, even for the relatively talent-free, like themselves.

I had no such qualms. This was a means to an end as far as I was concerned. In a short while I would be able to take up the threads of my life where I had left them, and in the infinitely superior position of a woman of means. Then, and not before I would re-emerge from my self-imposed exile and get on with my life in the way both Father and I would have wished. In the interim, I might as well enjoy myself as much as possible. This was a side of life I would be unlikely to see again, and it seemed important to me to relish every experience while the opportunity was available.

* * * * *

April 1937.

The Palace.

I was on my way to the theatre one evening when I happened to see a poster advertising a Sunday concert by none other than the London Philharmonic Orchestra, due to take place at the St. Andrew's Halls in a few weeks. Under their conductor, Sir Thomas Beecham, the orchestra were to give a selection of popular classics – Dvorak's New World symphony and the Mendelssohn Violin Concerto among them, with the talented young soloist Ruby Hall in the latter.

Ruby! How well I remembered her, my roly-poly fellow student from university. And of course, Finlay would be playing in the horn section of the orchestra. I was tempted to attend. Of course, there were bound to be people I knew in the audience, people from my past, people well-known in the Scottish musical world. But – surely there was little likelihood of me being recognised? I was now an adult, and my new appearance could hardly have been more different from that of the Evadne Hinge they remembered. I resolved to take the chance.

It was unlikely that any of my fellow dancers would have any interest in attending such an event. But when I mentioned the concert to The Divine Sarah, I learned to my surprise that she was a rabid 'classical' fan, and, indeed, had played the clarinet in a military band during her stint in the Armed Forces.

"Dvorak? Mendelssohn? – right up ma street, hen. Get a couple of tickets – good seats mind – and Ah'll come with you."

And that's what we did.

The St Andrew's Halls. Scene of my debut nearly five years ago. With what emotion I entered the lovely old building, and under what different circumstances.

The concert itself was a wonderful experience. I had not realised how starved of culture I was. Ruby looked well, if a little pale, and gave a scintillating performance of the concerto. Even so, I couldn't help noticing that she had not managed to shed any weight, always her ambition. If anything, she was even bigger than I remembered her. However, though she would never be a beauty – and certainly not a Beauty – or, frankly, even moderately attractive, she *had* slightly improved her grooming. But I had learned a lot about fashion and style in the last few months, and felt strongly that the high-necked shapeless gown she had chosen for her performance, in a bilious pea-green raw silk, did little to enhance her appearance.

On the other hand, handsome Finlay, in the depths of the orchestra, hadn't changed at all. And although I saw a few familiar faces in the crowd, no-one appeared to recognise the smartly dressed blonde on the arm of the military looking gentleman with the pronounced limp.

After the concert I was unable to resist. I gave Sarah some excuse and made my way round to the artists' exit. Concealing myself in a shop doorway opposite, I waited for just another glimpse of Finlay. I had no intention of approaching him. I just wanted to see him from a closer vantage. How foolish this decision was to prove.

The orchestra musicians poured out, followed by their renowned conductor. Sir Thomas stopped to sign a few autographs for an enthusiastic group of fans, and then made his way to the Rolls-Royce which was waiting to take him to his hotel. Finally, Finlay appeared. With him was Ruby, plump and matronly in tweed, and she was immediately surrounded by a small crowd of eager well-wishers, anxious to congratulate her on her performance. I waited, torn between the desire to make myself known to my old friends, and the necessity of remaining anonymous. How wise I had been to stay in the shadows became clear to me as I watched Finlay and Ruby kiss, and leave together arm in arm, laughing and joking affectionately between themselves.

The miserable end to a miserable evening occurred shortly thereafter. I didn't feel like facing my friends at The Palace, and decided to take a short stroll to gather my thoughts. It was a mild spring night, and the trees were just beginning to blossom. I let my feet carry me where they would. A few moments after I had stopped to admire some of the lovely Georgian architecture in Blythswood Square a car pulled up at the kerb next to me.

"Business, hen?"

I was not sure I had understood. I made my way towards the car.

"Can I help you, sir?" I said.

"Just wondering if you were looking for business, hen," the respectable-looking elderly gentleman asked me, with a conspiratorial wink.

I shook my head with a rueful smile. "It's very kind, but I already have a job."

He laughed. "Really? And what might that be, hen?"

"I'm in show business," I replied.

"Well, I've no doubt you could show me the business, if you chose to," he continued with a lascivious little smile. "What do you say? Hop in, the heater's on."

Just at that moment, I heard a voice behind me.

"Drive on sir, if you don't mind. Come on, blondie, move along; we don't want your sort hanging around here."

And the uniformed constable continued on his beat.

* * * * *

I had to accept the fact that, by cutting myself off as I had from my former existence, the inevitable price was that life went on for others as it did for me. I had no right to complain or expect people to put their lives on hold just because I chose to follow a different path. I was less important to the rest of the world than I had perhaps imagined I was. This was a salutary lesson. I was at first surprised and, yes, hurt, that Finlay seemed to have been able to replace me so quickly. But why shouldn't he? – it had been *my* decision to end our relationship. He had simply done as most people would. A little regret, surely, a little grieving, possibly, and then… life goes on. It was more than a trifle disconcerting to finally admit that, yes, somewhere in the back of my mind I had nurtured the thought that, if all else failed, if life became simply unendurable, he would be there, ready to welcome me back.

I wondered if my letter had reached him? – I had never received any reply. But that could easily have been because mine didn't find its destination. Or because he decided that he no longer wanted to remain in contact with me. Or perhaps his reply had gone astray… Foolish and pointless questions.

* * * * *

Elizabeth and I sat over breakfast the following morning in the kitchen of The Palace – Sarah was serving the paying customers in the adjoining dining-room. Mae was nowhere to be seen. I was in a quiet mood – I had indulged in rather too many gin and tonics in Mae's company after the revelations of the previous evening. We had run into each other when I was on my way home, and she had suggested we stop off at Paddy's, a well-known local speak-easy. Paddy was happy to serve drinks all night long if one could pay for them, and had no objections at all to ladies, accompanied or otherwise.

Elizabeth looked up from her crossword and remarked on my uncommunicative mood; but I didn't feel that I wanted to discuss the reasons with her, or indeed with anyone. I simply said I had had too much to drink the previous evening and was feeling a little the worse for wear. Elizabeth was just about to embark on a homily concerning the dangers of over-indulgence when we were interrupted.

Sarah reversed tidily through the swinging door that separated the kitchen from the guests' quarters, a tray in her hands, her face a study.

"Pregnant!" she whispered hoarsely as the door swung closed behind her. "Pregnant – Ah was pretty sure last night, an' now it's confirmed."

Elizabeth was unimpressed. "Pregnant? I hardly think so, Sarah, unless it's an immaculate conception. It's well-known that no man's riddled your grate since 1932."

Sarah placed the tray on the table. "No Liz, no' *me* – *her*! Oh – good morning, Eva."

"Good morning, Sarah," I said, only half listening, as I sipped my hot, sweet tea.

Elizabeth abandoned her boiled eggs and her crossword for a moment.

"*Her*? Her *who*, Sarah, for heaven's sake? *Please* try not to speak in riddles at this hour of the morning. It's more than Our Royal Head can stand!"

Sarah sat down at the table.

"Sorry, Liz. I mean *her* – the violin lassie – from last night – of course, you weren't there, but Eva remembers, don't you, Eva? Awfy guid, she wis, a real virtuoso. And now the poor soul's there wi her heid half-way doon the lavvy, and the wee fella wi' her, holding her forehead. It's her first, he was saying, and she's having a bad time of it."

Suddenly I was all attention.

"They'd asked for breakfast in their room, ye see, and ye know how long it takes me tae get up thae stairs, wi ma leg and aw…"

"Sarah," I interrupted, "You mean Ruby? Ruby Hall?"

She nodded. "Aye Eva, that wis the name right enough. Aye, Ruby Hall." Sarah poured herself a cup of tea. She became reflective. "Funnily enough, Ah was thinkin she was probably a lezzie – she's goat that look, did ye no think, Eva? Ah'd even decided oan a name for her – Henry Hall…"

"Or Albert Hall," suggested the ever-inventive Elizabeth.

"Anyway, whichever Hall it is, Ah wis wrang, it seems. And *that's* a rarity."

Sarah picked up a spoon as Elizabeth digested the news.

"Sarah." I tried to sound casual, even disinterested. "The chap with her – what does he look like?"

"Oh, he's lovely, Eva – young fella, fair hair, nice looking, and *so* concerned aboot her. Only married a few months too, he wis sayin'. Ah've jist phoned them a taxi, they've got a train tae catch, it seems, playing in Manchester or some place the night. The poor lassie's feeling a bit better, apparently."

Sarah added two spoons of sugar, and stirred het tea before continuing.

"But why dae ye ask, Eva – dae ye know them?"

"No, no, not at all, Sarah." I got to my feet. "I just happened to see her last night with a young man after you left, and wondered if it was the same one."

"Oh well, Ah couldnae say as tae that, Eva – but are ye no having a bit of breakfast?"

"No thanks, Sarah, I'm feeling a bit under the weather. Going to have a lie down for an hour or two."

"Best thing, Eva – Ah'll bring ye up some nice hot soup about eleven, OK?"

"Yes, thanks, Sarah."

Before I turned to go, I caught Elizabeth's speculative glance turned in my direction.

* * * * *

With a heavy heart I watched the departure of Ruby and Finlay from behind my bedroom curtain. Yes, I could see she was indeed pregnant. That was the source of her extra weight. And the unbecoming dress she had worn for the concert was, I realised, designed to conceal the fact as far as possible. Apparently Finlay's ambition to single-handedly repopulate the world was meeting with little opposition.

I felt better after a short sleep, and determined to stop torturing myself with 'what ifs' and try to put the whole matter out of my head. In the days that followed, I put all my energy into my performances and endeavoured to forget the scenes I had witnessed. And in truth, with three shows many days, I didn't have a lot of time left for brooding.

* * * * *

We were a happy little company on the whole. Mae was particularly pleased to be at the Queen's Theatre, as her regular boy-friend, Danny, was also employed there. Inevitably there were the occasional bouts of temperament from one or the other of the stars. This was due to the pressure of the job, and it was always a sore point if one of the leads felt that they were not being accorded the level of appreciation from the audience that they considered their due. The comics were the most culpable in this respect. They were very jealous of their material, and were always on the lookout for anyone who was, they felt, treading on their own territory. As support artistes we dancers were not really affected by this, but when one of these blow-ups arrived we relished the occasional row between the principals, and indeed, shameful to say, sometimes encouraged them.

I became particularly friendly with Joe Cameron, our second comic. It was he who had the unenviable job of warming the audience up with his front cloth monologues. Tall and good-looking, with a dapper sense of dress and a warm smile, Joe was a young lad who had only recently joined the theatrical profession. He and I hit it off straight away, and whenever he needed a support to feed him his gags, I was his partner of choice. He invited me out several times, but I declined. A well overdue realisation of my own minimal importance in the larger scheme of things had come over me on seeing Finlay apparently happy with another girl; indeed, married to her. But it was still painful, and said something about myself that I needed to absorb and come to terms with. The last thing I wanted to do was to cloud the issue by becoming involved with someone new.

* * * * *

May 1937.

The Winter Gardens, Rothesay.

I was booked to go into a summer season when the spring show came to an end. We were off to the Winter Gardens in Rothesay for four months, starting near the end of May. This would be my first time away from home – I had come to regard The Palace as my home – and, a new experience, I would be staying in theatrical 'digs'. Mae and I would share a small apartment, and she was very sternly warned by Elizabeth to look after me properly. Indeed, the latter fussed around me like a mother, and, in fact, were it biologically possible, I would have much preferred her in the rôle to the unfortunate example Nature had saddled me with.

We were somewhat disconcerted to discover that not one, but two of our dancers would be leaving us. Pregnancy was obviously in the air. Somehow both Deirdre and Mairi had contrived to be in 'an interesting condition' at the same time – and, Mae claimed, thanks to the attentions of the same gentleman. Or gentlemen. Mae explained that the two girls had been going out regularly with 'The Great Tamblinskys'. The latter were a four-man acrobatic troupe of allegedly Hungarian origin, despite their broad Scots accents.

"But which one?" I asked Mae. "Sandor? Gregor? Matiàs? Or the other one whose name I can never remember?"

"You mean Istvan." She shrugged. "No idea, angel. Any one, or two, or all four, for all I know. These boys share everything."

Whether this was true or not, I couldn't say, but Mae assured me it was the case. So two more blondes were co-opted into our group. The inseparable Sandra Slack and Phyllis Small (Slack and Small, as they were generally known) were still with us, but Mae and I were joined by Shona McCann and Mary Kelly, two pleasant girls whom Mae knew from previous engagements. I was pleased to see that young Joe Cameron, who continued to court me assiduously and unsuccessfully, was also on the bill, and that Vincent Murphy and his partner Lena Lorraine, '*The Sweethearts of Variety*', were our singing duo. I had first worked with them in *Goodie Two-Shoes*, and took a slightly malicious pleasure in the fact that these so-called sweethearts fought like cat and dog throughout the entire run of the show. Poor Vincent suffered mightily at the hands of his temperamental partner, and more than once had to go onstage heavily made up to try to conceal yet another black eye.

Our principal comic was Tony McLean, a new face to me. He was, I discovered, a very funny comedian in the low and vulgar style, and offstage a pleasant and agreeable man. Very popular with our audiences, both he and his feed, or straight man, Don Michaels, treated us girls well, and often used us in their routines when they needed a comedy woman for one character or another.

We had two speciality acts. Bertram and his Budgies I have mentioned, and the other was yet again The Great Tamblinskys, apparently none the worse for their experiments in paternity. And that, with the addition of an attractive young soubrette[1] and singer, Agnes Gibson, made up our company.

Agnes and I became friends, as she was around my age. Short and fair complexioned, she had an impish sense of humour, and constantly kept me in stitches with stories of her past *amours*, of which she seemed to have had a

1 Soubrette – a young female character actress, flirtatious and light-hearted, often too a singer in the light soprano category.

remarkable number, considering her youth. With my single experience of these matters, I could hardly compete.

Mae, however, who had worked with Agnes in the past, warned me to be a little cautious.

"Aye, nice enough lassie, Rina, a good laugh, sure enough, but Ah've heard a few stories. She pits herself aboot, Agnes – man mad, ma mother wid have called her. And of course, you'll say, why shouldn't she? But be careful – she bears watching, Agnes does, that's all Ah'm saying."

We played to mostly full houses throughout June, July and August. It was a glorious summer, and the many holidaymakers who were in Rothesay for their annual break were an appreciative and loyal audience. I continued to resist the invitations of Joe Cameron, against Mae's advice – "Well, Rina, he's no' a bad looking lad, and yer daeing nothing else". There was no denying this. Not only was Joe an attractive-looking man, as I got to know him better, I came to realise that he was a person entirely without malice, and with no trace of the devious and self-serving nature not uncommon in the theatrical profession. Indeed, I had just begun to come round to the idea that it might do no harm to allow him to take me out to the cinema or for a late supper, when the fateful evening of the brown eyes happened.

* * * * *

August 1937.

Rothesay.

They were astonishing. Eyes of a very light brown, hazel, I suppose, with a decided twinkle in them; an agreeable face, not handsome, but with regular features and a high complexion; a build in the Dougal McDougal mould – that is, short and compact with broad shoulders; older than me, probably mid-twenties; sharply dressed in a rather flashy style, but the clothes of good quality. Hair crisp and curling and of a mid-brown. I didn't take all that in till later, however. It was the eyes that did it.

"What's your story, hen?" he wanted to know. So I gave him the current version. I was becoming quite an adept deceiver in this area, and just had to ensure that today's edition didn't clash with whatever I might have told anyone else in the past. Mae was aware that my antecedents were something of a mystery, and always jumped in to support me if I got something wrong. But that was rare. I was skilled at presenting the character I wanted to be seen as, and I was far from the only person in our business to reinvent the past.

"Shove along one, hen," the new arrival asked Sandra. "Ah want tae have a wee chat wi' this lassie."

Sandra obliged, and Mr McCarthy sat himself down next to me.

"So – how long huv ye been a professional dancer, Marina?"

I was in an odd mood. This evening, I thought I might essay a little elaboration, God knows why…

"Oh, not long – just a year or so. Of course I trained with the Vic-Wells Ballet, but suffered an injury dancing in *Swan Lake*, and have had to lower my professional sights somewhat."

What a fluent liar I was becoming, I congratulated myself. Rather too hastily.

"Oh dear. Ye're a bit of a fibber on the quiet, aren't ye, Marina?" he responded with a smile, shaking his head from side to side. "Ah've seen ye dance, remember. Ye get by. Just."

I was momentarily at a loss. But he had more to say.

He laughed. "*Swan Lake*? – mair like *Duck Pond*, if ye ask me. Let me tell ye, Ah'm something of an expert on dancers and the choreographic art. Not that it makes any difference tae me, it's no yer dancin' Ah'm interested in."

I was mortified. Why had I not simply stuck to my usual 'local dancing school' story?

No point in hedging. "OK, guilty as charged, you're right, sorry. I don't respond well to idle curiosity, I'm afraid. Let's just say I prefer not to answer any more of your questions, Mr McCarthy. The fact is, it's none of your business anyway."

"Fair enough, hen. If that's the way you want it. And it's 'Rab'. Or 'Robert' if you prefer."

"Of the two, I prefer 'Robert'. 'Rab' is rather common in my opinion. Not that I imagine I will have much call to use either one."

Why was I being so unpleasant? He was just being friendly. He had caught me out fairly in a blatant lie. And his estimation of my dancing prowess was, if anything, generous.

"Oh, is that right?" He didn't seem discouraged in the least. "Well, Ah hope ye will, masel'. Ah wis wondering what you're doing later? Are ye going tae Mae's place efter?"

"Well, I don't have a lot of choice, since it's also *my* place," I snipped.

He stood up. "Good. Ah'll see ye there then, Marina. Maybe ye'll like me more when ye get to know me better? Who knows?"

And, crinkling into a smile, the brown eyes moved off to chat to someone else.

* * * * *

Later that evening, the standard of performance at the little get-together in our flat far outdid anything to be seen in *Doon the Watter.* Joe Cameron spent the entire evening gazing soulfully into my eyes and holding my hand (which I did nothing to discourage, shame on me), while Mr McCarthy flirted enthusiastically with pretty Agnes. She seemed flattered, if I was any judge, but it was easy to tell where *his* true interest lay. While whispering confidingly in her ear, his gaze sought mine constantly, and often found it. We were aware that we were playing a game and we were both enjoying it. Before he left, he took me aside.

"Breakfast tomorrow morning, Marina? – what d'ye say?"

I assumed a mildly regretful expression. "Sorry, Mr McCarthy. I'm attending to my hair. Which – you will no doubt be aware, expert on all things artistic as you are – is not naturally blond."

"OK. Lunch then? – and Ah've told you, it's Robert."

"Sorry again, Mr McCarthy, but I'm having lunch with Joe, here. He just asked me." I wasn't and he hadn't. "Why don't you ask Agnes instead? It would be a kindness, she doesn't get many invitations."

He hesitated. "OK, I will," he said eventually, frowning slightly and looking a bit nonplussed.

I smiled winningly. "Good. That'll be nice for you both."

He stepped back a little and looked me up and down. Mostly up, as I was a good four inches taller in my heels.

He gave a little theatrical sigh, his head moving from side to side. "Aye, you're something else, Marina, dae ye know that?"

"Oh yes, I know that, Mr McCarthy," I smiled again, and shook his hand. "Good night, it's been a pleasure."

* * * * *

I kept Mr McCarthy dangling for a good two weeks before I eventually accepted one of his invitations.

But before that I received another interesting proposition.

There was no question that young Joe, our second comic, was anxious to take our working relationship into other areas. But, while I liked him enormously, I couldn't see him as other than a friend. I made this clear, and, gentleman that he was, he accepted it. Many might have considered that tall, slim Joe would have made a better match for tall, slim me than would short, sturdy Robert McCarthy.

But, as someone later said, "The heart has its reasons".[1]

Oh, not that my heart was ever seriously engaged with Mr McCarthy. But I found him attractive physically, and almost more importantly, he made me laugh. He had a very typically Glasgow sense of humour, dry and self-deprecating. And I would be less than honest if I didn't admit that it gave me a selfish pleasure to imagine that, since he had been the one who did all the chasing, I would retain control of our relationship.

But to return to Joe. I was sitting in the empty green room one afternoon between shows, entertaining myself by picking out a couple of tunes on my banjo. It was one of the few possessions I had that dated back to my childhood, and I treasured it. Sometimes I would amuse the girls in our dressing room with a few choruses of popular songs of the day, in which they would join lustily. But today I was alone. Just as I came to the end of *My Blue Heaven*, humming along to the melody, I was startled to hear the sound of hands clapping. I turned round, and was slightly embarrassed to see Joe standing in the doorway.

"Hey, Rina, that was great. No idea you played the banjo – and you're really good."

"No, not at all." I was somewhat flustered. "Just a few chords I picked up, I'm no expert." My musical background was my most guarded secret.

He left the doorway and sat down next to me.

"I don't agree. I'm telling you, you're good. I've been meaning to mention something to you for a long time, and this just makes it all the more possible…"

Oh dear – not another invitation. "What's that, Joe?"

But no.

"A double act. You and me. What do you think? I'm sick to death of the comedy business; there's far too many others out there much better than me."

I started to pack away my banjo. "Nonsense, Joe, you're very good." Actually he was so-so.

"Thanks, Rina, that's kind. But I'm nothing special, *I* know that. However" – he paused – "I've been thinking of getting out of the comedy for a while now. How about you and me getting together and working up a wee double act? I play the guitar and the piano, plus I sing a bit."

He warmed to his theme.

"Yes, I can see it… You can play the banjo, you look good. You can dance; join in a song or two with me; maybe a few wee funny lines between us. I've seen you in sketches, you've got real comedy timing. We could be a success, I know it. What do you think?"

"Well, Joe…" The thought of getting out of the repetitive dance numbers and

1 'The Heart has its Reasons' – the title of the autobiography of the Duchess of Windsor.

perhaps earning a little more money was not unappealing. "But would we be able to find any work? There are endless double acts out there. We're no Clark and Murray[1]."

Joe laughed.

"Clark and Murray? Aye, sure, they're good. But I play the piano a darn sight better than Grace Clark, Rina. And I can sing better than Colin Murray."

I didn't think it was appropriate to mention that it was a safe bet that I myself could easily knock the piano playing of both Grace Clark and Joe Cameron into a cocked hat. Anyway, there was no stopping Joe.

"I could get us plenty of work as a double. The powers-that-be at Galt's Agency know me well, and I'm sure they would let us try out a few one nighters to break the act in. And I've got a really funny idea for a ventriloquist routine."

"Is there anything you can't do?" I smiled, as I snapped the catches on my banjo case. "I didn't know you were a ventriloquist, Joe."

"Oh, I'm not. No, my idea is that *you* are the ventriloquist. And I am the dummy!"

Yes, I could picture it. An original notion.

"Well – let me think about it, Joe. The season ends here in a week or two, and the Beauties – I mean, the Blondes – are not booked in again till pantomime. Maybe you're right."

The more I thought about it, the more the idea appealed to me.

"You know, Joe, I can play the piano a little bit, too. Perhaps a little piano duet could be worked in?"

"Wonderful, Rina – between the two of us, we can do a bit of everything. Now, here's how I see it..."

* * * * *

October 1937.

The Palace.

Doon the Watter closed at the end of September, and I found myself 'resting' until pantomime rehearsals were due to start at the beginning of December. So Joe and I had two months to work out our new double act and to try to get some bookings. First we had to come up with a name. The obvious *Cameron and Montpellier* we didn't think had the right ring to it. *Joe and Mo* suggested *The Two Stooges*. *Joe Cameron and Marina*, I felt, made me sound like the glamorous assistant to a stage magician. Eventually Joe came up with *Joe and*

1 Grace Clark and Colin Murray (Mr and Mrs Glasgow) were a fixture of the Scottish theatre scene for fifty years from 1926.

Co., which I agreed was suitably snappy. So, I had yet another identity – I was 'and Co.'

Mr McCarthy had been visiting Rothesay every weekend during the final month of our show, and bit by bit I let down the barriers I had erected since my discovery that I appeared to have been replaced painlessly in Finlay's marital projects. My new friend was likeable, amusing, and, at least in the early stages, undemanding. The only problem I had with him in the beginning was what to call him.

"What am I to call you?" I asked as I sat next to him. He had offered me a lift back to Glasgow in his car.

He took his eyes off the road for a moment. "Well, ye know ma name, don't ye?"

"Yes, but 'Robert' is a name that simply doesn't suit you. At least, in my opinion."

"Ah see," he said, with a little smile. "Never let my old mother hear ye say that, Rina, she'd be black affronted. 'Rab' then – that's what most people call me anyway."

"No, sorry, to my ear, 'Rab' sounds common. I couldn't possibly."

"There's nothing common aboot 'Rab', Rina – what aboot our national bard, Rabbie Burns?"

"Common. Correctly, he's *Robert* Burns." I successfully concealed my surprise that the very non-intellectual Mr McCarthy had even *heard* of Burns. He would surprise me in this way more than once in the future.

"OK, OK," he sighed, as he pulled up at some traffic lights.. "Call me '846793 McCarthy', if ye like. That wis ma army number." An idea seemed to occur to him. "Or maybe just 'McCarthy' will do? That's whit Ah wis in The Bar L."

It was a long time before I learned that 'The Bar L' was common Glasgow cant for its notorious Barlinnie Prison. I imagine Mr McCarthy was counting on my ignorance, or why would he have mentioned it?

Whatever, from that day on, to me, he was simply McCarthy.

* * * * *

When Mae and I returned to The Palace in October, he became a regular visitor. The Divine Sarah and the rest of the 'ladies' were thrilled that I had finally found a boy-friend ('*And such a good-looking one!*' breathed Sarah, dewy-eyed), and it was obvious that McCarthy's looks set more than one maiden heart a-flutter in that company. Only Elizabeth was relatively unimpressed.

"Yes, nice lad, that Rab. Nice looking too, no question. But are you sure he's the kind of fella you should be going around with, Eva? God knows, I'm no snob in spite of my aristocratic lineage. But really dear, he's not your class. You could do better."

I explained that McCarthy and I were not 'serious' and that I simply enjoyed his company.

"Well, as long as that's the case. And as long as he sees it the same way you do, that's fine. Just be careful, that's all I'm saying. Have you never wondered what he does for a living? He's never short of money, I grant you that. But ask yourself where it comes from."

Indeed, I had wondered about that. McCarthy was always vague when I raised the subject. Buying and selling, apparently was the name of the game. He was often away for two or three days at a time, 'doing a bit of business' as he put it. Details were scant, however.

Of course there was one more dissenting voice amid the general chorus of approbation that greeted my new swain. Joe Cameron was definitely not a fan. Naturally, I put that down to his resentment at not being the favoured suitor. Indeed, I finally had to make it clear to him that I considered that he was playing the spurned lover a little too relentlessly.

"You're jealous," I said, baldly.

"Of course I'm jealous, Rina. Naturally. But if I thought he was worthy of you, I would step aside and be glad to see you happy." He frowned. "It's not that. He's a wrong 'un, your McCarthy. I've met his type only too often before. All ghastly charm and flashing dentures on the surface, but underneath…" He didn't continue.

Poor Joe, I thought. I hoped that his attitude wouldn't cause problems when it came time to work out our plans for the projected double act.

I had other things on the go at this time. I never forgot Mother's list of Father's alleged frailties, and was determined to get to the bottom of the mystery eventually. The drugs and plagiarism nonsense had been proved to my satisfaction to be totally without foundation. There remained the Case of Jeannie Dunt. Somehow I would track her down and get the truth out of her one way or another. But even more troubling was the mysterious Mary McGuire. What had Mother said?

"*Don't imagine that the money he left to you was come by honestly. It should have gone to his cousin Mary. But your dear Father contrived to have the poor woman put away for a crime she didn't commit.*"

* * * * *

I had recently received a communication from Father's solicitors, Bartington and Hunt, to inform me that old Mr James Bartington, whom I remembered well from his visits to the Castle in bygone years, had retired, and that his son, Mr Jonathan Bartington, would be looking after my affairs in the future. Also to let me know that the securities in which the firm had invested my inheritance were doing well, and that I could look forward to a moderate increase in the amount when my eighteenth birthday, now less than a year away, rolled around.

After much heart searching, I decided that I would see if it was possible to find out some of the details concerning Father's enigmatic cousin. Solicitors after all were in the legal business, where they not? Mr Jonathan Bartington was personally unknown to me, as was I to him. The firm charged significant fees for administering Father's estate. Why should I not make them work for their money?

With this in mind, I wrote to arrange an appointment with young Mr Bartington under the name of Eva Lestrange, at the company's offices in Prince's Street, Edinburgh. I was reluctant to commit the details of my enquiry in writing, and felt strongly that a face-to-face encounter was likely to prove more productive. I considered that I was by now something of a woman of the world – few young ladies from my background had had the variety of experience that I had. I was certain I could handle young Mr Bartington sympathetically but firmly.

I heard back from the firm a few days later, arranging an appointment for the beginning of November, and began to lay my plans.

* * * * *

McCarthy had practically moved into The Palace. We were by now recognised as a couple, and he spent as many nights in my cosy bedroom as he did in his own. He had a small flat in the Townhead, a raffish and rather rough area in the centre of Glasgow. He was eternally trying to persuade me to move in there with him, but I had no intention of giving up my independence, and I was quite happy in Hill Street with all my friends. I felt secure there with Sarah and Elizabeth, and though McCarthy pressed me to fall in with his ideas, I told him firmly that there was no possibility at present.

How strange our relationship was. I didn't love him, *tout court*. I did feel a tolerant affection for him. I enjoyed his company, both privately and publicly, and took pride in having this boisterous but loveable pet that only I, it seemed, could control. It was a new and heady experience for me to feel that I was finally *in charge* of something or someone. How illusory this novel sensation would prove to be, and how ill-founded was my smug self-satisfaction, would be brought home to me before too much time had passed..

And *he* certainly didn't love *me*, although he occasionally claimed to. I was a complete riddle to him, I think, one he was always trying unsuccessfully to solve. That, I am sure, was the root of his attraction to me. Physically, he knew me as well as it is possible to know anyone. But mentally, I was an eternal challenge that continued to resist his efforts, and this was a source of endless fascination to him. Some instinct – and he was far from stupid – told him that I was not quite what or who I appeared to be, and this riddle nagged at him constantly. He would try from time to time to catch me out in a contradiction, but by now I was completely used to concealing my origins, and had realised that needless elaboration only led me into difficulties. In general we got along well, but now and then I was made aware of his frustration and his bafflement. In nature he was generally mild-mannered and pleasant. Certainly, with me, he was the ever-agreeable gentleman. But I occasionally saw quite another side to him. He could be aggressive and even physically violent if he felt his masculinity was being threatened, or if some other man expressed more than a passing interest in me. It took me some time to become aware of this, and very gradually I came to realise that I was, in a sense, dancing on the edge of a volcano. But, content to imagine that I was in charge of our relationship, I contrived to put these misgivings out of my mind. If I am completely honest, I suppose I even took some sort of bizarre pride in being The Beauty who had tamed The Beast.

McCarthy had no problem with Joe, however. Naturally he saw himself as the victor in that particular contest, and considered that a certain magnanimity should be extended to the vanquished. Joe, however, as I have indicated, while always polite and even friendly on the surface, actually nursed a deep mistrust and even a dislike of my new beau.

* * * * *

November 1937.

Glasgow Green.

An incident illustrating McCarthy's character is probably better than any amount of analysis. One Saturday evening he suggested we pay a visit to the fairground at Glasgow Green. I was delighted to accept – I have always adored fairgrounds – the smells, the noise and bustle, the crowds of people, the shrieks of delight mingled with terror from those rash enough to sample the Waltzer or the Dive Bomber. I loved the rides, and luckily have a very strong stomach, but McCarthy began to look alarmingly queasy after our second circuit of the Big Dipper. Taking pity on him, I suggested that we slow down the pace and visit one or two of the sideshows which ringed the outer edge of the fairground.

After McCarthy had demonstrated his prowess at the shooting range and the coconut shy, we ended up outside an attraction whose banner announced the imminent appearance of *The Charlita Sisters*. A fifty-something hard-faced blond stood on a small platform, microphone in hand, giving the 'spiel'.

"Ladies and gentlemen, don't miss this, the last show of the day, your very last chance to see the performance of the lovely Charlita Sisters..."

The latter were obviously the two youngish women stood to one side of the 'barker' – one blond, short and skinny, the other tall, dark and plump. If they were sisters, it was under the skin. Both were clad in flimsy leotards and a plethora of goose-pimples – the temperature must have been near zero. These two shuffled from foot to foot not quite in time with the tinny music which accompanied the announcement.

"...Yes, The Charlita Sisters will demonstrate for you Grace, Charm and Flexibility. And if you behave, ladies and gentlemen, if you show your appreciation, Rita may even show you her Bare Behind! – Yes, ladies and gentlemen" – I was just about the only person present who could have been described, even loosely, as a lady – "Yes, her Bare Behind. Come along, now, positively the last chance today to see them – don't miss this act – The Charlita Sisters, presenting Grace, Charm and Flexibility."

We couldn't resist.

The 'show' was so dreadful it was almost good. A few inexpert cartwheels and handstands; an illusion – *The Woman Kept Alive for Twenty Years Without a Head*; an ill-executed mind-reading speciality; and the climactic *Bare Behind* moment, the short skinny blonde turning around and holding a stuffed teddy bear across her meagre sequinned buttocks.

I was intrigued to discover that there was a level of show-business even lower than that in which I was currently employed.

Just as we left the tent, a happy drunk gentleman made no bones about pinching my bottom quite frankly and openly, and quipping:

"Aye, there's one behind Ah wouldnae mind baring. How's about it, gorgeous?"

He had hardly got the last word out when a white-lipped McCarthy turned on him, punched him squarely on the jaw, and after the intrepid bottom-pincher collapsed to the ground, gave him two hard kicks in the head.

Turning back to me, as if the incident had never taken place, he took my arm and said, "Well, yon show was a waste of time. So what now Rina? Another go on the Waltzer?"

Chapter Ten
Unexpected Encounters

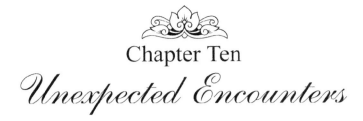

November 1937.

The Palace.

Housekeeping standards at The Palace had, I am sorry to say, slipped somewhat since I was in charge. Although the surface appearance remained acceptable, a closer inspection of the less accessible areas revealed a lamentable lack of application. Keith was now my replacement – Elizabeth had put him in charge after my retirement from the position, and as far as I could judge, their relationship appeared to be progressing well.

Keith was a pleasant, quiet young man in his thirties. He was, surprisingly, of a rather religious disposition. I would have thought that any true believer would have looked on The Palace as about one step behind Gomorrah, and one past Sodom. But he seemed able to reconcile his beliefs with his lifestyle without any apparent difficulty – something I believe many of us manage to do fairly easily. I decided that a humorous approach might be best.

"Keith, dear," I said to him one morning when we passed on the stairs. "I know you are a good Christian. Tell me – do you believe, as the Bible says, that when we're born we come from dust?"

"Certainly I do, Eva."

"And that when we die we go to dust?"

"Yes, of course."

I nodded. "In that case, Keith, do have a look under my bed. I think someone's either coming or going."

I'm pleased to say that my light-hearted approach seemed to do the trick.

* * * * *

Early in November, Joe and I presented *Joe and Co.* to a paying public for the first time. We had tried out our ideas before an appreciative audience at The Palace, but I was aware that this was no reliable criterion. Joe had used his influence with Galt's Agency to get us a series of 'split weeks' at some of the smaller and more remote theatres in order to break the new act in. We played three nights here, three nights there in such unlikely locations as The Empire, Galashiels; His Majesty's, Fortrose; and the Opera House, Lochgelly. Famously difficult to please, the audiences at these smaller venues made no bones about expressing their disgruntlement if they felt the quality of entertainment they were being offered was not up to their expectations. We were understandably nervous as our début approached.

We had worked out two 'spots', that is, two different ten-minute routines, one for the first half of the show and one for the second. Our opening act was basically musical, with Joe on the guitar and myself on the banjo, performing a few popular songs of the day, along with the traditional Scots selections which are as close as it is possible to get to a guaranteed success with Scottish audiences. We had rehearsed a couple of duets such as the much-loved *The Crooked Bawbee* and *The Deil's Awa' wi' the Excise man*[1], but for some reason Joe felt that my vocal efforts were perhaps too subtle and artistic to appeal to the market we were playing to. And so on his advice I left the vocals to him. I've always felt that I had a pleasant and agreeable singing voice, but for some reason few other people seemed to be of the same opinion. Joe himself had a sweet and tuneful baritone, and, importantly, the legs for a kilt, and the audiences seemed to enjoy our performance. I wore a traditional tartan crinoline-style outfit and my elaborate banjo solo, *The Wee Cooper o' Fife*, for which Joe moved to the piano, was very well received. He had devised some light-hearted banter between us, slightly saucy in places, but never crossing the bounds of good taste. In general our reception was all we could have wished for.

For our second appearance we had decided to try out Joe's idea for a ventriloquist act with a difference. For this, I was dressed conservatively in a sober, almost school-ma'am-ish outfit. I played the piano-teacher, Miss Quaver, while Joe was my pupil, Cheerful Charlie Chalk. I was seated on the piano stool, which was draped in black fabric down to the floor. Joe knelt behind this, so that he was seen only from the waist up. Thus the top half of Cheerful Charlie was Joe, while from the waist down, the rest of the 'dummy' was a false piece attached to my costume. We had worked out a bright and jolly cross-talk routine, with myself as the simple 'foil' and Joe, as Cheerful Charlie, ribbing me in a light-hearted way, and flirting shamelessly with the respectable lady on whose knee he appeared to be sitting. I was supposedly young Charlie's professor, giving him guidance on his piano technique. The audiences particularly enjoyed our finale, in which I played on the piano Rimsky-Korsakov's *Flight of the Bumble Bee*, with Joe, still apparently sitting on my lap contributing the occasional chord or counter-melody, and keeping up his bantering remarks. This *tour de force* frequently brought our audience to its feet.

All in all, *Joe and Co.* was a notable success, and Joe felt sure we would be

---

1 Literally, 'The Devil has carried off the customs officer', song based on a poem by Robert Burns, who for a period was himself employed as an 'excise man'.

offered more work in the future, perhaps even in pantomime for the Christmas season. He confessed himself astonished at my proficiency on the keyboard – I had to cover up by speaking vaguely of childhood piano lessons and a retentive memory.

He continued to be uneasy about my on-going relationship with McCarthy, convinced that Rab's regular absences and 'wee bits of business' were a sign of something dishonest, or even criminal. I managed to persuade myself that his attitude had its roots in a jealous resentment. I suppose I was to some extent burying my head in the sand, for, when I look back, there were indications that Joe's surmises were all too accurate. The only excuse I can offer for what I now see as my wilful blindness is that I had other matters on my mind at that time. The first appointment with my solicitor was looming.

* * * * *

November 1937.

Edinburgh.

I presented myself at the premises of Bartington and Hunt in Edinburgh on a Friday afternoon in November, and was shown into the inner sanctum, the office of Mr Jonathan Bartington himself. Joe and I were appearing that week at the Pavilion Theatre in Leith so I didn't have to make a long journey. I had dressed for the occasion in what I considered an appropriately sober style, a navy blue ensemble with touches of white, discreet jewellery (a present from McCarthy) and a smart little hat perched on my rather too blond hair.

Young Mr Bartington proved to be an agreeable gentleman in his thirties, and welcomed me warmly into his office.

"It's a pleasure to meet you, Miss Lestrange. Do take a seat."

I did as he asked, and perched myself demurely on the edge of the chair opposite him.

"I don't believe we have met before?" he asked.

"No, Mr Bartington, we have not. But I find myself in need of some advice of a legal nature."

He smiled. "Call me Jonathan, Miss Lestrange, please."

I hesitated. "Mr Bartington. Jonathan. There is a matter you can help me with, if you will."

"Certainly, Miss Lestrange. Just name it – I will be glad to assist if I can."

"It's a family matter, Jonathan."

Somehow I explained the few details that I knew. That a certain lady to whom I was distantly related had apparently been imprisoned for some unknown crime. When this had taken place, I knew not. The nature of the offence, the victim, the sentence – of all of this I was ignorant. The most I could state with any certainty was that the date was likely to have been in the fifty years between eighteen-seventy and nineteen-twenty. And one more thing. The condemned woman was called Mary McGuire.

Jonathan looked dubious.

"I don't think it's the kind of matter I can help you with. The details are very vague. You have no further information?"

I hesitated once more.

"There is a possibility" – I wondered if I was saying too much? – "that the father of a friend of mine may have been involved in some fashion."

"I see." He paused. "I'm sorry. I doubt if we would be able to achieve anything."

"But there must be records, surely? It can't be impossible to track down the details. All I want is information. And I can pay."

Jonathan continued to look uncertain. I crossed my legs and raised the hem of my skirt an inch or two.

"Please, Mr Bartington. You will never know how important this matter is to me."

I took a tiny lace-edged handkerchief from my handbag and dabbed my dry eyes. He sighed.

"Very well. I can guarantee nothing. But I will see what I can do, Miss Lestrange."

"Oh, Eva, please," I breathed.

"Eva, yes. Well, I make no promises, none whatever. But I may be able to find out a few details. Leave it with me. I will be in touch if I have anything to pass on to you."

"Oh, Jonathan, that is all I ask. Just some information." I added a discreet sob or two.

He turned slightly pink and coughed uncomfortably.

"Please, Eva, don't upset yourself. Let me look into it."

"How can I thank you?" I smoothed my skirt down over my knees.

"No need, really, no need," he smiled. "But if you want to thank me, come out and have some afternoon tea with me. I'm finished here for the day, and would like a bit of company."

* * * * *

Jonathan and I enjoyed a delicious tea at the North British Hotel. He was, I discovered, a charming and interesting man, well-travelled and sophisticated. And, contrary to my initial expectations, he made no attempt at all to flirt with me or suggest we continue our afternoon more privately. Spending an hour with him made a pleasant change from the level of masculine company I had been accustomed to recently. And the afternoon was about to get even better.

"More tea, Miss?" our waitress asked.

"Oh, yes please," I replied, and looked up into the face of Jeannie Dunt. She poured the tea and moved off towards the kitchens.

Unsurprisingly, she hadn't recognised me. I hastily told Jonathan I had to powder my nose and left the table. I waited in the hallway outside the restaurant, hoping Jeannie would appear. But, obviously busy with her duties, she continued to move in and out between the kitchens and the dining room.

I made my way to the main entrance of the hotel, and presented myself at reception.

"Can I help you, madam?" asked the imposing figure behind the desk.

"I hope so. I have an urgent message for a member of your staff. A family matter. I need to speak to Jeannie Dunt. One of the waitresses in the restaurant."

He frowned. "I'm sorry, madam, we're not allowed to pass messages to employees. Not from here. Go to the staff entrance. Outside the main door, turn left, and then left again. They should be able to help you there."

And the rather grand gentleman turned away to attend to another customer.

I followed instructions and eventually found the staff entrance. The doorman there took my message, and two minutes later Jeannie appeared, wiping her hands on her apron.

"You have a message for me, Miss? Not bad news, I hope?"

"No Jeannie. Not bad news." I waited. "Don't you recognise me?"

She peered into my face.

Her jaw dropped. "Miss Eva? But – whit's happened to ye? Ye look – well – different."

I was aware that I did. Blond, permed, made-up, fashionably dressed… But I hadn't realised that my transformation was sufficiently complete to prevent recognition by someone who had known me so well.

"It's a long story, Jeannie." I could hardly control my impatience to question her. Did I have a half-brother or did I not? But I felt that even in this situation the niceties must be observed. "And how is the baby? And your husband?" I couldn't for the moment remember who the man in question was.

She seemed to have recovered from her surprise. "Oh, the baby's very well, Miss. And Johnny too." Of course – Johnny Kerr, our local car mechanic. Nice man. "Wee Hector's nearly three now, walking and chattering away the whole day long. We've a nice hoose doon Leith Walk. Johnny's business is doing great, and Ah love ma job here. They treat ye well, and the tips are good. It was the best thing we ever did, leaving the old place."

Most of this passed me by. Two words rang in my head. *Wee Hector.*

"And how's yourself, Miss?" she went on. "Doing well, I hope? And your Mother?"

"Yes, yes, fine." I could wait no longer. "Jeannie – there's something I need to find out. I wouldn't ask, but it's really important. More than you will ever know."

"Well, of course, Miss. Whit is it?"

I hesitated momentarily. "You won't like it Jeannie. The last time I mentioned it, you wouldn't say. But – please believe me – I don't ask lightly. It's not idle curiosity. And I'm afraid I already know the answer…"

"Yes?"

"Who was the baby's father?" I asked baldly.

Jeannie smiled. I waited on tenterhooks.

"Oh, that, Miss. I don't mind who knows that now. It was Ron McKenzie. Was. And still is."

I thought I had imagined her response.

"Ron McKenzie? Who's he?" The name meant nothing. Then – "Oh – yes… of course…" Ronnie McKenzie. The village Lothario. Husband of Janet McKenzie, our local shop owner and number one gossip. Imagine that! "But – when I asked you last time…"

She raised her eyebrows. "Well, I couldn't say then, could I, Miss? Not in the shop. Not with him and his wife stood three feet away from me."

One thing was puzzling me. "But – Wee Hector?"

Jeannie smiled. "Yes, Miss – after yer Dad. I hope ye dinnae mind?" An idea seemed to occur to her. "Wait – ye don't mean to say ye thought?…" She burst out laughing. Wiping her eyes she went on, "I called him that after yer Dad, sure enough. I always liked the name, and yer Dad was always good to me. But as for anything more…" Once again she laughed in genuine amusement. "Set your mind at rest on that score, Miss, nothing ever passed between me and Hector Hinge that couldn't have been laid before the minister and the entire church congregation."

I threw my arms round Jeannie and kissed her soundly on the cheek.

"Thank you, thank you, Jeannie…"

I left her, after taking note of her address, and returned to the restaurant, where Jonathan must have been wondering what had happened to me. He must have wondered too, at the broad and uncontrollable smile on my face.

I took my seat at our table. Time, I thought, to lay my cards on it.

"Jonathan, you will think I am quite mad..."

He looked at me quizzically. "Oh? And why should I think that, Eva?"

I took a deep breath and plunged in. "I am not Eva Lestrange at all. My name is Eva Hinge. Evadne Hinge."

His jaw dropped, and he stared at me. "No! Really? Your Hector's daughter? But why didn't you say? Why the charade?"

I sighed. "It's hard to explain – there are reasons. But now I have met you, I feel sure I can trust you."

He reached across and patted my hand.

"Of course you can. If you want to keep your identity a mystery, then I'm your man. We solicitors are very good at keeping secrets. It's part of the job."

"Thank you," I said, relieved.

"But can I ask why you thought it necessary? As you know, Bartington and Hunt have handled your family's affairs for a very long time; so I'm glad you got in touch, however unusual the circumstances. It's important, I think, for us to get to know our clients on a personal level as well as a business one."

"Of course, I appreciate that. But as I said, I had my reasons."

He hesitated for a moment. "I'm sure you did." He paused again, and looked at me speculatively. "Your mother has been in contact from time to time. She has been anxious to get in touch with you, it appears. Naturally, following your written instructions, I was unable to provide her with any information."

I nodded. "And that is the way it must stay, Mr Bartington, if we are to continue to do business together," I replied. "The reasons are private and have no bearing on our affairs here. I trust I may rely on your continued discretion?"

"Certainly you may, Eva. And please – call me Jonathan."

Our conversation went along predictable lines. He was anxious to discuss the details of my inheritance, and wondered if I could give him any information as to any plans I might have made. I explained that at present they were fluid and that I would keep him aware of any decisions I reached. He discussed the figures, and explained the investments he had undertaken on my behalf. All this appeared satisfactory.

After we had covered these business matters, we reverted to our previous wide-ranging conversation. He was obviously a man of many interests – for example, he was surprisingly knowledgeable about music, and was, he claimed, an admirer of my father's work.

"Such a loss," he said, "your dad. But gratifying to know that his music has become so popular since he died."

It was true that the resurgence of interest in Father's music had only slightly abated in the last year. One of his operas, *Phaedra,* had recently been staged in Edinburgh, and the Royal Opera House in London would première his *Lysistrata* in September 1938. An event at which I fully intended to be present.

As we rose to leave, he shook my hand.

"One more thing before you go, Eva. That other matter we discussed – Mary McGuire? Your relative, I think you said?"

I looked up as he helped me on with my coat. "My father's cousin, apparently, yes."

"Ah, I see." After a pause, he went on, "Let me pass this matter on to my wife, Marion. She is a barrister, and would be much more likely to be able to unearth the information than would I. May I have your permission to give her the details?"

I hesitated. Then, recognising that the expression on his face was one of concern, not prurient curiosity, I agreed that he might do as he had suggested.

He promised he would be in touch as soon as he had anything to tell me. I left the hotel, and made my way back to the theatre for the evening performance with a spring in my step, and the knowledge that I had found a friend and an ally.

* * * * *

January 1938.

The Gaiety Theatre, Ayr.

Joe had good news for me too. We were booked to appear in pantomime at the Gaiety Theatre in Ayr for the Christmas season. The subject was *Cinderella*, and amazingly, we were to have actual rôles in the production. We would be playing the Broker's Men (or Broker's Man and Woman on this occasion), and not only have speaking parts and comedy scenes, but also our own spot in the second half of the show. We were delighted with this upturn in our fortunes. We would be paid more than we had been earning previously, and if we were successful, we could look forward to an unending stream of work in the future. I resolutely put out of my head the knowledge that in only a few months' time I would have no further use for 'show business', and would be leaving all my new friends behind. For the moment I was enjoying myself, and resolved to continue to 'live for the day' until that time came.

There was only one problem. The Gaiety Theatre was in the holiday town of Ayr, and was only about twenty miles from my former home near Kilmarnock. I had not been in touch at all with Mother or anyone in the village since my departure eighteen months previously, and I was anxious to keep my whereabouts unknown until such time as I was ready to make my move. But I consoled myself with the thought that, even if someone who remembered me from my old life were to attend the pantomime, it was very unlikely that they would associate the glamorous, blonde comedienne, Marina Montpellier, with the mousey, quiet music student, Evadne Hinge.

* * * * *

Although the scale of the production was necessarily smaller than my previous pantomime, nevertheless, an excellent cast had been assembled, and I met up with several colleagues with whom I had appeared on past occasions. My good friend, pretty Agnes Gibson, was the Cinderella; Buttons, the comedy rôle, was played by Tony MacLean; and as luck would have it, the dancing troupe was yet again the Betty Barnard Blondes.

I had been replaced in the dance line-up quite painlessly. As Betty herself put it when I explained my new status, "Okay-dokay darling, best of luck. It's no great loss – yer hardly Pavlova."

This meant that Mae and I would once again be able to share digs for the season – I resisted Joe's suggestion that it would be 'nice' if he and I were to find accommodation together. We might be a double act in public, but not in private.

In private, indeed, McCarthy was still very much in evidence. He continued to disappear from time to time on his 'business' ventures, but our relationship went on smoothly for the most part. He was a naturally generous man, and there was always a small gift for me when he returned from the latest of his trips – perfume, chocolates and even from time to time a small piece of the rather gaudy jewellery he favoured. He never, at least as far as I was aware, showed any interest in other girls. Occasionally I became slightly concerned that one day there might be a reckoning between us, as he certainly did not feature in my future schemes. But I reassured myself that I would simply be able to disappear without trace when the time was right.

* * * * *

He was usually down in Ayr for the weekend, spending a couple of nights in the flat Mae and I were renting for the season. And I was on his arm on the memorable occasion when, on leaving the stage door after our evening performance, I was greeted by a small knot of enthusiastic well-wishers. This in itself was not unusual – the audiences for *Cinderella* were responsive, and largely made up of children, who often wanted to add yet another autograph to their collections. But on this particular evening, I was aghast to recognise among the small crowd my sister Lavinia. She was now fourteen, and had blossomed into a tall, attractive young woman, very much in Mother's mould. We had not seen each other for some years, but the family resemblance was unmistakable. I froze.

"Whit's the matter, Rina, yer as white as a sheet?" said McCarthy.

"No, I'm fine, just a bit tired," I replied, taking an autograph book from the trembling hand of a young lad.

"Ye were really great, Miss," he mumbled enthusiastically through his chewing gum. I signed and handed the book back to him. But he hadn't quite finished. "Ah was wondering, Miss – dae ye wear knickers under yon wee short skirt?" he asked.

"No, of course not," I replied absently, moving on to the next grubby outstretched hand, never thinking that in all probability I had inadvertently provided material for five years of fantasy.

I signed again, unseeing, and finally came face to face with my sister. Just at that moment there was a shout from a large car parked by the kerb.

"Come along, dear, hurry up. And don't get too close to these people, you might catch something." Mother's tones were unmistakable.

I was on the verge of panic. I took the autograph book from Lavinia's hand.

She addressed me politely. "I just wanted to say how much I enjoyed the show, Miss Montpellier. And you were the best thing in it, really lovely, and so talented. I'm hoping to be an actress myself, one day."

She appeared to have no idea who I was.

Nonetheless, I avoided meeting her gaze. "Thank you dear, I appreciate it. I wish you the best of luck."

Then the devil somehow got into my head. "But no doubt your mother will have something to say about that," I smiled as I signed the book – '*To Lavinia, with all best wishes, Marina Montpellier.*'

She smiled. "Oh yes, I'm sure she will. But I can always get round her. My mother's not as smart as she thinks she is."

My forgotten sister, it appeared, was no fool.

"Thank you so much, Miss Montpellier." She shook my hand politely. "I hope we will meet again." And Lavinia took the book and returned to the waiting car.

I smiled to myself. *'Imagine – Lavinia practically grown up'*. I had handled that well, I thought.

But I hadn't. I had signed '*To Lavinia*' without asking her name.

* * * * *

I was struck by the bizarre parallel between my recent encounter and the plot of my current show. Cinderella goes to the ball, disguised in the finery provided by her Fairy Godmother. Her sisters and step-mother are there, but fail to recognise her. Life imitating art, perhaps?

No. The letter arrived two days later at the stage door.

"Dear Sister

Did you really think I hadn't recognised you? I knew who you were as soon as you appeared on the stage. Mother wears glasses at home these days, but refuses to when she's out in public, so sees nothing. She had no idea, of course. Anyway, she wasn't very interested in the show and spent most of the evening in the bar – some things never change, n'est-ce pas? You looked wonderful, I thought – quite a stoater[1]*, as the common people say. And I always thought I was the beauty of the family!*

I know you recognised me too, or how would you have known my name? – not a common one, I'm pleased to say.

If you don't want to reply, I understand. But if you do (and I hope you will) write to me care of Andrew Anderson, 9 Mill Street, Kilmarnock. I have all my correspondence sent there – Mother opens everything that comes to the house, as you can imagine. Don't worry, I haven't said a word to her (and won't). The less she knows the better.

Oh – and who was the handsome gentleman? Your boy-friend I bet!

Your loving sister

Lavinia Hinge."

I went to bed late that evening, and after reading a few chapters of Daphne du Maurier's wonderful new novel, *Rebecca*, fell into a troubled sleep.

I had a vivid dream. In full bridal attire, I stood next to Dougal McDougal at the altar. Mother was behind us pointing a loaded shotgun in my direction. We were, I realised, in the Auchterarla Post Office. Betty Barnard and Mae Hockshaw, dressed as bridesmaids, stood behind me. Vicky Dean sang Schubert's *Ave Maria* to Janey Dawson's organ accompaniment. Janet McKenzie, in a dog-collar and a smart black two-piece, conducted the ceremony. Over to one side, Elizabeth and The Divine Sarah sniffed delicately into matching lace handkerchiefs. '*You can never go back to Manderley, Miss Montpellier,*' Lavinia's voice whispered from the gloom. '*You may now kiss the bride,*' intoned Janet. As Dougal bent over me, I realised he was actually McCarthy. '*No, no, that's the wrong one!*' shrieked Mother. '*Do I have to do* everything *around here?*' She fired. McCarthy fell at my feet, bleeding. '*Quick –*

1 A stoater – a vulgar Glasgow expression for a striking woman, a beauty.

bring on the understudy – the baby must have a father,' went on Mother in a perfectly natural tone of voice. Mona McCafferty emerged from the shadows in top hat and tails, and as Janey Dawson preluded the Wedding March on her wheezing harmonium, Mona took my arm and led me from the Post Office. The crowd waiting outside showered us with pound notes, which Mother proceeded to gather up avidly.

Obviously recent events were preying on my mind. Should I or should I not write to my sister? This could easily be a plot concocted by my eternally devious mother. Lavinia might be an innocent pawn, or a party to the conspiracy.

Suddenly reality struck home. '*What can Mother actually do? Short of kidnapping me bodily and forcing me at gunpoint, as in my dream, the answer is* nothing.' Her blackmail attempt was virtually exposed as a tissue of lies. There remained only one piece of the jigsaw to be put in place – the riddle of Mary McGuire. I resolved to take a chance and answer my sister's letter.

I kept it brief and to the point. Scant on details, I gave her just the most general outline of my life over the past eighteen months. I said how pleased I was to be in contact with her, but trusted her discretion in the matter of Mother. I would see her again soon at a time of my choosing. Until then, I would be delighted to hear further from her.

Our clandestine correspondence continued, and I found myself in the delightful position of, for once, being the one 'in the know'. Lavinia was able to pass on all sorts of snippets, and I soon was up to date with current events at home. After my disappearance, Mother had raved for days about my defection, my attempt to poison her, my destruction of what she termed 'my private papers', and what she described as my 'complete lack of family loyalty'. She had been further discomfited when her father, Grandpa Max, unexpectedly recovered from the stroke which had incapacitated him subsequent to his motoring accident, and proceeded to take the reins of the family concerns back into his own hands. Just in time, it seemed, as Mother, I learned, had practically succeeded in bringing the distillery business to the verge of bankruptcy. Since this had occurred, she seemed to have lost all interest in regaining contact with me. From that I deduced that it was through her own deplorable mismanagement of the business that her sudden desperate desire to entail my inheritance had its origins. Perhaps most surprisingly, Lavinia passed on the news that my mother had actually been compelled to find a job.

All very positive and encouraging. However, I was saddened to learn that still no word had been received concerning Leicester, my missing brother. *He*, it appeared, had disappeared without leaving any trace behind him.

* * * * *

February 1938.

Miss Rombach's Restaurant, Glasgow.

Pantomime came to an end early in February – the length of the run was shorter in rural Ayrshire than in the big city of Glasgow. *Joe and Co.* were booked for the spring show in the small Theatre Royal, Dumfries, a short run of just a couple of months commencing mid-March. Then, Joe told me, it would be off to summer season in the holiday resort of Largs, on the Clyde coast.

I was in something of a quandary. I hated the idea of letting Joe down, but I had no intention of continuing my present way of life one day longer than was necessary. Should I simply disappear? In July, when my eighteenth birthday would allow me to finally claim my inheritance? *No,* I thought. There were people to whom I owed a great deal – Joe himself, of course, but also Mae, who had been like a sister to me, and most of all, to Elizabeth and Sarah at The Palace, to whose kindness I owed, I felt, my very survival. And of course – McCarthy.

It was at this point that I decided to confide the whole situation to Elizabeth and Sarah. The former already knew something of my true history, so before setting out for Dumfries, I arranged to take them out for an afternoon tea at Miss Rombach's Restaurant, scene of my less than triumphant début as a piano entertainer. I laid the entire story before them, omitting nothing of any consequence.

"Well, hen," said Sarah, settling back in her chair when I had finished, "thon's quite a story. More tea, Liz?"

"Yes, please, Sarah," Elizabeth replied. "So, Eva – that *is* your name, isn't it? – I got a bit confused in the middle there for a moment – so – you are going to be leaving us?"

"Yes, I shall. In July."

Sarah was still breathlessly caught up in the tale. "And that mother of yours – whit an awfy cow!"

"Now, now, Sarah, we're not qualified to judge," remonstrated Elizabeth. "She must have had her reasons."

"Mother doesn't need reasons," I pointed out. "Indeed, sometimes I think she's not quite sane."

"Well, *that* wid be a reason, I suppose," mused Sarah. "Even so, Elizabeth, you must agree, it's hardly the behaviour of a mother."

"No, granted, Sarah," Elizabeth concurred. "But I just wonder what possessed her, that's all. But to get back to what I was saying… What are your plans, Eva? You know you are welcome to stay with us as long as you want."

"I'm not sure I know, Elizabeth. But I will definitely be moving on. I have lots to do. One thing I ask you: please don't breathe a word of what I've told you to anyone. Particularly…

"McCarthy," finished Sarah. "No, of course we won't. Nor to anyone else. Isn't that right Liz?"

"Of course, Sarah. Don't worry, Eva, you can rely on us."

And I knew I could.

* * * * *

March 1938.

Theatre Royal, Dumfries.

The spring show in Dumfries was a small affair. But it was exceptional in one respect. Joe had asked to be allowed to write and produce it – he was always buzzing with ideas – and his notion was to invent a new format, one in which the entire production would focus on a single theme, in contrast to the loosely constructed series of individual acts that was then popular. In many ways he was anticipating the later 'revue' type of show, which was to enjoy an extended vogue twenty years in the future – the kind of show where all the work was done by a few talented performers in brief sketches and songs.

The show was called *Behind Every Man*, and the theme was designed to illustrate the utter incompetence of the heroes of history, had it not been for the support and encouragement of the ladies behind the scenes. A troupe of four dancers and only four other supporting players composed the entire cast, and most of the sketches featured principally Joe and myself. Mae sadly, for once, was not in the company.

A brief snippet of some of the sketches will give an idea of the style of the show. I was Eve to Joe's Adam in *Paradise Lost…*

***Adam**: "Good morning Eve – I must say, that's a lovely juicy pair you have there."*

***Eve**: "No, Adam, that's an apple.".*

I was Josephine to his Napoleon in *Not Tonight!…*

***Napoleon:** What's this I hear, Josephine? You have been disporting yourself with a lover during my absence! Take care! I am the Emperor of France, and I'm not playing second fiddle to anyone.*

***Josephine:** Boney dear, with your instrument, you're lucky to be in the band!*

I was Poppaea to his Nero in *Roman Flames.*

***Nero:** Poppy, my darling, where is that warped old lyre?*

Poppaea: *Sorry, dear – didn't you say you'd left your mother in Pompeii?*

Nero: *Ah yes, of course. Now, my beloved, you'd better shed some of those heavy clothes, because –* (he sings) *– "There's gonna be a hot time in the old town tonight..."*

We had some trouble with the local Watch Committee about the level of vulgarity in the show, as you may well imagine! Joe was able to reassure them that he would remove the more offensive lines, and we did. For about two performances, as I recall.

Our grand finale was in quite another tone. Banking on the Scots delight in patriotic emotion, and the ever ready Caledonian tear, I played Flora McDonald to Joe's Bonnie Prince Charlie. The set represented the craggy shore of Kilbride on the island of Skye. We 'sailed' onto the stage in a tiny rowing boat and full Highland dress while the rest of the cast, offstage, rendered *Over the Sea to Skye*. Flora bids a tearful farewell to Charlie, and collapses on the 'shore' as her beloved Prince sails away. Two kilted pipers enter along with the rest of the cast. Reprise of *Over the Sea to Skye*. Not a dry seat in the house.

I did point out to Joe that, historically, Charlie had actually arrived on Skye disguised as Betty Burke, Flora's maid. While Joe was alive to the comic potential of appearing *en travesti*, he realised correctly that any hint of burlesque would undermine the sentimental appeal of the scene.

It was during the run of *Behind Every Man* that a letter was forwarded to me from Jonathan Bartington, asking me to contact him to arrange a meeting. I duly did so, and it was fixed that when I finished the show in Dumfries, around the middle of May, I would travel through to Edinburgh and call on him at the company offices. I hoped fervently that he would have some news for me.,

But before that, I had another surprise in store. Joe and I had naturally been spending a lot of time in each other's company. When we weren't onstage together, we were eating together, socialising together, indeed everything except sleeping together. A gap that Joe seemed intent on filling.

"Let's get married," he said, as we shared high tea at Susan's Restaurant, the Dumfries equivalent to Miss Rombach's.

"What?" I nearly dropped my Empire biscuit.

"Let's get married. I'll make you happy. You might not think so now, but I would. I'm a nice chap, kind, generous, talented, considerate and of course very good-looking. Give it a go – what have you got to lose?"

"Well..." Just for that moment I couldn't think of anything.

He put his elbows on the table and stared at me. "We work well together onstage, you like me, I like you – it's obvious, don't you think?"

I was almost lost for words. "Obvious? Joe, aren't you forgetting about...?"

"Him, you mean? McCarthy? He's not been around much recently, has he?"

He nodded. "He's playing away, trust me. And I know that for a fact."

It was true that McCarthy had not been down to Dumfries for several weeks.

I picked up the teapot. "He's away on business," I protested. "He told me he would be gone for a while. That's all there is to it. Business." I poured some more tea for both of us and put the teapot back on its rest.

He reached over and took my hand. "Monkey business, Rina. Him and Agnes Gibson. You know she's at the Pavilion in Glasgow? And he's been seen around with her a helluva lot. I know – I hear all the gossip from the city. I've told you – he's a worthless little crook. To him you're just some kind of prize he thinks he's won. The best of a not very inspiring bunch." He gave my hand a squeeze. "You need a man who will care for you, who will provide for you. Who understands you, and loves you."

Joe was utterly sincere. And if McCarthy *was* actually taking a more than friendly interest in the lovely Agnes, did I *really* care? No, not to any great extent. Our relationship had been – why not admit it? – a convenience to me. And it would soon be over. In fact, this information might prove just the excuse I needed for terminating the affair. So, to my shame, I decided to play a rather devious game.

"Joe," I said, "I'm truly touched by your proposal. And I suspect that you may be right about – that other man. I don't know. I'm very fond of you, you know that. We get on well, we never argue, I know I can trust you. But that's not enough, surely?"

"Only one way to find out, Eva…"

"I don't know, Joe. I'll have to think about it."

"Don't take *too* long, Eva – you know how much in demand I am," Joe smiled, as he lifted my hand and kissed it.

Chapter Eleven

McCarthy's Last Stand

May 1938.

Edinburgh.

I sat in the offices of Mr Jonathan Bartington, only half-paying attention as he droned on about taxes, interest, investments, reversions, recoveries and the like. After he had achieved his peroration he smiled and said, "So – as you will have gathered, Eva, everything is in order. I have some papers here you need to sign, and then in July we will open an account for you and provide you with the necessary documentation. The total now is close to twelve thousand pounds – minus our fees of course." He grinned ingratiatingly.

"Thank you, Jonathan, that all sounds satisfactory. I will arrange to come back in July. I'm not sure of the exact date – I have other commitments. But I will be in touch."

I rose to leave, and stretched out my hand in farewell.

"Just a moment, Eva. I have some more news for you. About that other family matter we discussed."

I sat down again immediately.

"Yes? What have you managed to find?"

"I think it might be best if you heard it from someone else, someone who can give you all the details. Someone who remembers the whole sorry affair as if it happened yesterday. Will you step into the parlour?"

'*Said the spider to the fly*,' I thought. I followed Jonathan from his office into a cosy little sitting room close by. A very old white-haired lady sat in a comfy armchair sipping a cup of tea.

"Eva," said Jonathan, "I want you to meet Mary Andrews."

With some difficulty, the old lady rose to greet me.

"So you're Eva, Hector's girl? How lovely to meet up with you at last."

"How do you do?" I said automatically. "Mary Andrews? Sorry – should I know you?"

"Mary McGuire was my maiden name. Then Mary Laskaris. Currently, Mary Andrews, widow."

Good Heavens! So this was Father's mysterious cousin. I didn't know what to say. So I said the first thing that came into my head. "Father's cousin? So – you are my first cousin – er – once removed?"

"No, dear, it's more complicated than that," the lady replied, sitting down and setting her teacup on a nearby table. "We're not actually related at all. I was married to your father's cousin, Dionysus Laskaris. May he rot in hell." She said this last with no change of tone, and with a complacent equanimity. As if she had said it, or at least thought it, many times in the past.

"Sorry, I am confused. Who?"

"His mother was born Artemisia Paskalis, and she was your grandmother Aliki's sister. Artemisia married Kostas Laskaris, and my husband was their only son. *He* is your father's cousin, not me. Rather, he *was*. Not anymore. I killed him, you see."

"What?" Was I imagining this conversation, or was this pleasant eighty-something lady a certifiable lunatic? And I wasn't sure if I had managed to follow all these complicated family interrelationships – so she was the daughter-in-law of my grandmother's sister? I thought so...

"Why don't you sit yourself down dear, and have a cup of tea? I'll tell you the whole story."

I did as she suggested. Mary settled herself and poured another cup of tea, along with one for me.

"Milk dear? Perhaps you'll help yourself, my hands are not too steady these days. So sorry to hear about your dear dad, by the way. I was very fond of him, you know. Long, long ago."

Jonathan, I noticed, was not partaking. But he sat down on a chair behind us.

"Now, where do I start? With Madeleine, I suppose. It was all Madeleine's fault, really. She got away with it, and I thought I might too. You remember Madeleine Smith, I'm sure? It was in all the papers – a long time ago of course, long before you were born."

I vaguely remembered reading about the famous murder trial. Madeleine Smith of Blythswood Square, Glasgow, was charged with poisoning her French lover, Emile L'Angelier, with arsenic. The jury returned the peculiar Scottish verdict of 'Not Proven',[1] and Madeleine was released. But this was all surely ancient history, a hundred years or more in the past.

"Eighteen-fifty-seven, it was," Mary went on, as if answering my thoughts. "The murder, I mean. I would have been seven. I remember Madeleine well, although I was only ten or thereabouts when she and her family moved away. The scandal, of course – although she got off, most people knew she had done it.

1 In Scotland, the 'Not Proven' verdict is offered as an alternative to 'Guilty' or 'Not Guilty'. Effectively it means 'we think she did it, but there is not sufficient evidence to prove the matter'.

We McGuires lived a few doors away from the Smiths, in Blythswood Square, and young Madeleine often took me out as a child, first in my perambulator when I was tiny, and when I was older, for walks. I had sharp eyes and sharper ears. So I was the only person who knew that she was using these excursions as an excuse to meet up with *him*, the Frenchman."

She paused and sipped her tea before continuing.

"Of course, I was too young to be called as a witness in the trial, but I could have told them a thing or two, believe me. Not that I would have – Madeleine was my friend, a lovely girl, and that nasty Frenchman was blackmailing her – what else could she do? He was a low character, goodness knows what she was thinking to get involved with him. He was a rogue, and worse, a foreigner. Deserved all he got in my opinion."

She paused again for a long moment and looked down into her cup.

Neither Jonathan nor I dared to say anything. '*Had she finished?*' I wondered. But this explained nothing, nothing at all. Then she looked up with a little smile. "Now wouldn't you think I would have taken the lesson to heart? But no – I went and made the same mistake. I married a foreigner, too. But worse. A Greek."

I was considerably taken aback by her equanimity. '*The attitude of another era entirely,*' I thought. Fascinating as this all was, I wondered where my father fitted into the story.

Mary turned her cup round and round in its saucer. She frowned to herself, and seemed to momentarily lose her thread.

"And you knew my father?" I prompted.

She immediately brightened. "Oh, yes, knew him well. Of course he was only a wee boy at the time. I was eighteen when I got married. Your Dad would have been nine or ten. He used to visit our house with his mother, your grandmother, and play the piano. So talented, so talented. I looked forward to his visits. And his mother, your grandmother – she was a real lady, even though she'd been in the theatre – opera singer, I seem to recall. Of course, by the time I knew her, she had retired."

Once again, the frown, and a downward glance. I resisted the urge to prompt again, realising that this lady would tell her story in her own time and at her own pace.

Suddenly she set down her teacup, and looked up.

"My married life wasn't a happy one, you know. We became good friends, your father and I."

I felt I ought to say something. "And your husband – Mr Laskaris – he – er – he died?"

She sighed heavily. "Dionysus. That he did, my dear. At my hands. Oh yes, I don't mind admitting it now. After all, I've paid the price, cleared my debt to society, as they say." She nodded with deliberation. "My husband was a monster. Not in public, of course. Ever the handsome charmer. Everybody admired him. Clever, good-looking, talented. But behind closed doors… He kept me a virtual prisoner. Abused me, physically and mentally. Forced me to be present when he consorted with other women. Women of the lowest type, too – prostitutes, actresses and the like."

I wondered what Mary would have thought if she had realised that I, too, was currently a kind of actress.

By now she was in full flow, reliving the past.

"But all *that* I could have coped with, I suppose," she went on. "I was very young. No-one knew the truth. What went on in the home was kept in the home in those days. I was probably not the only woman in that position. I resigned myself. Never said a word to anyone. But then I discovered I was pregnant."

"Pregnant? But didn't you say…"

"Oh yes – but he still forced himself on *me* whenever the notion took him – there are stories I could tell you, dear, that a young girl like you shouldn't have to hear. And you won't from me. But when I discovered I was expecting, I thought, '*Perhaps this will change everything…*' I felt consoled, comforted. For perhaps the first time since my marriage, the future seemed to hold the faint promise of better times to come. To have a baby…"

She picked up her cup again. "I thought he would be pleased, proud.. But no. He told me he didn't want children, ever. He pushed me down the stairs, deliberately. I lost the child."

The awful recital was all the more horrifying for its baldness.

"Oh – you poor woman," I murmured, inadequately. "And…?"

She held up a hand to quiet me.

"It was when I was getting rid of the perambulator – my own old one, the one Madeleine had taken me out in as a child. I didn't want to see it, not then. I was in a bad way, after the miscarriage; my head wasn't quite right…"

"No, I can imagine," I breathed.

"I decided to clean it thoroughly. It was in good condition – perhaps I could pass it on to someone? It was then I found the packet, hidden in the lining. Just a little brown envelope. On the front, "*Arsenic. Madeleine Smith. For rats. Poison.*"

I remembered that Madeleine had purchased the arsenic she used in her crime quite openly, saying it was for use against rats.[1]

Mary sat pensive, as if reliving the dreadful moment.

1 At her trial, however, she claimed she had been too embarrassed to tell the chemist the truth, that she wanted the arsenic as a wash for her complexion.

"And I certainly had a rat to deal with. It was as though it had been delivered into my hands just for that purpose. I fed it to him slowly. In his whisky. He suffered. Eventually he died."

I began to feel a little light-headed. The quiet matter-of-fact tone, the horrible intimacy of the revelations, all this delivered over a cup of tea in my solicitor's quiet, discreetly furnished office… But there was something more I needed to know. "When did this happen, Mary – what year, I mean?"

"Eighteen-seventy-one. I was twenty-one. I had been married for two years, just."

Eighteen-seventy-one? Father would have been twelve.

"What happened, Mary?"

"I was arrested and charged with murder. I hadn't been clever, you see. But I wasn't worried. Madeleine hadn't been clever either, and she got away with it. As I said, my mind was a bit disturbed at the time – if I had really thought about it, I could have done it much more cunningly. That's my only regret. Not for what I did. But for getting caught."

I didn't like to ask, but had to. "You went to prison, I suppose?"

She shook her head. "No, not to prison. My lawyer at the trial managed to convince the court that, since I had suffered dreadful abuse during my marriage and had recently lost a child, I had acted while the balance of my mind was disturbed. As indeed, it was. But where was the proof, you might ask? All these things happened behind closed doors, after all, so who could stand up for me? Only your dad. He had seen things that no-one else had. Who pays any attention to the presence of a young child? He was called as a witness at my trial. It was his evidence that saved me. Instead of the rope or prison, I was sent to an institution for the criminally insane. I was twenty-one. I was there for thirty years."

Thirty years. If my calculations were correct, she would have been released around the turn of the century. What a dreadful, horrible story. I wanted to stop my ears. But there was one thing I had to know.

"Mary – tell me about the money. Father inherited some money, and I believe that had something to do with you."

"Oh yes – the money. It was my husband's money. With all his personal faults, he was a brilliant businessman. And he himself had inherited from his own father, who died shortly after we were married. And *he* was *rich*."

"So how did this money find its way to Father?"

"Well, I think I can explain that. I was naturally disqualified by law from benefitting from my crime. So the money went to his mother. Then when she passed away, to her sister, your grandmother. And thence to your dad. Best place for it. He deserved it, if anyone did. It will come to you now, I imagine. Make the most of it dear, won't you?"

"I would hope to, Mary, certainly. But… what about you?"

"I was lucky. After I was released, I married again. David Andrews was a wonderful man. We had thirty-seven happy years together. He passed away only last year, and left me well-provided for. So, if you're thinking – and I suspect you are – that poor old Mary McGuire is short of money and could do with a bit of charity, please don't. I want nothing to do with that money. You're welcome to it. Some more tea, dear?"

I eyed my cup rather dubiously.

* * * * *

After Mary left, Jonathan and I exchanged a few words.

"An odd woman, that. But nice, in a slightly scary kind of way," he said.

"A very scary kind of way. So pleasant and agreeable on the surface. So matter of fact, even when she is recounting horrors."

"Yes," he went on. "You put it very well. Anyway, the question is – did you get the information you were hoping for?"

Yes. I had. The final nail in Mother's coffin. Not literally, of course. Well, not yet.

* * * * *

June 1938.

Barfield's Pavilion, Largs, Scotland.

Joe and I opened in the summer show at Barfield's Pavilion in Largs at the beginning of June. I had come to a decision. I would play out the show until my birthday arrived in July. Then I would simply vanish. I had considered telling Joe the whole truth, but, aware that there are no secrets backstage in a theatre, I decided against this. Joe was still awaiting my answer regarding his proposal, and although I hated the thought of hurting him, I came to the conclusion that the less people who knew my plans the better. At present, only Sarah and Elizabeth were aware of my intentions, but I determined to make sure that they would explain the situation to all my other friends after I had gone.

There remained the McCarthy situation to resolve. I had come to believe that Joe was right, and that Rab was indeed seeing someone else on a regular basis. When I tackled him about it, he was, on the surface, engagingly frank.

"Sure, Rina, Agnes and me huv been out a few times. Yer always away working, so what am Ah supposed tae dae? – sit in every night on ma own? She's a nice lassie, good company, but we're just friends, there's nothing going on between us. It's not as if Ah'm trying to keep it a secret, am I? If Ah'm oot wi her, it's in a crowd, and it goes no further than a few drinks."

I wondered. Maybe he was telling the truth. But I had gradually come to realise that Agnes, pleasant and friendly as she appeared, was a somewhat 'sleekit'[1] character. I remembered how Mae had warned me against her long ago. And there was no doubt in my mind that McCarthy would say whatever he thought I wanted to hear.

He put an arm round me. "If ye wid just move in wi' me all this could be settled, Rina. Give up the stage, Ah'm no short of cash, there's no need for ye tae work at all, really. Think aboot it, why don't ye?"

I crossed my fingers, and said I would.

* * * * *

Thursday 7th July 1938.

Largs.

The summer show was a large-scale affair – Largs was a popular holiday destination, and many familiar faces were in the show. Joe and I had moved up the bill, and were now a featured act, but Mae and the rest of the girls were in the company and Betty Barnard was yet again the principal dancer.

Joe decided that we would celebrate my eighteenth birthday in style, so on the day itself, a Thursday, he arranged for the entire company to join us for a meal in Largs' première hotel, 'The Moorings'. It was a wonderful evening, although tinged with sadness. I realised I would not have all these dear friends for much longer. Everyone had clubbed together to buy me a birthday present – of all things, a piano-accordion. Second-hand, obviously, but in good condition.

"There you are Marina," said Joe. "You'll master that in no time at all, and then we can introduce it into the act."

I was incredibly touched. For a moment or two I thought to myself, '*I could just stay here. I could marry Joe. We have a successful and popular act. He's honest and kind. We wouldn't want for money. Why not?*'

Then I seemed to hear Father's voice: '*I can see a day when the name of Evadne Hinge will be known throughout the world.*' The name of Evadne Hinge. Not the name of Marina Montpellier. No, I had to be strong. I was doing the right thing.

---

1 Sleekit – sly and cunning, two-faced

I had arranged to call at the offices of Bartington and Son on Monday 11th July to finalise the paperwork, and take charge of my inheritance. So after the second show on the 9th, I told Joe that I had been urgently called back to Glasgow, as my mother was sick. This last was true, of course, but not quite in the way Joe understood it. I assured him I would be back for the evening show on the Monday. He drove me to the station at Largs, kissed me *au revoir*, and I boarded the train for Glasgow.

* * * * *

Saturday 9th July 1938.

The Palace.

It was late when I arrived at The Palace, where Elizabeth and Sarah welcomed me warmly, and we had a long and cosy chat over a drink or two. It was a rather tearful evening, unsurprisingly; I was saying goodbye, and who knew whether we would ever meet again?

"Elizabeth. Sarah," I said. "I need you to do something for me. I will be gone on Monday. Would you, please, get together all the people important to me, and tell them the truth. Explain, if you can, that I took no pleasure in deceiving them; that it was just to keep myself safe that I hid my real past. Can I rely on you for that? Mae, of course, and Joe Chapman. Phyllis, Sandra, the rest of the girls; all our friends from here – Mary, Joanna, Desdemona – whoever you feel ought to know."

"Of course we will," said Elizabeth, "You can rest easy. They'll hear just enough to set their minds at rest. We don't want them to be sending out search parties for you, or dragging the Clyde, do we?"

"What about McCarthy?" asked Sarah.

"No, not him. I will deal with that myself," I said.

So I had a piece of unfinished business to attend to on Sunday the 10th of July.

* * * * *

Sunday 10th July 1938.

Townhead, Glasgow.

Although I had never visited McCarthy's flat, I had the address. I had come to the conclusion that I owed him some kind of explanation, although not the true one. I planned to tell him that I had decided to marry Joe, and that henceforth he must consider our relationship at an end. I expected some resistance to the idea, but felt I was quite capable of handling the situation.

It was a beautiful summer morning. I took a taxi to the Townhead district, at that time a warren of mean streets surrounding Glasgow Cathedral, and eventually located the tenement in which McCarthy's one room apartment was situated. I made my way up the three flights of steep stone stairs, and arrived on the top floor to find the door of his flat ajar. I could hear music from inside. After knocking firmly, and receiving no response, I pushed the door open and entered the little hallway, thinking I would surprise him. But the surprise was to be mine.

Through the half-open door of the main room, I could clearly see, reclining on a sofa, none other than the lady herself, Agnes Gibson. Loud music blared from the radio. Agnes was dressed in a gaping and grubby pink satin peignoir and mules, her hair was in curlers, and she hummed along and tapped her foot in time to the music. Periodically she dipped into a large box of chocolates, and occasionally sipped from a glass of whisky. All the while flicking through a fashion magazine. Multi-tasking is, I believe, the modern expression.

I pushed the door wide and entered.

"Good morning, Agnes. Lovely day, isn't it?"

Agnes choked on a chocolate, and almost dropped her glass.

"Rina! Thought you were in Largs! What are you doing here?"

I smiled agreeably. "No, I think that's *my* question, don't you, Agnes?"

Agnes pulled the sides of her pink wrap together and succeeded in covering most of her bosom.

"Oh – you'll never guess, Rina…" she started nervously. "I missed my last bus last night and Robert very kindly offered to put me up. He's such a kind soul, isn't he?"

I sat down in a chair and made myself comfortable.

"Robert? Yes, isn't he? Do anything for anyone, McCarthy would. Apparently."

"Yes." She gulped. "Er – he's just popped out to get some milk. He'll be back in a minute." Agnes set down her glass shakily. "You know men, Rina, never got anything in, not even the necessities." She grinned confidingly in a 'we girls know best' kind of way.

I smiled and nodded agreement. "Absolutely, you're *so* right Agnes. Not like us girls, eh? – always have everything we need, isn't that the way?"

"We do, don't we?" Agnes, smiling back, seemed to be recovering her composure.

"Yes," I agreed. I crossed my legs. "As they say, *'Fail to plan, and you plan to fail.'* Like yourself, for example, Agnes. How *sensible* of you to carry slippers and a nightdress with you wherever you go. Not to mention a negligee and curlers. Bet you've got a toothbrush too. Oh, you're an example to us all." I laughed light-heartedly. "Unless, of course, they're McCarthy's."

As Agnes appeared to consider this improbable explanation, right on cue, I heard the front door bang closed, and McCarthy himself entered the room carrying a bottle of milk.

He nearly dropped it when he saw me. "Rina! – what are you doing here?"

I stood up.

"Agnes has already done that one, McCarthy. Want to try something else?"

"Agnes missed her last bus…"

"Yes, she's done that one too. Anything more to add?"

His guilt was written all over his features. He took a deep breath and turned to Agnes.

"You'd better go, Agnes. I need to talk to Rina here."

Agnes scrambled to her feet, nodding vigorously.

"Of course, OK, Rab – I'll just get dressed…"

"No time for that. Get yourself gone."

"But Rab… I'll catch ma death…"

"You heard me, Agnes. Out."

"But what'll folks say?..."

McCarthy was becoming enraged. His fists clenched and unclenched. I helped myself to a chocolate.

"It's a lovely sunny day, Agnes," I said, over my shoulder. "No doubt the neighbours will just think you are setting a new trend in summer wear. You'll be fine." I couldn't have cared less if she caught pneumonia.

Agnes hesitated. "Please, Rab…

"Ye've got five seconds, Agnes. One…" McCarthy raised a hand.

The terrified Agnes scampered from the room, pausing only to scoop up her chocolates and the whisky bottle. Once again, the front door opened and closed. Seconds later I could hear the clacking of her kitten-heels as she made her way down the stairs to the street.

'*This is working out perfectly*,' I congratulated myself.

"Rina, I can explain…" he said, setting down the bottle of milk.

"Yes, I'm sure you can. But really, spare yourself the trouble, McCarthy, I'm not interested. I just came to say goodbye, anyway. I'll be off now."

I stood up, turned on my heel, and prepared to follow Agnes. I had got as far as the hallway when he grabbed my arm as I reached for the handle of the front door.

"Wait, Rina, wait. OK. I admit it. Ah *have* been seeing Agnes. Just now and then. It meant nothing, nothing at all. But wi' you being away all the time, Ah wis lonely." He put on an unconvincing 'poor me' kind of face. "I wis jealous. Rina, Ah suppose, if ye want the truth. Ah'm thinking, '*Whit's Rina up to wi' that Joe fella…*' Ah know ye like him, and he's been after you for ages…"

I rounded on him at that.

"Don't you *dare* bring Joe into this, McCarthy. Unlike *you*, he's a decent, honest man. Oh – and thank you for the kind suggestion that I am no better than you – virtually accusing me of being up to hanky-panky behind your back. That just shows how little you know me."

Suddenly he seemed to deflate. He let go of my arm.

"No, you're right there, Rina. I don't know you. That's part of the problem. You've never let me."

In spite of my disgust at the whole sordid scene, I had to admit to myself the justice of this remark.

But this was no time for back-peddling. A golden opportunity had been handed to me. I had to seize it. Onward and upward.

"No, I haven't, you're right. So let me enlighten you. Joe and I are going to be married. You and I are finished. Is that clear and simple enough for you to take in?"

Once again I reached for the door handle.

The expression of astonishment on his face was almost comical. "Marry Joe? Are ye mad? Ye don't love Joe."

I paused.

"How can you be sure of that? You just said you don't know me."

He hesitated.

"*I'll* marry you, Rina."

"What?"

"Yes. Ye know how I feel aboot ye, how Ah've always felt aboot ye."

However intrigued, I had to keep up the pressure. "I know exactly how you feel about me. You want to own me, not marry me. So the answer's 'no'. Sorry. It was fun. But it's over. I'm going."

Yet again I turned to leave. But, moving in front of me, McCarthy barred my way.

"Yer no goin' anywhere," he said hoarsely. "No, yer no leaving here until we've sorted this out, Rina. Don't push me – ye'll be sorry."

This was the other McCarthy. One I had only seen rarely, and that from a distance. How was I to get out of this? I'd seen the level of violence of which he was capable. I thought of the last act of *Carmen.* And of how she ended up.

Suddenly there was a heaven-sent interruption. A loud banging at the flat door. Agnes, I thought. Obviously forgotten something vital. Her brain, perhaps.

"Come on, in there. Open up!"

The manly tone certainly didn't sound like Agnes.

McCarthy turned towards the door for a second. I slipped past him and opened it.

"Police, miss." Two very large uniformed constables stood on the threshold. "We're looking for Robert McCarthy. This is his place, I believe?"

In spite of my shaking knees, I struggled to regain my composure. "Look no further, officers. You've found him."

I let out a sigh of relief. '*Saved by the Bill'*, one might say today.

I stood aside, and the representatives of the law entered. McCarthy, backing into the main room of the flat, had gone rather pale.

"Robert McCarthy?" one of the policemen asked.

"Aye, that's me," he replied politely, nodding, all innocence and eagerness to help.

"We've a few questions for you, Mr McCarthy. Concerning a robbery at a jewellery shop in Alloa. Last night, around midnight."

"Oh? Alloa, ye say? Never been there, masel'. Sorry boys, Ah can't help ye." McCarthy spread his hands and smiled deprecatingly. "Ah was here aw' night. A quiet night in wi' ma girl-friend here. Is that no right, Rina?"

He looked at me imploringly. For a second, I wavered. But this had to end.

"No, it isn't right, McCarthy." I turned to the two policemen. "I was in Largs last night. I've never been here before today. And I only arrived ten minutes ago – I just came to deliver a message."

I turned back to McCarthy. "Good heavens, McCarthy, what a terrible memory you've got. *I* wasn't here last night, it must have been your *other* girl-friend." I smiled meaningfully in his direction – it was the least I could do. "Does the name *Agnes* not ring a bell?"

He caught on immediately. "Agnes, aye, ye're right. Sorry, we had a few drinks, it wis a long night." Shaking his head, he turned away. I addressed the two policemen.

"So do you mind if I leave, gentlemen? I have an urgent appointment, and I am sure you would prefer to interview Mr McCarthy in private."

The one who was obviously in charge nodded. "Aye, ye can go, hen. Just leave your name and address in case we need to get in touch with you."

"Of course, of course, delighted, officer. It's Marina Montpellier, care of the

Stage Door, Barfield's Pavilion, Largs. That'll always get me."

The second officer noted the details I had given.

As I turned to leave, I added, "It's a great show, by the way. Why don't you boys come down and see it? Bring the children – it's a family show. I will be happy to provide the tickets – I have such admiration for the police. Just drop me a line if the idea appeals."

"Rina…"

I waved a hand amicably in his direction. "Sorry, McCarthy, got to dash. I'm sure these nice gentlemen will take care of you. Good-bye."

* * * * *

Leaving the building, I passed Agnes standing at a bus-stop in her night attire. She still maintained a death-grip on the whisky bottle and the chocolates.

As I approached, she tucked the box under her arm, and stretched out one hand beseechingly. "Rina, Ah've nae money. Can ye spare a copper or two for the bus?"

"No, sorry, Agnes, I can't." I looked back over my shoulder. "But you'll find a couple upstairs with McCarthy."

Agnes's unusual attire was drawing some attention from a few fascinated children.

"Ur ye a hoor, you?" one grubby urchin asked her, poking her midriff with his finger.

Agnes recoiled slightly and dropped her chocolates on the ground.

"Yes, that's exactly what she is, sonny," I confirmed with a smile, patting him on the head.

The boy suddenly kicked Agnes hard in the shins, grabbed the whisky bottle, scooped up the chocolates, and raced off down the street.

"Good-bye, Agnes," I smiled as I flagged down a passing taxi. "Must do this again sometime. Such fun."

* * * * *

The taxi dropped me off at Queen Street station where I boarded the first train for Edinburgh. I had some money saved from my wages and had decided to treat myself to a night of luxury, something I had not enjoyed for some time. I booked into the North British Hotel in Princes Street, which I had last visited for tea with Jonathan Bartington, and reserved a table for dinner. I was pleased to see that Jeannie was on duty, and we were able to share a friendly chat as she served me. Then it was back to my comfortable room and a sound night's sleep.

* * * * *

Monday 11th July 1938.

Edinburgh.

I arrived at the Bartington premises punctually at 10 AM as had been arranged, and was ushered into his private office by Jonathan himself, his manner even more obsequious than was usual.

"You're looking well, Eva," he said. "Well – today's the day. I have all the paperwork here ready for you."

I signed endless documents, of which he provided copies.

"Here are your bank books, Eva. There's two thousand in the savings account, and one thousand eight hundred in the current account. The other eight thousand I will keep invested for now, as we discussed. That alone should bring you in an income of about eight hundred a year, enough to live on very comfortably. If you want any changes to these arrangements, just let me know." He smiled agreeably as he passed the paperwork to me.

"Thank you, Jonathan, you have been very helpful in all this." I tucked them into my handbag. "Now I need another favour."

"Anything I can do, Eva. You know that."

"I want you to pass on a cheque for one hundred pounds[1]. Several cheques, actually. One each for the people who have helped me. My friends."

"Yes, I can attend to that. If you care to write out the cheques and give me the addresses, I will see that they reach their destinations."

I proceeded to fill out a cheque for the said sum to all the people I knew who would appreciate it. One to Elizabeth and Sarah – I had to ensure this one was made out correctly to Frederick Lyon. One to Joe Chapman. One each to Mae Hockshaw and Jeannie Dunt. And one to Lavinia Hinge.

Jonathan provided me with envelopes which I proceeded to address carefully. He said he would be happy to deal with them, and I left them in his care. He assured me they would go in the post that very day.

"Before you leave, Eva," he said. "I was wondering if you would care to join me for a bite to eat this evening? There's a new French restaurant in the Old Town that I hear good reports about. Just a nice little get-together – no strings attached."

---

1 Worth around four thousand pounds (2002)

"Are you sure about that, Jonathan?" I smiled doubtfully.

"Of course. I'm very happily married, Eva. I truly wasn't suggesting anything untoward. Just a pleasant evening with a good friend. I hope you see me as that?"

How unfair I was being. '*I must try to lose this mistrustful attitude, imputing dark motives to every simple question,*' I thought. '*Thank you, Mother...*'

I covered our slight embarrassment with what I hoped was a light-hearted tone.

"Jonathan, I was joking. Yes, of course, I *do* see you as a friend. And yes, I would be delighted to have dinner with you this evening. Collect me about eight outside my hotel? I have some urgent business to attend to this afternoon."

* * * * *

I imagine I would have been unrecognisable to any of my recent acquaintances when I left Jenner's, Edinburgh's most exclusive department store, later that day. A selection of smart outfits, shoes, underwear, blouses, jumpers and coats would be delivered to my hotel later. Several handbags and a set of matching luggage; a range of fine cosmetics and perfumes; some modest jewellery; these too would arrive courtesy of the distinguished establishment. My hair had been cut and styled, and its colour completely altered from the brilliant 'dance-hall gold' I had recently favoured. It was now a warm chestnut brown as of old. In the mirror I looked at Evadne Hinge. Doctor Evadne Hinge, in fact. I was glad to see her again.

Jonathan and I enjoyed a splendid meal that evening, after he had walked past me twice at our agreed rendezvous – eventually I had to introduce myself. Over dinner I gave him the lightest possible *aperçu* into my recent past.

"Family problems, Jonathan," I said, picking up an oyster with the implement provided. "I have been avoiding contact with them, for reasons I won't go into."

"Your mother, maybe?" asked the perceptive Jonathan, sipping his Chablis.

"Indeed. That and – other things."

He sat back in his chair. "Yes. I have had some dealings with your mother in the past, and she's not a lady to be trifled with. A character, certainly. But I confess she scares me a bit. A fine-looking woman, of course, and charming when she wants to be. You're very alike, you know. In looks, I mean – not – er..."

"No, I hope not, Jonathan, I hope not."

Mother and I alike? I was getting a bit tired of hearing this.

At the mention of her, I suddenly realised that my mother was now approaching forty. I wondered if age had mellowed her? I doubted it.

As Jonathan and I continued to chat over our coffee he asked me what my immediate plans were.

"I will be leaving Edinburgh tomorrow, Jonathan. Going home. At last."

Home? No, it had not been that since the hour Father died. But I was going back there anyway, however briefly. I had to face my mother for what I fervently hoped would be the final time.

"Eva," said Jonathan, "If you like, I can take a day off tomorrow and drive you there. It would be a pleasure."

"No, really, it's very kind of you…"

"It's absolutely no trouble at all. In fact I will enjoy seeing the place you grew up in. Dean Castle – my Dad mentioned it often. And I believe the Ayrshire countryside is beautiful – I've never actually been there. Marion, my wife, would enjoy the trip too. Allow us this pleasure?"

I acquiesced with some uncertainty. It would of course spare me the awkward train journey, and it might not be a bad idea to have some kind of support, just in case Mother proved to be in one of her less tractable moods.

* * * * *

Tuesday 12th July 1938.

Dean Castle.

Jonathan and his wife, Marion, an attractive (and natural) blonde, collected me from my hotel the following morning. The journey passed quickly and Marion and I chattered away to each other like old friends. It was explained to me that it was she, rather than her husband, who had taken on the task of tracking down the elusive Mary McGuire, and she, too, who had managed to persuade the old lady that, however painful recollections of her past might be, there was someone who was owed an explanation.

Thus it was on a blazing July afternoon that I arrived with my friends at the portals of 'Castle Hinge' for the first time in over two years.

Chapter Twelve
Home

The main house appeared to be deserted, although the French windows onto the terrace were open and the curtains swung in the gentle summer breeze. Cautiously, the three of us crossed the threshold into the lounge.

"Hello?" I called out. But there was no reply. It appeared the grand entrance I had envisaged was turning into something of a slinking intrusion.

"Wait here, Jonathan, Marion," I said. "I'll try the servants' quarters – there's bound to be someone there. Have a seat, shan't be long."

I pressed on into the hall and down the long passage to the kitchen. It too appeared to be empty. But through the window I could see Eileen Angus in the garden, pegging out some washing on the drying green. I opened the back door and called out to her.

"Miss Eva!" she cried, dropping a large bundle of sheets at her feet. "What a surprise! – I didn't know you were expected. The mistress said nothing about it." Calling over her shoulder – "John! Billy! Look who's here!" – she came towards me full of smiles, and threw her arms around me. "It's so lovely to see you again, Miss, and so unexpected! "

"Well, Mrs Angus, I just thought I'd look in and say 'hello', it wasn't planned."

Just at that moment both the Old and the Young Anguses appeared together from the direction of the kitchen garden.

"Good Heavens, Miss Eva, where did you spring from?" said Young Angus.

His father took up the refrain. "We had no idea you were getting out of hospital."

Out of hospital?

"Does the mistress know? And Miss Lavinia? They'll be so pleased. But your mother never said anything. Are you planning to surprise her?"

I was certainly planning to do that.

"Come away into the kitchen, dear, the kettle's on, we'll have a cup of tea," suggested Eileen. "We can have a good catch-up."

"Thank you, that will be lovely. And I have some friends with me – I'll call them in a minute." I followed the little group towards the house. "But – where *is* Mother?"

Eileen replied, "Oh, she's out at work, she'll be back later. But Miss Lavinia is around somewhere, with her wee friend. Have a cup of tea first, and then we'll find them and let them know the good news. I must say, you're looking wonderfully well. You'd never know you'd been so ill."

Ill?

Inside, I left them and went to call Jonathan and his wife to join us, and we all settled down in the cosy kitchen. From the preceding conversation, I had an inkling of the story Mother must have put about to account for my absence. I had apparently been in hospital with some mysterious complaint, that much was clear. More information percolated through during subsequent chat. I had suffered, it was said, from some kind of nervous breakdown and had been having treatment, details unspecified and prognosis uncertain. Very typically Mother, of course, the whole thing. I thought I had better introduce my friends.

"And this is my doctor, Doctor Bartington," I couldn't resist saying. "I owe him everything, you know. The man is a saint. And this is my private nurse, Nurse Hamstring – er – Hamilton."

Jonathan looked at first a little confused, as well he might. Marion, more adept, merely smiled and checked my pulse, with a quiet, "Mustn't over-exert ourselves on our first day, must we, dear?". Jonathan eventually caught her wink in his direction and then played up to his rôle manfully.

Over a strong cup of tea I was able to glean all the details. It seemed that the combination of my heavy workload, the strain of Father's death and the worry over Leicester's disappearance had finally caused me to have a complete collapse. My solicitous mother had made sure that I would have the best of care, and advised that visitors would not be permitted until I had recovered to some extent. I was in some kind of rest home, distant, precise location unspecified, and it was thought that it might be some considerable time before I was able to re-join the family. In the meantime, all must pray for me.

I had to smile at Mother's relentless ingenuity, and decided to play along for the time being. Even so, I was a little surprised – though I shouldn't have been, knowing my mother's talent for corroborative and convincing detail – to hear Mrs Angus comment, "And your lovely hair – how well it has grown back. You would never know. That must have been dreadful for you, having it all shaved off for the – well, you know – the electric thing."

Old Angus interrupted hastily. "Good heavens, Eileen, that's enough, I'm sure Miss Eva doesn't want to be reminded of such matters. Let us all just be thankful that she's recovered and is back with us where she belongs."

We enjoyed our tea and shortbread, and the conversation soon took a more general tone.

After we had finished, I said, "Mrs Angus, I must go and find Lavinia and tell her the good news. Will you do something for me? When is Mother generally in from work?"

"Oh, around seven, as a rule, Miss."

I knew from Lavinia's letters that Dougal was still here, performing his chauffeuring duties.

"Well, would it be possible to prepare a very special dinner for us this evening? If you get Dougal to drive you into Kilmarnock or wherever, to do some shopping? Nothing but the best. Lobster, venison, caviar – the very finest and most expensive you can buy. I will pay for it all – just let me know what it costs. This is a celebration – the prodigal's return, in fact."

"Indeed it is, Miss. Yes, of course – John, get hold of Dougie and let him know Miss Eva's wishes. You go with him, make sure he gets it right. Billy, finish pegging that washing out – I've got too much to do around the house. Miss Eva's room to make up, and – for the doctor here? – and Nurse Hamilton…?"

"Oh, yes," I said. I turned to Jonathan and Marion, "You will stay over, won't you, both of you, for the night?" I said.

"Oh, we wouldn't miss it for the world, would we, doctor? It'll be a pleasure," Marion smiled suavely. "Just the one room for the doctor and myself, Mrs Angus. We know each other *very* well."

Mrs Angus hesitated almost imperceptibly. "Certainly, yes, how very modern." Then, immediately ready for action, she disappeared off into the depths of the house, muttering. "Dear, dear, so much to do, but oh, what a treat. One room? Well, well… Oh, your mother will get such a surprise…"

Yes, I thought, she will, won't she?

* * * * *

I left the Bartingtons in the kitchen, and soon found Lavinia in the Italian garden, heads together with a boy I didn't recognise.

"Eva," she shrieked, bounding to her feet. "You're back! Oh frabjous day, calloo, callay," and she fell into my arms.

"I'm just passing through, really," I smiled after we had shared a warm sisterly embrace. "I won't be here long. Just needed to sort a few things out." I looked over. "And, may I ask, who is this young man?"

"This is Andrew Anderson. Andy, meet my wonderful sister, Doctor Evadne Hinge, otherwise the glamorous Miss Marina Montpellier of the variety theatre. But according to Mother, of course, patient X of some mental hospital somewhere."

The pleasant-looking young man shook my hand, looking understandably confused.

"How do you do, Miss, it's very nice to meet you. Lavinia has told me all about you."

"Not quite all, I hope." I smiled significantly in Lavinia's direction. "And call me 'Eva', please."

My sister was unstoppable. "Andy's my boyfriend, the one whose address I was using. Of course, Eva, as I wrote to you, I never for a minute swallowed that stupid story of Mother's. Not even before I saw you in Ayr. As if you, my sensible sister, would do anything so undignified as to have a mental breakdown. There's only one lunatic in this family…"

"She seems to have convinced the Anguses, however…"

"Yes, but they're not the sharpest knives in the box, are they? Dougal, of course, knew the truth, and it didn't take long for me to get it out of him. How you got away, Mother's tricks and schemes…"

I interrupted. "Yes, I was meaning to ask you – how is Dougal?"

"Just the same as usual, you know Dougal. Mother's dear Dougie. He's all right really, Dougal, when you get to know him."

"Still dancing to Mother's tune, no doubt?" I asked.

"I suppose so," said Lavinia. "Although these days it's sometimes hard to tell who is dancing to who's, if that makes sense. Anyway, he keeps an eye on her."

"And I hear she is working – how did that come about?"

"Well…" Lavinia took a breath. "Andy, I will see you later – got some serious chat to do with my big sister. You'll be here for dinner?"

Andy nodded. Lavinia linked her arm through mine and we strolled together in the warm afternoon sunlight.

"Well," she started, "you remember I told you that Max – Grandpa Max – finally started to recover from his stroke? After the car accident?"

"Yes. That was good news, the best."

"Not for Mother. But for McWhirter's, definitely. Mother had somehow managed to run the business into the ground. I'm not quite sure how. She may be peculiar, but she's not stupid. Anyway, gradually Grandpa Max regained almost his full health. Still a little shaky, from time to time, inclined to forget things now and then, but in general, back to his old self. And in a month or two he was well enough to take over the reins again. He managed to save the day, although I believe it was a close thing. We were completely penniless, Mother and I, but Max helped out with that until things improved."

"I see," I said. "So where is she working?"

"That's just it, Eva – for *McWhirter's*. Grandpa said that as she was going to inherit the lot one day, and had made such a mess of things, she'd better learn how to run the business properly. So he gave her a job. Something to do with sales. Sales manager, maybe? Anyway, the truth is, I think she is actually enjoying it. She has cut right down on the drink, she's into work every morning at nine, home by around seven. Quite the reformed character these days, Mother. But you will be able to judge for yourself later, won't you?"

"I suppose so," I replied. "I look forward to it, though I doubt if she will feel quite the same. Well – that is a surprise." Changing the subject, I said, "And who is this young Andy, then?"

My sister coloured slightly. "Well, Andy and I have been friends since we were ever so young, from our days at the village school. Now he's my boyfriend. I suppose."

I smiled. "You suppose? Are you not sure?"

She giggled. "Well, Eva, you know how it is. He thinks so, certainly. I haven't really decided yet. I'm only fourteen, remember."

I recalled vividly my own tussles with Finlay when I was fourteen.

"I hope you're being sensible, Lavinia. I mean…"

My sister roared with laughter. "Oh, I know what you mean, Eva. Don't worry. I assure you, I don't permit liberties. Now, if it was that delicious gentleman I saw you with in Ayr, I might be tempted. Whatever happened to *him*?"

McCarthy. "Not enough, Lavinia, not enough…"

I wondered, briefly. He might be anywhere. Or nowhere.

And my sister and I continued to chatter and exchange confidences for the rest of the afternoon.

* * * * *

"Come in, Mother, come in. Have a seat. We were just wondering what was keeping you, weren't we, Lavinia?"

Indeed, she *was* looking well. A tailored suit. Minimally made-up. Her hair in a becoming chignon. And business-like spectacles.

We sat down at the dinner table – Mother, Lavinia, myself, Jonathan and Marion, and young Andy, who was, Lavinia had explained, something of a permanent fixture currently.

Mother did not appear all that surprised to see me. If she was, she concealed it very well.

"I see. It's you, Mona. I was wondering how long it would take you to show your face. I thought it would be sooner – when was your birthday? Thursday? What kept you?"

"Ah yes, that. Medical matters, I'm afraid, Mother. You must remember how it is, signing oneself out of a doctor's care? The endless paperwork, the forms, the lectures, the medication? And I'm sure you remember Doctor Bartington? And Nurse Hamilton? What long chats you three must have shared about my condition, my treatment, my prospects."

I registered Lavinia's ill-concealed smile and young Andy's bemused look.

Mother raised her eyebrows. "I remember Jonathan, of course. But let's not play this silly game any longer, Mona. We all know the truth. All of us here, that is. But it has suited me to keep outsiders in the dark."

I had forgotten how shamelessly, quickly, and with what equanimity Mother would abandon her fabrications once they had ceased to serve her purposes.

"Very well, Mother. In that case let me introduce Jonathan's wife, Marion." Mother at first tried her *grande dame* routine on Marion, but realising quickly that it was not having at all the desired effect, soon abandoned it.

"In the meantime," I continued, "I suggest we all enjoy our dinner. Mrs Angus has gone to a lot of trouble, let's not waste it. Think of it as the condemned man's last meal, Mother. You and I are going to have a little chat later."

"Just as you like, Mona. You're in charge, it appears." And Mother commenced to eat with her accustomed hearty appetite as if this were the most normal evening in the world.

Certainly Mrs Angus had done us proud. Lobster in a delicious sauce, venison braised in red wine with juniper berries, a selection of Scottish cheeses, and the dessert known as 'Cranachan', a kind of syllabub made with raspberries, cream and whisky. I noticed that Mother drank only a glass or two of water as an accompaniment.

Conversation was inevitably a little stilted initially, but gradually assumed a more normal tone. Mother chatted to Jonathan and Marion amicably, and apart from occasionally rebuking Lavinia mildly on her table manners, seemed in a high good humour.

"And how is Grandpa Max, Mother?" I asked over the coffee. "I hear he is out of hospital and back in the saddle again?"

"Oh, Dad is just grand, Mona. Made a complete recovery, quite his old self. He and I are getting on really well these days. And we've not always, as you know."

"Yes, as you say. And Grandma?"

She put down her cup. "Well, there's something you'll *not* know, Mona. Believe it or not, she's very much improved. The hospital is even talking about maybe letting her out again some day. Not too soon, I hope." Mother laughed light-heartedly. "I doubt Dad could survive another of her wee accidents."

I thought I had misheard her. "What?"

Mother raised her eyebrows, reached for the coffeepot, and continued airily, "Who knows, Mona, who knows? More coffee, Marion?"

* * * * *

It was nine-thirty or thereabouts when Mother and I sat opposite one another in the little room she referred to as her study. She seemed relaxed and comfortable. Which was more than I was.

"I must say, you're looking well, Mona. Wherever you've been, you've certainly picked up a few tips on dress and grooming. You must have been spending time with people of some taste and distinction."

I briefly wondered what Mother would have made of the denizens of The Palace and they of her.

"So – what are your plans then?"

"I've not entirely decided as yet, Mother. I intend to buy a house somewhere nearby. Just somewhere small, for myself. Near enough to keep an eye on you, at least. After all, you're getting on, aren't you? Forty next year, isn't it?"

She smiled. "Yes indeed. Life begins then, don't they say that? Let's hope so. It's not been much of a life up till now."

How ridiculous. And how typical. I was understandably amused. "Don't be melodramatic, Mother. You've had a better life than most."

"Is that how you see it?" Again the quizzical little smile. "Strange, that. How little you know me. But I probably didn't make that easy, all things considered."

An off-road trip down memory lane was not on my agenda.

"You're right, Mother, you didn't. But never mind that, it's not relevant. I'm here to talk about Father."

She smiled and sighed.

"Oh yes, of course, always your father. He came first with you. Just like mine did with me."

And no, I thought, we're not going to be side-tracked onto the Life and Philosophy of Maureen.

I forestalled yet more general reminiscences. "What was all that rubbish you came out with about Father? His drugs, his mistress, all that nonsense. Why?"

Completely unembarrassed, she admitted, "Yes, it was nonsense, as you say. But you must understand, I was desperate."

'Desperate' suggested to me something mild, such as an urgent need to avail oneself of the facilities.

"Really? Desperate enough to try to blackmail me into a marriage with your own lover? The lover you were also blackmailing? The one who seems to be about the only person who actually cares about you, for some unfathomable reason? What circumstances, Mother, however *desperate*, could justify that?"

She held up her hand.

"If it's any consolation, Mona, I regret it. I regret lots of things. But I didn't know where to turn. I would have done anything, anything at all, to save the business."

Her typical, casual self-justification infuriated me. "So you would happily contemplate ruining my life simply to get your hands on some money? Blackmail is a crime, you know." '*Time for a few home truths*,' I thought. "Of course, criminal behaviour is something you are not unfamiliar with, as we know."

She lowered her head and looked at me over the top of her spectacles. "I was waiting for that one to come up, Mona. Maybe it's time you heard the full story instead of the odds and ends Morag has given you."

In spite of my urgent desire to get this scene over with, I decided to let her have her say.

"All right, Mother, let's hear it. But keep it short, I haven't got all night."

"Dear dear, ever in a rush. But don't worry, this won't take long."

She settled herself and sipped her coffee.

"Once upon a time…"

Why had I even allowed her to start? "Really, Mother, let's just have the facts."

She removed her glasses. "Bear with me, Mona, please." She resumed. "Once upon a time there was a family. A well-to-do family, respected and admired. Comfortably off too. They lived in Cambuslang, a nice little town, quiet and rural. There was a father, hard-working and successful, and a mother, a pillar of the community and the church, and two children, a boy and a girl. The boy was the elder by a couple of years. The little girl adored her brother – something you will understand, Mona – and he loved his little sister in equal measure. They went everywhere together and shared everything. Never was there a more contented and happy little family."

In spite of my impatience I was drawn in.

"Then something happened. The boy changed as he grew older. Oh, he loved his little sister and his parents no less, but something happened inside him. He realised he was different. Different from other boys, that is. He didn't feel able to discuss this with his family, it was too deep, too personal. And they were too close to notice this change in him. But others did. And they were often unkind. They called him nasty names, most of which he didn't understand. But it troubled him in spite of that. He was very unhappy indeed. His little sister knew he was unhappy but couldn't understand why. This made her unhappy too."

"Then, one night something terrible happened. Two men who didn't like her brother, because he was different, lay in wait for him. They attacked him, and beat him badly. He was seriously hurt. When the little sister heard about this, she stopped being unhappy and became angry. She knew where her father kept his rifle, so she took it and went to look for the men who had hurt her brother. She found one of them in the Post Office."

In spite of – or perhaps because of – her unusual narrative method, it was all incredibly vivid to me.

"I see, Mother. But you didn't..."

"Oh, I would have. But someone knocked the rifle from my hand just as I fired. He was hurt, but not killed. Fortunately, I suppose, although that was not what I thought at the time."

I considered Mother's story. I knew how mendacious she could be. But this had the ring of truth. There was none of her usual self-dramatising in it, she told the story plainly and simply. I asked myself how I might have acted in a similar situation, at fourteen. Would I not have done the same thing? No, indeed. I would have dug a concealed pit, trapped the miscreants, and let them slowly starve to death, while Leicester and I danced around the edge hurling rocks at them. But the end result would have been exactly the same. A bit messier, perhaps.

"Shall I go on?" Mother asked.

"Yes."

"Conan recovered, of course, and left home to join the Navy. I went to prison for two years, as you know. When Conan came back, things were never the same between us. It was like the past had cast a shadow over our relationship. And Dad never forgave either of us. That was the worst of all, in a way. I adored my father, just as you did yours. He barely spoke to me for years. I promised myself that one way or another I would regain his love and make him proud of me."

"Years went by. I married your father. Never did there seem to be an opportunity I could make use of. But when Dad had his accident, I saw my chance. I would run the business, and when he recovered – assuming he did – I would be able to present him with my success and prove that he had made a mistake in considering me of no account all those years ago."

A great deal about Mother was suddenly clear to me. I had never pictured her as a young girl – I think I somehow believed that she had sprung to life in all her glory, like Athena, fully armed, from the head of Zeus. I could imagine how I would have felt had my father not loved *me*.

"But things didn't work out with the business, Mother? You weren't able to make a success of it?" I felt a sudden twinge of sympathy for her, probably for the first time in my life.

Mother laughed bitterly. "I had no chance, Mona. What my dad didn't know was that your grandmother had been withdrawing huge sums from the business account. There was practically nothing left. Dad never bothered with the books much, he left that side of things to her. The business had always done well. Why would it not continue to do so? Orders were as large and as regular as ever. He thought he was rich."

Once again Mother gave her sour little laugh.

"But why did Grandma take all that money, Mother? What did she do with it? What did she buy with it?"

Mother smiled. "Buy? If only she had, one might have understood, in a way. But no, she bought *nothing*. Nothing at all. She gave it away. Every last penny. To her religious causes – missionaries in Africa, bibles for China, babies in India, Jehovah's Witnesses, Christian Scientists… You name it, she supported it."

"I see. So you decided you must have *my* money. Father's money, that is?"

"Yes, I did. If you married Dougal, we would have been able to raise a loan on your inheritance prospects and get the business out of trouble."

I had to interject. "But why didn't you simply explain the problem to me and ask *me* to do that. I would have helped."

"Really? Would you?" Mother looked sceptical. "I doubt it. You've always despised me, I know. Wouldn't you just have said, '*You've made the mess, mother, you can clear it up*'? I didn't trust you, Mona. Sorry, but that's the truth."

Was she right? Perhaps she was.

"I've never really trusted anyone. Not in a very long time," she went on.

"Not even Father?"

Mother smiled slightly. "Ah, yes. Your dear father. It all comes back to fathers, doesn't it?"

She lit a cigarette. "Yes, him I did trust. At the start anyway. He was so much older than me. Like a father in many ways. A substitute for my own father, maybe? No doubt that's what Mr Freud would say. And yes, at first I did trust him. We were happy in our odd way. Then you children came along and everything changed."

"What do you mean, changed?"

Mother paused for a moment.

"I'm not an intellectual, Mona. I never have been. As you yourself have pointed out on more than one occasion. Stupid, uneducated, ignorant. I've heard you use these words in reference to me many times. You think I didn't know what you and your father were sniggering about? Not in detail, perhaps, but the gist was clear."

I suddenly felt embarrassed and guilty. It was all too true.

"But your father, of course, *was* an intellectual. When it was just the two of us it didn't seem to matter. We were opposites, and they say that opposites attract. I was proud to be the wife of such a famous man, and he was delighted to have a wife with my looks and family connections. But after a few years, here were these two smart little mini-Hectors to add to the mix. Two little satellites revolving round the Great Luminary. As soon as you could talk, your father indulged you shamelessly. Leicester too, although *you* were his favourite, always. Gradually I became the outsider. Not a member of the club. Not Wanted On Voyage."

Suddenly my whole picture of our childhood and Mother's place in it seemed to shift. As in a shaken kaleidoscope, the pieces were the same, but the pattern was different.

She went on, "So – I had to make my own life. Find my own amusements. Leave you three to enjoy your exclusive little party."

I had to say something. Mother's voice had dropped, she seemed to have shrunk into herself, reliving the past.

"Mother. I had no idea. None at all. I thought *you* had chosen to give up your family, not the other way around."

"Well – I suppose it all depends how you look at it. Whose was the initial fault? Mine or your father's? In the end it made no difference. When Lavinia arrived, I thought, '*Here is my moment. Another chance. This one will be mine.*' And at first she was. For some time. But eventually, she too moved on."

"All children do, Mother," I said gently.

She continued as if I hadn't spoken. "So – I drank a lot, went out a lot, did other things I prefer not to go into. The family never needed me. But there were others who did. Or seemed to."

"But we *did* need you, Mother. We just didn't *know* we did."

"Maybe. Faults on both sides, as I seem to recall saying to you once, long ago."

"Yes." I smiled as I remembered the one time we had been joined in conspiracy. The Leicester disappearance. My smile faded as I remembered how that had turned out.

"Anyway," said Mother, stubbing out her cigarette, "It's all in the past. Now you know everything. Why I acted the way I did, said the things I said. I'm not proud of it, not now. But it's done. You're an adult now. We have to go forward. Whether it's together or separately… That's up to you."

I didn't know what to say. For the first time in my life, I wanted to give my mother a hug. But didn't quite dare.

Eventually, "You've given me a lot to think about, Mother. I can't make any decisions now. We'll talk again soon, I hope," I said, as I rose to leave.

Mother stood up too, and, oddly, shook my hand.

"Just as you like, Mona. But don't leave it too long, will you? I've another piece of news. I'm getting married again. Next month."

* * * * *

I didn't sleep much that night. Mother's revelations went round and round in my head. Could I believe her? I wanted to, that was certain. If all was as she had said, I could dimly understand her for the first time in my life. Yes, it was certainly the case that my father and I – and Leicester too, to a lesser extent – had been members of what we ourselves considered a privileged and favoured band. But had we excluded Mother intentionally? Or had she excluded *us*? Chicken and egg, I thought. I remembered my conversations with Dougal, and how he had given me an unexpected insight into the behaviour of my brother and myself all those years ago, a view of that period that had never struck me before. And his defence of Mother which I had so airily dismissed. Could I have been that self-absorbed? And was my view of Mother just another example of my own snobbish self-centredness? Was her vindictive and unpleasant behaviour in some measure the result of my own actions? And those of my father? Had we made her into what she became? I remembered the rare occasions when I had seen another side of Mother. Was *that* the real person, or just another mask she had contrived? Who knew?

There were no easy answers to these questions; at least none that I could formulate without much deeper reflection. I decided that for now the only thing was to let matters lie and wait.

* * * * *

Wednesday 13th July 1938.

Dean Castle.

I had naturally assumed that Mother's approaching nuptials involved Dougal. A final regularisation of a long-standing union. I mentioned this the next day, as we sat in the garden enjoying the balmy July sun. But once again she surprised me.

"No, no, Mona, God, you wouldn't wish that on the poor lad, surely? He's far too young for me. What is he now, twenty-two?"

That was about right, I supposed. But if he'd not been too young a couple of years ago, why was he now considered *hors concours*?

I thought it perhaps unwise to go into that question further.

"So, Mother, who is the lucky man?" If I intended some irony by the epithet, naturally Mother recognised none.

"Monty. Well, that's what I call him. In full, Manuel Esteban Montero. Mexican. Everyone at work calls him Montezuma, just a little joke. But to me, he's Monty."

"His name is Manuel? Then why not call him Manny?" I wondered.

She raised her eyebrows. "Good heavens, Mona – he's *Mexican*, not Jewish."

The fortunate bridegroom, it was explained, was an architect – wealthy, talented and handsome. Mother's order. He was currently working for Grandpa, designing and overseeing the construction of a new malting plant, or some such.

"I see. And how old is this Monty, then?"

"Oh, just a year or two younger than me," Mother prevaricated vaguely. "I'm not sure exactly. Thirty-seven, thirty-eight maybe."

Mother had more to say. "And I was wondering – how would you feel about playing the organ for the ceremony, Mona? I've always thought you play quite nicely, myself. Lavinia will be bridesmaid, naturally. And Dad will give me away."

"Well if he chooses to, he certainly knows all the facts." I couldn't resist.

"Naughty, Mona," Mother smiled roguishly. "I thought we'd agreed to leave all that in the past?"

I forbore to mention that I had agreed to nothing. Mother sailed on regardless.

"Your grandpa and I are the best of pals these days, as it happens. He's put me in charge of sales – you know, meeting up with the reps, entertaining new clients, finding new business openings. And it may surprise you to learn, Mona, your silly old mother is very good at it."

I knew quite well that entertaining gentlemen and getting them to agree to her plans was a field Mother had cultivated assiduously in the past. So it was not astonishing that she was making a success of it. But credit where it's due, I thought.

"So – what do you say?" she went on. "About the wedding, I mean?"

I hesitated. This was a situation that I had never, in my best or worst moments, considered I might have to deal with.

"Certainly, if it's what you want. But it will depend on the date. I have plans of my own."

"The sixth of August, a Saturday. Oh – say you will, Mona, for me."

The dewy-eyed expression and the wheedling tone were a little disconcerting. But what could I do?

"Yes, Mother. I will, since you seem to have your heart set on it."

"Good, good, that's all settled. And wait till you meet Monty. You'll be impressed. Just the kind of man I would want for you, one of these days." Her tone suddenly changed from the enthusiastic to the intimate. "Speaking of which, am I to understand that there's no-one in your life at the moment?"

But sharing girlish confidences with Mother was a step further than I had any intention of going. And the McCarthy matter, if raised, might provide all too much ammunition for future confrontations. I took a leaf from Mother's conversational textbook and didn't answer the question.

"Mother, I should tell you that I have projects of my own. I intend to take a holiday. A month, no more. Abroad, I'm not sure where. Italy, Austria, Switzerland perhaps. And I want to take Lavinia with me."

"What a splendid idea, Mona. Oh, she'll be thrilled, I've no doubt."

What? I had expected opposition. I had foreseen arguments about Lavinia's schooling being interrupted, her being too young, me being too irresponsible, and much more.

"And," Mother went on, decisively, "It will get her away from that wee Andy. They see too much of each other, in my opinion. Nice enough boy, but I don't trust him with Lavinia. Eyes too close together, probably got all sorts of nasty ideas in his head. *You* know what boys are like. That young horn-player chap who was all over you a few years ago, for example. What became of him? You've never said."

Mother gave me a worrying, conspiratorial smile. I wondered if Lavinia had possibly been rather more indiscreet with my correspondence than I had anticipated.

"Oh, that reminds me, Mona." She reached into her handbag. "These came for you while you were – away. From London, it seems. A friend, I suppose? A gentleman friend, by the sound of it?" Her tone was calculated to convey a helpful but disinterested ingenuousness. "Desperate to get in touch with you, at any rate. Not signed, so no idea who they were from. I would have forwarded them, naturally, if you had done me the kindness of letting me know where you were."

She drew out a small bundle of envelopes. Opened, I noticed.

She passed them to me, and I glanced briefly at the topmost. It was from Finlay, I would have recognised his writing anywhere. I realised that Mother knew exactly what the story behind them was, despite her assumed air of innocent ignorance.

"Did you have to open them Mother? Nose bothering you, was it?"

Her expression changed to a kind of helpless and bemused indignation. "Really, Mona! What else could I have done? They might have been something important. I suppose I *could* have forwarded them to the hospital…"

"No, stop, stop. You're losing my sympathy. Mother, there *was* no hospital, you're getting confused. Don't they say that the first thing you need to be a good liar is a good memory? You're slipping, it appears."

As usual when she was caught out, Mother didn't bother to answer. I tucked the letters into my pocket. I would read them later.

As if this scene were not already sufficiently surreal, the next thing she drew from her capacious handbag was a piece of knotted fabric.

"Crochet, Mother?" I could scarcely believe my eyes.

"Macramé, actually, Mona. I'm doing a table runner. An Aztec pattern. Anyway, to get back to what I was saying…. Monty and I are off to Mexico for the honeymoon. He's looking forward so much to introducing me to his parents – he hasn't told them yet. I can't wait – can you imagine their surprise? *¡Ay, caramba!*" She gestured flamboyantly as though manipulating an invisible fan.

I could indeed imagine how *la familia Montero* might react to Monty's child bride. With a '*Madre di Dios!*', more likely.

My mother commenced a series of intricate moves on her table runner.

"Whom do you plan to invite to the wedding, Mother? Will this be a big affair, or just a family thing?"

"Oh, a big 'do', no question. I want everyone from work there, all the locals, the servants, maybe one or two of your father's musical friends, anyone you want to ask…"

I foresaw complications. "Hang on a minute, Mother. Might it not be wise to leave out one or two of the locals? Those who have – er – perhaps known you too well in the past? Ronnie and Janet McKenzie, for example?"

"Och, Mona, never you worry your head about the McKenzies or any of their set." She smiled grimly in the old familiar manner. "I know far too much about that lot for them to risk opening their mouths."

Some things, I thought, never change. Mother continued to knot industriously. After a few moments, she laid her work to one side.

"Now, Mona." She was in business mode suddenly. "I need your advice. About clothes, I mean. I couldn't help but notice how you've smartened yourself up. And you've filled out, too – it's clear to anyone where you get your figure from. Now – I was thinking of something neutral for the wedding dress. Ivory or cream, maybe. Écru, perhaps? Not sure these washed-out colours suit me, though. Be honest now, Mona, do you think I'm too old for white?"

Chapter Thirteen
And Away

As soon as I was alone, I made my way into the garden, and took out the bundle of letters Mother had passed on to me. As I had surmised, all four were from Finlay. The first sent merely told me that he was settling down in London, was in the process of looking for a small flat for us both, and that he missed me terribly. Would I write soon?

The second wondered at my silence – perhaps *his* had gone astray? Anyway, he had found a suitable one-bedroom apartment in Pimlico, would I *please* write soon and let him know I was well, and when I expected to join him. He loved me very much, and couldn't wait to see me and introduce me to the sights of London.

The course of the third and fourth were predictable. Obviously, he had never received my own letter. His gradual disillusionment was clear. The tone of the third was anxious, that of the fourth bitter.

It was all too sad. I could read clearly his hurt. It upset me to think of the impression I had inadvertently created. I had loved him, certainly, at one time. I could only hope he would be happy in his new life. With his new wife. And baby by now, I supposed…

* * * * *

Thursday 14th July 1938.

Dean Castle.

I liked Monty from the very first, although Mother was surprisingly nervous about introducing us. On reflection I can understand her qualms. Had I chosen to, I could have given her intended a rather illuminating insight into the antecedents of his bride-to-be. Jonathan and Marion had returned to Edinburgh, and Mother and I were in my bedroom, where she was helping me to unpack, when she first broached the subject.

"You'll not say anything, Mona, will you? I mean, not anything that… well, let me put it this way, there are things in the past that Monty doesn't need to know about, aren't there? I mean – I suppose you have every reason, if you wanted to be difficult…"

She was actually at a loss for once. I took advantage of this unaccustomed hesitancy.

"Difficult, Mother? Me? What do you mean?" I asked innocently, continuing to empty my suitcases.

Mother sat down on the edge of the bed. "Come on, Mona, you know exactly what I mean. The wee misunderstandings that came between us for a while." Her tone was half exasperated and half wheedling.

I smiled as if in sudden comprehension. "Ah, I see – you mean the lying, the drinking, the men, the blackmail, the Dougal business – that sort of thing?"

She was in a corner, and she knew it. Not that that stopped her trying to find an escape route. She attempted a deprecating and light-hearted tone. "Well, if you insist on sensationalising matters, and forcing me to be frank, yes, that *is* what I mean."

A sudden inspiration struck. I turned to her.

"I'll tell you what, Mother, let's make a little deal, shall we?"

She was immediately suspicious, "A deal? What kind of a deal?"

I opened the wardrobe and began hanging my clothes away. We had agreed that I would remain at the castle until after the wedding had taken place.

"Oh, a very simple deal. Here it is. I don't say anything at all that could embarrass you in front of Monty. And in return, you stop immediately calling me 'Mona' and use my proper name – 'Evadne' – can you manage that, do you think?"

Amazingly, she hesitated.

"Well – I suppose I could try…"

I closed the wardrobe door firmly after placing my empty suitcase inside it, and turned to face her.

"No, Mother, you won't *try*. Let me make it easy for you. Keep this in mind. For every 'Mona' you utter, I spill the beans about one of your escapades. I have ammunition enough to last me a very long time, as you know."

She appeared to consider for a moment. She tried a final wriggle.

"This is blackmail, Mona."

I nodded agreeably. "Yes, mother, so it is. I wonder where I picked that up from? Oh – and you just made your first slip-up. Now, let me see…."

Mother rose from the bed. "Oh, very well, *Evadne*. It feels as if I'm talking to a stranger! I will try, honestly I will. But I might make the odd mistake, by accident, so you mustn't be *too* harsh."

"OK. Try 'Eva', if that's easier."

"Yes, *Eva* – well, as I say I'll try."

I sighed. "They say God loves a trier, Mother." I supposed this was about the best I could hope for. "Now – when are we to meet this prodigy?"

* * * * *

It had been arranged that Monty would have dinner with us that evening. I managed to persuade Lavinia that *her* suggestion, that we all greet him at the castle entrance, dressed in sombreros, and singing *La Paloma* – though it was not without merit – might be best left until we knew him better. I didn't want the man to feel uncomfortable, and reminded my sister that, since he was doing us the unimaginable favour of taking Mother off our hands, nothing must be allowed to discourage or alienate him.

We dined *à la Mexicaine*. And he was charming. I don't know what I had expected – maybe a horse blanket and an Emiliano Zapata[1] moustache – but Monty turned out to be more American than anything else.

"My father is Mexican," he explained, "He was a diplomat, now retired, but my mother is from Albuquerque. I was born in Tijuana, but was educated in the States, so I'm pretty much a Yank."

In spite of this, Mother insisted on slipping the odd Spanish expression into her conversation. She must have bought a phrase book, I thought.

"*Otra enchilada, querido*?"

Monty indulgently responded in kind.

"*Sí, gracias, mi pelirrojita*," as their hands met over the bowl of *salsa*.

I caught Lavinia's eye, and looked down before we disgraced ourselves.

A handsome man. Not quite as tall as Mother, but with an imposing presence. Soft brown eyes and an engaging smile, both very Latin; beautiful teeth, no doubt American; and a sun-tanned complexion. And patently nowhere near the age she had claimed for him.

Quite unexpectedly, Mother herself provided the opening.

"I had forgotten to mention it, girls, but it will be Monty's birthday, *su cumpleaños*, next month. The same day as the wedding. A double celebration," she remarked with a girlish smile in his direction.

"Really, Monty? How lovely. And how old will you be?" Lavinia asked.

"Thirty," said Monty, and, "Don't be rude, Lavinia," said Mother, simultaneously.

"*No*, Monty!" I remarked, as I helped myself to some delicious *guacamole*. "You don't look that old."

1 Emiliano Zapata – leader of the Mexican revolution of 1910, later immortalised in the 1952 film 'Viva Zapata'.

"Please, *Eva*! Don't embarrass the man!"

"Oh, I don't mind, Maureen." He smiled, and gazed soulfully into her eyes. "It's knowing you that has made me young."

"What a pity that doesn't work both ways," Lavinia muttered into her *frijoles refritos*.

* * * * *

"So what do you think of him?" I asked my sister later that evening.

"Oh, I think he's just lovely, Eva. Don't you?"

"Yes, I do. I wonder what he sees in her, though?" Young Monty certainly appeared to be besotted. Mother had been looking well. And in truth, the ten-year age gap wasn't nearly as blatantly obvious as my sister and I had implied.

Lavinia paused. "Well, she's the boss's daughter, isn't she? And he isn't to know how near the edge the business is. Or was."

I laughed. "Lavinia, don't be so cynical, please! According to Mother, he's from a wealthy background, anyway."

Lavinia frowned slightly. "Yes. Or so he's *told* her."

"No." Possible, but unlikely, I decided. "Trust me, Lavinia. I know Mother. She will have had his family thoroughly checked out. Whatever else she may be, our mother is no-one's fool."

* * * * *

August 1938.

Dean Castle.

The wedding day dawned dull and overcast, but extremely close. Luckily, by the afternoon, the clouds had disappeared and the sun shone from a perfect blue sky.

I had managed to persuade Mother that, no, white was hardly the appropriate choice for a woman of her years and marital history. She briefly considered black ('*Well, I'm officially a widow, of course*') but that notion, too, I managed to head off. Eventually we settled on a becoming apricot silk, and the cliché 'radiant' actually described her appearance pretty well. Monty looked dashing in his wedding apparel, and Lavinia had chosen an outfit in the same shade as Mother's. For myself I had picked out a pale *eau de nil* with a matching hat, while Grandpa Max, whom I had not seen in a very long time, was resplendent in his pearl-grey morning suit. I had neglected to ask who was going to act as 'best man', and was not a little astonished to see Dougal McDougal, in full Highland dress, playing the rôle as to the manner born, and with apparent enthusiasm.

I was able to survey everything clearly from my eyrie in the organ loft. The ceremony went off smoothly (although I was overcome by a well-nigh irresistible urge to contribute at the 'if any person here present' bit) and my mother left the church as Señora Montero, or 'Mrs Monty', as she referred to herself. She had engaged extra help for the occasion, and the reception was held in the Castle grounds, where a huge throng enjoyed the splendid supper prepared by Mrs Angus, and a considerable amount of the family beverage was consumed. I threw my arms round dear Grandpa Max, and we had a long chat; although it was a little disconcerting when almost the first thing he asked me was how I was doing, now that my long illness was past. '*Damn Mother*!' I thought, '*Why does she always leave these ends dangling, instead of tidying up after herself*?' But I was able to wriggle out of the situation by claiming that I was now very well, and preferred not to discuss what had been a difficult and unhappy period in my life.

"I perfectly understand, dear, perfectly," he said. "After all, I should – I'm still recovering myself."

"And how is Grandma?" I went on. "Mother mentioned that there is a good chance that she will be – er – re-joining us some time soon."

"Over my dead body, Eva!" said Max, shaking his head. "And I dare say that's how she would prefer it. No, I doubt your grandmother will be seeing the light of liberty for some considerable time, if ever. And if she does, it will be a long way from wherever I am. But I can't see it happening, myself. She's completely batty, you know. Always was, in fact."

Oh dear. It looked as though Mother's bizarre conjecture might have some basis in fact. I decided to let the matter lie.

Max linked his arm through mine, and we surveyed the happy scene.

"Not married yourself yet, Eva? What's keeping you?" he continued, smiling. "It can't be a lack of offers surely?"

I laughed. "No indeed, Grandpa. Don't tell Mother, but I have actually been proposed to three times. Once by a criminal, once by a comedian and once by a *corniste*."

"No! – three times? Just never the right man, then?"

"Who knows, Grandpa? I certainly didn't think so at the time."

He squeezed my arm. "And you were no doubt right, Eva. You've plenty of time for that. And trust me, dear, marriage is not necessarily the great institution it's made out to be."

And with that he excused himself and wandered off.

I eventually found a quiet corner near the little chapel where my brother and I had played together so many years ago. I sat down in a sunny spot, on some steps, and sipped my champagne. In some ways it felt as if I had never been away. Very little had changed. There was the old swing over the stream where Leicester had almost drowned me, encouraging me to swing out further and further over the water, until the rope broke. There was the paddock where my little mare, Nellie, had been kept. Nellie had to be about twelve by now, but she still ambled round happily with one or other of the local children on her back if she was in the mood. She had got fat, I had noticed. Over in the far corner there grew a patch of the nettles which I had so unkindly encouraged Dougal to gather and push down his trousers. The sun was hot, and I began to drowse. At any moment, I thought, I might hear Leicester calling me… *"Eva, where are you?..."*

"Ah, there you are, Eva. I wondered where you had disappeared to."

I sat up. "Oh – hello, Dougal. Sorry – I was nodding. It's very warm."

"Yes, isn't it? Great day for the wedding. Mind if I join you?"

"No, sit down."

I was oddly pleased to see him, handsome in his kilt. We had not had the opportunity for a chat since my return. It would be nice to share a moment with someone else who remembered those childhood days, albeit with rather different emotions.

"How are you, Dougal?" I asked.

He sprawled beside me, after dusting the steps fastidiously with his handkerchief, which was more than I had bothered to do. "I'm just grand, Eva, really well. And yourself?"

Looking at him, I couldn't help but notice how totally suited his physical appearance was to the kilt.

"If I'm honest, I'm not sure, Dougal." I shrugged, and took another sip. "Oh, I'm fine, really. It's just strange being back again."

He stared at me intently. "Yes, I can imagine. After the last time you were here."

"Yes. But it's not just that Dougal. So many memories. Happy memories, sad memories. Both at the same time, even."

He took out a cigarette and lit it. "I know what you mean."

We lapsed into a companionable silence.

After a moment or two I said, "By the way – I was surprised to see *you* as best man. Do you know Monty well?"

"Hardly at all," he admitted. "But he doesn't have many friends over here, it seems. It was Maureen's idea." He raised his eyebrows quizzically. "Which won't astonish you, I dare say?"

I smiled. "No, by no means. So – the best man thing – a sort of consolation prize, was it, Dougal?"

He laughed heartily and unaffectedly. "For her not marrying me, do you mean? Not in the least. I would *never* marry your mother, even supposing she had suggested it. I'd have run a mile. Good God, talk about a life of servitude! That laddie's got a hard road ahead of him with Maureen at his side, don't you think?"

I giggled. "Yes, you're right. It was just that – I thought you cared for her."

He pondered. "I did. And I do. But *marry* her?" He shook his head. "I was there for her when she needed someone. And she for me, though not in the same way. She's happy now – at least for the moment. I wish her luck. Him too – he'll need it!"

He drew on his cigarette and leaned back.

"And what about you, Dougal. What are your plans?"

"Oh, nothing special. Your mother has asked me to stay on here to keep an eye on the place. The Anguses too. Apparently she intends to divide her time between here and Monty's place, Mexico, or wherever it is. It will be nice and peaceful here with her gone. A bit duller maybe…" He laughed loudly as he stubbed out his cigarette, and then continued in a more intimate tone.

"I was wondering, Eva – it's none of my business, of course, but – did you ever make it to London? That was your intention, as I recall."

I looked away, remembering the night I had fled from him – more than two years ago now.

"No, Dougal, I didn't. My plans changed." I thought it best to keep the details of that part of my story to myself.

"I see," he mused. "And" – he hesitated – "the boy friend? What became of that?"

"These plans changed too." I paused. "What about yourself, Dougal? Anyone in your life at the moment?"

He smiled. "Oh well, maybe… Nothing serious though. I'm only a lad, Eva. Twenty-two, just. No plans to settle down. I may never get married, you know. Don't like the look of it from what I've seen."

I had to agree. He stood up.

"But," he went on, "I *am* planning a wee holiday. Don't know where yet. Maybe drive up north and see Dad. Maybe try abroad, who knows? I've got the use of Maureen's car. The world's my oyster."

"I'm planning a holiday, too," I said. "But *I've* got it all worked out – you know me, Dougal. And I'm taking Lavinia with me. Italy. Austria, maybe."

He helped me to my feet, and used his handkerchief to wipe the dust from the back of my dress. An oddly intimate gesture.

"No! Really? Sounds wonderful. Tell me all about it!"

I slipped my arm through his, and we made our way back, chatting together, towards the crowd on the lawn.

* * * * *

Everyone, it seemed, was there. Dougal and I shared a few reminiscences with Effie Burns, my old music teacher, who, arm in arm with her friend Miss Hodgetts, was sauntering around dispensing wisdom and reviewing her memories of her long association with the family. Mr Jones the chemist (Aloysius, or maybe his son) gave me a friendly wave from the refreshment tent. Jonathan Bartington and Marion, along with Jonathan's father, James, offered their congratulations to Mother, who beamed graciously on all. Monty looked as proud as possible of his new wife, and made me promise I would visit them in Acapulco or Cancún one of these days. Everyone seemed to be in a happy and mellow mood. The sun shone. Lavinia danced with young Andy, he a little self-consciously, she gracefully and with remarkable assurance. '*She would have done far better than me,*' I thought, '*as a Betty Barnard Beauty.*'

But rounding a corner with Dougal, I almost ran full-tilt into a small knot of locals, in time to overhear Janet McKenzie holding forth to a couple of her cronies.

"...and of course, the grandmother is locked away in a mental home. Completely round the bend, or so I hear. That's where the Eva one gets it from. Bad blood. They've just let *her* out from some institution or other, a nervous breakdown or some such nonsense. The whole family's peculiar. And as for the blushing bride – oh aye, there are stories I could tell you about her. Let's just say she's well past the blushing stage. Oh yes, she's put herself about and no mistake. She drinks, of course, that's an old story. But her morals! Off with this one or that one, up to God knows what. And all the while, the poor old husband – the music chappie – the first husband, that is – had no idea what was going on. Now him – he was a nice man. Didn't deserve that sort of treatment. But apart from him... Oh, and there's a brother too – or there *was*..."

I interrupted, smiling graciously.

"Good afternoon, Janet, so pleased you could be here. Have you all had enough to eat and drink? Delightful weather, isn't it? So lucky for Mother." I let go of Dougal's arm and eased my way into the middle of the group.

"Oh – good afternoon, Miss Eva, I was just saying..."

"Yes, Janet, I heard what you were saying." Although furious, I affected a light-hearted laugh. "You were discussing my mad family, isn't that right?"

Janet tittered nervously, "No, no, you misunderstood, Miss. I was just bringing Susan and Doris here up to date – you know, explaining who everyone was, that sort of thing…" She trailed off into inaudibility.

"Yes, I understand, of course, Janet." I turned to her. "And tell me – have you also given them the latest on your *own* family history? Oh, by the way, how is your little – what shall I call him? – step-son? No, that's not right. Wee Hector, at any rate?"

Janet's brow corrugated. "Who?"

"Ah," I went on, with a smile, "I see you haven't. Allow me, please." I turned to the rest of the company. "Susan, Doris, what wonderful news. You don't know, obviously, that Janet has a new addition to the family. And at her age too – isn't that amazing?"

The two in question looked baffled and stared at Janet. As well they might.

"No, no, don't misunderstand me," I continued. "*That* would indeed be a medical miracle! Sorry, Janet, it's not *your* son, of course not. It's *Ronnie's* son. The one he had with young Jeannie – you all remember Jeannie Dunt, surely?"

"Oh, yes, of course," chorused Susan and Doris.

"Jeannie?" exclaimed Janet, aghast.

"Yes, yes, Janet, Jeannie. Do keep up, please. And don't interrupt. I can see that Sylvia and Dolly – sorry, Susan and Doris – can't wait to hear the rest."

Indeed, they were hanging on my every word.

"You see, ladies, it seems that Ronnie – oh, hello, Ronnie, I didn't notice you there – it must be useful for a philanderer to look so insignificant. Anyway, Ronnie here, it appears, was getting rather fed up with harrowing the same old furrow, the lovely Janet, and decided to do a bit of ploughing in a different field. Not exactly virgin territory, by all accounts, but no doubt a pleasant change from turning over the old home sod – nothing personal, Janet. Anyway to keep it brief, the unexpected result was Wee Hector – named after my dear father, as it happens – a lovely little boy. You must be so proud, Janet, and you too, Ronnie. Although I hear from his mother that you are a bit sparing with the maintenance payments, not to mention the visits."

The look on Janet's face warmed my heart.

"Oh – didn't you know, Janet? Boys and their secrets, eh? Anyway," I smiled, "I can't stop, so much to do today. But I'm delighted to be the first to share the glad tidings with you all. Spread the word, won't you, Susan? You too, Doris?"

I nudged Dougal, and we strolled off together.

After we rounded the corner, he had to stop, holding his sides with laughter.

"Eva – has anyone ever told you how like your mother you can be?"

"Only too often, Dougal, I'm afraid." And we each collapsed against the other in uncontrollable merriment.

* * * * *

When I told Lavinia that we were off together on holiday, I thought she would burst with excitement.

"No! Eva, really? You're going to take me on holiday with you? When do we leave? Where are we going? Oh, I'll need some new clothes, new shoes…"

"Well you can afford them now, can't you?" I smiled. "You must have received a little present in the post, surely?"

Lavinia looked embarrassed. "Oh my God! Of course I did – and – I forgot to say 'thank you'! Eva, how could I, forgive me. I meant to, but it just went out of my head. There's been so much happening round here recently."

Indeed there had. Mother, a second Cortés, had embarked on the conquest of Mexico some days earlier. I had been spending the time looking at properties in the area. Dougal was happy to drive me wherever I wanted to go, and I thought I might have found just the place that would suit me. The little two-up, two-down cottage was situated in the tiny village of Moscow[1], only a short distance from Dean Castle. I wasn't sure if it was the property itself which allured me most, or the idea of living in a place called Moscow. I had practically made up my mind to go ahead with the purchase. The house would need a lot of work, but I planned to have this carried out while my sister and I enjoyed our continental trip.

"Now, Lavinia, I was thinking of visiting Italy first. Would you like that?"

"Would I like that? *La Bella Italia* – do you have to ask? And where next?"

"I had thought perhaps Vienna, but with all the problems there recently, I'm not sure[2]. Germany is, I suppose, not a good choice either these days. Spain, maybe? Oh, no, they're having a civil war or some such there at the moment, I believe. We'll have to make some enquiries. But we must be back in London by the end of September at the latest. You know they're presenting Father's *Lysistrata* at the Royal Opera House – a world première?"

"Oh yes, I'd heard – and I understand that we will be invited as honoured guests. How splendid. Really, I don't mind where we go, Eva. Oh, we will have a wonderful time!"

I had been giving our holiday lots of thought. It had come home to me that perhaps, with matters in Europe being somewhat unsettled, two young ladies travelling alone might benefit from some sort of chaperone, perhaps someone who drove. I broached the idea to my sister.

---

1 Moscow, East Ayrshire, about 4 miles from Kilmarnock. Population circa. 200.

2 The annexation of Austria by Nazi Germany had taken place a few months earlier.

"Lavinia, I wonder – would you mind terribly if I suggested to Dougal that he come with us? I know he is planning a holiday himself, and I bet he would jump at the chance. He actually mentioned to me…"

My sister smirked knowingly. "Now, why am I not surprised, Eva? Of course I *have* noticed how friendly you two have been recently, but I hadn't realised…"

I could feel myself blushing. "Don't be silly, Lavinia, it's nothing like that. I just thought it might be better for us to have a man around, just in case… well…"

"Yes, of course, Eva, a man, just in case."

"He drives, and I mean, that might be useful…"

"Yes, of course he does. Very useful. Potentially. What a good idea. He's a lovely driver." She paused. "No other reason, then, for your suggestion?"

"No, of course not… Stop it, Lavinia!

But there was no stopping her.

"Of course not, as you say. Well, personally, I shall be delighted to have Dougie around. I like him. Just as long as you two don't keep disappearing off and leaving me on my own. Maybe in some sleazy bar…"

My sister had the cheek to look hopeful.

"There's no chance of that, Lavinia, I assure you," I said firmly. "None at all. So don't get your hopes up."

"No, sister, of course not," she said, looking down demurely. I was unimpressed by this sudden assumed meekness. There was a touch of Mother in it.

"Anyway," she went on, "You'd better talk to Dougie about it. He may have other plans, you never know."

Indeed he might. I needed to speak to him right away.

* * * * *

His reaction surprised me a little. I had imagined he would be astonished by the invitation. But on the contrary…

"I was wondering if I should suggest it to you, myself. I've been thinking about it. You're what, eighteen? And Lavinia? – fourteen?"

"Yes, that's right."

He smiled. "Hardly enough to make one sensible adult between you. Yes, I think it would be best if you had someone more mature along on the trip."

"Hang on! You're only twenty-two!" I interposed.

He grinned. "Maybe, but I'm old beyond my years. And you know what these Italians can be like…"

I had to laugh.

"No, I don't, Dougal." The only Italian I had ever known even slightly was the ice-cream man who had delivered occasionally at The Palace. "But I have a suspicion that Lavinia intends to find out."

We were sitting in his cottage, sipping the delicious home-made lemonade that the remarkably domesticated Dougal had prepared.

"Yes," he mused. "I bet she does. Terrible age, fourteen. You'll remember what I was like at fourteen, I'm sure?"

I had a sudden vision of the adolescent Dougal McDougal and his ever ill-fastened trousers…

He saw my blush and laughed.

"God, what a little swine I was, eh? One thing on my mind. I'm amazed you didn't hit me with something, Eva, I deserved it!"

I simply ignored this. Mother's trick. I returned to my topic.

"We were thinking how useful it would be that you drive. Maybe we can find a car from somewhere and do a bit of touring? What do you think?"

He laughed again. "I think you want to change the subject, that's what I think. But I see. I'm invited along as chauffeur to you two ladies, is that it? Not as a member of the party. More the hired help?"

I wasn't sure if his expression of disdain was sincere or not.

"Oh Dougal *no*! I just thought… There's no need. I'm sure there are plenty of trains. Forget I mentioned it, I'm sorry."

"Eva, Eva – don't you know when I'm joking? You'll have to get to know me better. Of course I will drive. If we can find a car, that is. Even give you some lessons, if you like."

I wasn't sure about that. I had no skill with mechanical things except for pianos.

"One other thing, Dougal. This is my treat. I will pay for everything, I insist."

This time he was genuinely offended. "Indeed you will *not*. Then I *would* feel like a servant. The rôle of the kept man is not one I relish playing." He suddenly grinned. "Not these days, anyway." His tone became serious. "No, Eva, I won't hear of it. I'm not short of money, so we will split everything down the middle, if you don't mind."

"I don't mind at all, Dougal. Just as you say. Oh, I'm so glad you're coming with us."

"Me too. More lemonade, Eva?"

* * * * *

I signed the contract for the purchase of my little cottage on the 10th of August, and from that day on I seemed never to have a free moment to myself. There was furniture to buy, tradesmen to engage, décor to decide on. On top of this, preparations for our holiday occupied a lot of my time – booking tickets, arranging hotels, shopping for suitable clothes. Then, almost at the very last minute, we realised that none of us actually possessed a passport, so *that* brought on a narrowly averted crisis. Dougal was a godsend, driving me here and there to arrange matters, while my sister was absolutely no help at all. Bless her, all she could think about was whether she had enough clothes of the right type, should she pack bathing wear, was it likely to be very warm, or very cold, or very wet…

I had suggested that she might invite young Andy, her friend, to join us on *le nostre vacanze*, but she was decidedly of the opinion that this was not a good idea. I was aware from our conversations that she had no very strong feelings for him, other than a firm friendship, but I had nevertheless wondered if it might be fun for her to have someone of her own age along on the trip. Her response was tactful, but, I suspected, rather calculating…

"Well, imagine the scene, if you will, Eva. Me and Andy, you and Dougal. We would look like two couples. And you wouldn't want that, would you? Heavens, they might even try to put us in double rooms! Or worse, what if they saw us as a *family*? Mum and Dad and two children?"

"Lavinia," I snorted, "Even on my worst days, I could hardly be taken for your *mother*."

She grinned conspiratorially. "No, of course not. But you could be a second wife, Dougal a recent widower, we your two step-children…"

In spite of myself, I had to laugh. "Stop it Lavinia – Dougal is *twenty-two*."

She remained irrepressible. "Yes, but he's very mature, don't you think? And the Italians marry young, I believe. Yes, I think the scenario is quite possible. And you wouldn't want to be forced to share a room with Dougal, Eva, would you? I can imagine how embarrassing you would find that." Her tone became studiedly casual. "Yes – very *mature*, our Dougie." And then, slyly – "But of course, you *like* 'mature', don't you Eva? How old was that chap you were seeing in Glasgow? About thirty, maybe?"

"Lavinia," I said firmly, "I don't want to hear any more of your little hints and innuendoes. One more – just *one* – and I may decide to cancel your ticket!"

My sister had me there. "But you can't do that, can you, Eva? Imagine the scandal – you and Dougie off on holiday together without benefit of clergy! Think what the McKenzies could make of *that*!"

"Don't you be *entirely* sure that I wouldn't risk it, Lavinia…"

* * * * *

But at last everything was finalised. We would leave by train from Glasgow and travel to Southampton, where we would board ship for Italy. And then onward and upward to the land of Verdi, Bellini, Rossini. And Mussolini.

Postlude

August 1938, Positano, Italy

Midnight. Dougal and I stood on the terrace of the little cliff-top villa we had found, our arms round each other. A bottle of vintage Barolo stood on the stone table behind us, and as we gazed out at the reflection of the stars glittering on the sea off the Amalfi coast, I began to relax. How many more scrapes was my sister going to get herself into on this holiday? Luckily, Dougal had been able to see off the importunate young man without too much difficulty – the sight of an enraged Dougal would have struck terror into stouter hearts than that which beat in the breast of our Italian waiter. Lavinia had been firmly lectured, and packed off to bed. For a wonder, Dougal and I had an evening to ourselves, and meant to make the most of it.

'Maureen' stood parked just below us. The little car we had bought for the equivalent of around two pounds (hiring a vehicle seemed to be an impossibility in rural Italy) had been thus named by Dougal, due to its absolute determination to go where *it* wanted to go, and not where *we* wanted it to go. Luckily, Dougal seemed to have mastered it's eccentricities and was able to subdue it most of the time.

"Just as you did with the original," I couldn't resist remarking, with a smile. Although for how much longer 'Maureen' would continue to transport us safely and successfully was, according to Dougal, a matter of some uncertainty. We didn't care…

The first part of our Italian trip had not been short of incident. We had docked in a baking hot Naples ten days earlier, and had enjoyed a splendid evening at the famed San Carlo Opera House, where they were presenting *Madama Butterfly*. We had relished several wonderful meals, including my favourite – a delicious *spaghetti marinara* – in a busy and popular local *trattoria*. But oh! the crowds and the noise! We had decided we needed to find somewhere quieter.

'Maureen' had somewhat reluctantly carried us up the west coast to the Amalfi region, and we had been incredibly fortunate to alight on 'Le Fragole', a small stone-built cottage perched high on the cliffs above Positano. A cosy *salone*, tiny *cucina*, and, best of all, a large and shady terrace. Two bedrooms. One for Lavinia and me, and another for Dougal. Well, that had been the original plan…

We had been here almost a week, and planned to move on to Florence, Rome, Ravenna and Parma in a few days' time. I was particularly anxious to visit the last, as I had learned that a very young English soprano, who had been causing something of a furore throughout the Italian peninsula, was scheduled to appear in *Tosca* at the Teatro Regio. A curious name, I seemed to remember… Hilda Bracket…

Parma, I had been told, was a beautiful city.

'*And if the voice is disappointing*,' I thought, '*at least we'll enjoy the ham…*'

I was to discover that the unknown soprano usually supplied generous helpings of both.

As I mused on our future plans, my beloved, it appeared, was in a light-hearted and amorous mood.

"Guarda. Dorme ogni cosa…" he sang softly in his light and pleasant tenor.

"Ah! dolce notte! quante stelle!…" I responded.

Dougal continued the lines of the famous duet: *"Vieni! Vieni!"* [1]

And suddenly I felt tears trickling down my face.

His arms went round me and he pressed me to his chest.

"What's wrong, sweetheart, what's the matter?" he murmured in my ear. He took hold of my shoulders firmly, and regarded me at arms' length. "Why are you crying? What's wrong?"

"Nothing. Nothing at all."

I kissed him on the lips, long and lingering.

As I withdrew, I smiled. "Nothing's wrong, Dougal. For once, maybe for the first time, everything is right."

He wiped away my silly tears with the tip of his finger. "Of course it is. You're where you belong. I love you. I've always loved you. I always will."

"And I love you, Dougal. So much. But I must be stupid. Why did it take me so long to realise?" I wondered.

Arms entwined, we sat down on the old stone bench. I touched his cheek with my fingers and looked into his beautiful eyes. Grey eyes, sooty lashes...

I was truly puzzled.

"Why did I not know it was you? That it should always have been you? Look at the time we wasted…"

He gave the little laugh I loved so much.

"Eva, you're eighteen. We're young, both of us. What does it matter that it took you a while to catch on? I never doubted that you would eventually."

He turned away and reached for his glass.

1 These lines are from the love duet that ends the first act of Puccini's Madama Butterfly. **Pinkerton**: Look around – everything is asleep. **Butterfly**: Ah! Sweet night! So many stars! **Pinkerton**: Come! Come!

"Never? Really? *Una tale arroganza*!" I teased. Then, hesitating, "But you must sometimes have wondered how long it would take?" I added.

He stretched back on the bench, smiled and sighed contentedly. "Maybe I did, once or twice. Just for a moment. When things got complicated."

He turned again to me and gazed into my eyes.

"But none of that is important now. We have our lives ahead of us. *This* is our time, Eva. The last few years have been difficult, I know. But next year – that will be our year."

He was right, of course – 1939 would be our year...

And, of course, much more than that.

TO BE CONTINUED

14080395R00136

Printed in Great Britain
by Amazon.co.uk, Ltd.,
Marston Gate.